LOYAL UNTO DEATH

NEW ANTHROPOLOGIES OF EUROPE

Matti Bunzl and Michael Herzfeld, editors

Founding Editors

Daphne Berdahl

Matti Bunzl

Michael Herzfeld

LOYAL UNTO DEATH

Trust and Terror in Revolutionary Macedonia

KEITH BROWN

Indiana University Press

BLOOMINGTON AND INDIANAPOLIS

This book is a publication of

Indiana University Press
Office of Scholarly Publishing
Herman B Wells Library 350
1320 East 10th Street
Bloomington, Indiana 47405

iupress.indiana.edu

Telephone orders   800-842-6796
Fax orders   812-855-7931

LIBRARY OF CONGRESS CATALOGING-IN-PUBLICATION DATA

Brown, Keith, [date]
  Loyal unto death : trust and terror in revolutionary Macedonia / Keith Brown.
     pages cm. — (New anthropologies of Europe)
  Includes bibliographical references and index.
  ISBN 978-0-253-00835-0 (cloth : alkaline paper) — ISBN 978-0-253-00840-4 (paperback : alkaline paper) — ISBN 978-0-253-00847-3 (ebook) 1. Macedonia—History—1878-1912. 2. Macedonia—History—Autonomy and independence movements 3. Vnatrešna makedonska revolucionerna organizacija—History. 4. Revolutionaries—Macedonia—History. 5. Macedonia—Politics and government—19th century. 6. Macedonia—Politics and government—20th century. 7. Nationalism—Macedonia—History. 8. Trust—Political aspects—Macedonia—History. 9. Political violence—Macedonia—History. 10. Political culture—Macedonia—History. I. Title.
  DR2215.B76 2013
  949.5'6072—dc23   2012047306

                    1 2 3 4 5 18 17 16 15 14 13

For Peter Loizos 1937–2012

History can only make her pictures and rebuild the past out of the things she can save from a shipwreck.... The memory of the world is not a bright, shining crystal, but a heap of broken fragments, a few fine flashes of light that break through the darkness. And so, history is full of tales half-told, and of tunes that break off in the middle; she gives us snatches from the lives of men, a peep at some corner of a battlefield, just enough to make us long for a fuller vision.

—HERBERT BUTTERFIELD, *The Historical Novel*

CONTENTS

ACKNOWLEDGMENTS

This book is based on the Evans-Pritchard lectures I delivered at All Souls College, Oxford, in fall 2004, with the title "The Structure of Loyalty in Revolutionary Macedonia." I owe that opportunity, at least in part, to the two mentors who wrote my letters of recommendation: the late Peter Loizos, to whom this book is dedicated, and Jane Cowan. I am also indebted to the fellows, faculty, and students who attended and provided generous and constructive feedback. In particular, I would like to thank the then-Warden Professor John Davis, Professor Wendy James, Douglas Johnston, Noel Malcolm, and Dimitar Bechev for their engagement and encouragement.

Commitments to other research priorities since 2004 have slowed the project but also enriched it. As a visiting fellow at the University of Connecticut Humanities Institute during 2005–2006, my primary focus was on patterns of labor migration from Ottoman Macedonia to the United States. Director Richard Brown and Associate Director Françoise Dussart nonetheless created space and impetus for reflection that allowed me to realize the central importance of long-distance circuits of travel in Macedonia's modern history. At the Watson Institute for International Studies at Brown University, my involvement in research projects on U.S. democracy promotion and counterinsurgency has also generated new perspectives on the importance of flows of resources and ideas. Amid the more recent turmoil of mission restructuring and academic receivership at the institute, Director Michael Kennedy and Interim Director Carolyn Dean, in very different styles, nevertheless provided effective encouragement and support to see the project through. And the staffs at all three institutions made things run more smoothly, especially Mary Yoe at All Souls, Jo-Ann Waide at UCHI, and Deborah Healey at the Watson Institute.

I have benefited from enthusiastic and critical responses to the project from undergraduates and graduate students at both the University of Connecticut and at Brown, and from colleagues at a number of conferences and workshops. I would like to thank the students in "Anthropology and the Archive" at the University of Connecticut in Spring 2006, and in "Political Anthropology: Peasants, Tribes, Terrorists and Other Enemies of the State" at Brown University in fall 2011—in particular Matt Vining, Saskia Brechenmacher, Reuben Henriques, Julia Potter, Juan Ruiz, and Derek Sheridan—for their suggestions. Pamela Ballinger, Kristen Ghodsee, Milica Bakić-Hayden, Melissa Bokovoy, Maria Bucur, Emira Ibrahimpašić, and Mary Neuburger provided congenial company and valuable feedback on a composite version of chapters 3 and 4 presented at "Spiritualities and Secularisms in Southeastern Europe: An Interdisciplinary Workshop" at Bowdoin College in October 2009, and Nida Gelazis, Dana Ponte, John Lampe, and Dragan Ristovski posed important questions in response to a presentation drawn from chapter 6 at East European Studies at the Woodrow Wilson Center in Washington, D.C., in February 2012.

As ever, the circles of obligation extend too widely to thank individually all those colleagues who provided insight since I began working with the Ilinden archives in Skopje in the early 1990s. James Fernandez was among the first to urge me to spend more time in the world they conjured; in a slightly different vein, Gale Stokes advocated for history over metahistory. Victor Friedman's unflagging and generous support extended all the way from shrewd graduate school advice to reading and commenting on this book's page proofs. Jovan Donev, Toše Čepreganov, and Irena Stefoska continue to provide scholarly hospitality in Skopje, and I am grateful to Zoran Todorovski for making access to the national archives so straightforward. I have benefited from wide-ranging discussions with and/or specific reading or writing recommendations from Peter Andreas, Omer Bartov, Ulf Brunnbauer, John Comaroff, Jane Cowan, Loring Danforth, Victor Friedman, Dragi Gjorgiev, Chip Gagnon, Drew Gilbert, Vasilis Gounaris, Hannes Grandits, Michael Herzfeld, Michael Kennedy, Kostis Kornetis, Martha Lampland, Dimitris Livanios, Catherine Lutz, Milčo Mančevski, Tchavdar Marinov, Vladimir Milčin, Marija Pandevska, Biljana Risteska, Marshall Sahlins, Philip Shashko, Ann Laura Stoler, Maria Todorova, Žarko Trajanovski, Anastas Vangeli, and Susan Woodward.

Anusha Venkataraman provided invaluable research support on the text; David Manning created the maps. I am especially grateful to Svetlin Rusev for granting permission to reproduce his 1966 painting, and to Viliana Borisova and Tchavdar Marinov for making that possible. I was not able here to incorporate the data and insights of two new archivally-based books on the armed struggle in early twentieth-century Macedonia; Dimitris Lithoxou's *The Greek Anti-Macedonian Struggle* (Salient Publishing, 2012), and Ipek Yosmaoglu's *Blood Ties: Religion, Violence, and the Politics of Nationhood in Ottoman Macedonia, 1878-1908* (Cornell University Press, 2013).

I am grateful to the series editors Michael Herzfeld and Matti Bunzl for their support for the book, to the two external readers for their smart suggestions, to Nancy Lightfoot and Drew Bryan for meticulous copy editing, and especially to Indiana University Press editor Rebecca Tolen for her close reading, patience, and advocacy.

My greatest debt is to Shelley Stephenson, who has been there from the beginning, and has listened to or read every word here as well as all those that broke off along the way. When we are old and gray and full of sleep, and nodding by the fire, take down this book, and remind me I owe you, Chloe, and Leo a summer. At least.

NOTE ON TRANSLITERATION
AND PRONUNCIATION

The primary language of research for this book was Macedonian, which is a Slavic language codified in 1944. Macedonian is normally written in the Macedonian Cyrillic script. The main text uses the following system of transliteration, except when citing from sources that used their own.

Standard literary Macedonian is based on dialects spoken around Veles, Prilep, and Bitola. Standard Macedonian is spoken throughout the modern Republic of Macedonia, although different regions have their own specific dialects (one of the most identifiable being the Strumica dialect). The Ilinden pension biographies were largely written in standard Macedonian in the Cyrillic script, though there were some nonstandard elements.

For the limited Bulgarian that features, a similar system is used as for Macedonian.

Cyrillic	Latin	Note	Cyrillic	Latin	Note
А, а	a		Н, н	N	
Б, б	b		Њ, њ	nj	as in venue
В, в	v		О, о	O	
Г, г	g		П, п	P	
Д, д	d		Р, р	R	
Ѓ, ѓ	gj	gj as in argue	С, с	S	
Е, е	e		Т, т	T	
Ж, ж	ž	zh as in measure	Ќ, ќ	ḱj	kj as in cute
З, з	z		У, у	U	
Ѕ, ѕ	dz	as in lids	Ф, ф	F	
И, и	I		Х, х	H	as in hello
Ј, ј	y	as in year	Ц, ц	C	ts as in bits
К, к	k		Ч, ч	Č	ch as in chat
Л, л	l		Џ, џ	dž	as in grudge
Љ, љ	lj	as in value	Ш, ш	Š	sh as in shoe
М, м	m		Ъ	û	as in but

NOTE ON SOURCES

This book draws primarily on two sets of archival sources. The first is the records of the British Foreign Office in the late nineteenth and early twentieth century. These are designated by the series reference FO 195, which identifies records from embassies and consulates in the former Ottoman Empire, followed by the file number and page.

These records were consulted on microfilm at the Museum of the Macedonian Struggle in Thessaloniki Greece, which also houses French, American, and Austrian records from the same period.

The second source is the Ilinden Archive, stored at the National Archives in Skopje in the Republic of Macedonia, which consists of forty-three boxes of pension applications. Individual records are identified by box number, first letter of the applicant, and sequential number within the box.

CHRONOLOGY OF KEY ORIENTING DATES

1832	Greece recognized as independent
1839–76	Tanzimat reforms in Ottoman Empire
1869	*Cathechism of a Revolutionary* published in Russia
1870	Establishment of the (Bulgarian) Exarchate
1877–78	Russo–Turkish War
1878	(March) Treaty of San Stefano, creating a large Bulgaria
	(June) Formation of (Albanian) League of Prizren
	(July) Treaty of Berlin, restoring Ottoman territory in Europe and including provisions for local autonomy
	Establishment of Bulgaria as autonomous principality within Ottoman Empire
1881	Annexation of (Ottoman) Thessaly by Greece
1885	Unification of Bulgaria and Eastern Rumelia
	Serb-Bulgarian War
1887	Formation of Hunchak Armenian party
1893	Formation of the MRO in Salonika
1894	Sasun Massacre in southern Armenia
1895	Formation of Vrhovist Committee in Sofia
	Bulgarian incursion into Ottoman Macedonia, briefly occupying Melnik. Boris Sarafov was a participant.
1896	MRO statutes written down
	Armenian revolutionaries bomb Ottoman bank, Constantinople
1897	(January) Former British prime minister William Gladstone coins the phrase "Macedonia for Macedonians"
	(February) Cretan Revolt, and Greek-Turkish War
	(September) Vinica Affair, leading to Ottoman discovery of the MRO's existence
1898	(January) Sultan grants the Exarchate three new bishoprics in Macedonia, bringing the total of Exarchate bishops there to seven

1899   Establishment of the MRO *četa* system

1901   (January) Salonika Affair leads to multiple arrests and Garvanov's takeover of the MRO

(September) American missionary Ellen Stone kidnapped by the MRO and held for ransom over the winter

1902   General Končev's incursion into Macedonia from Bulgaria

1903   (January) The MRO's Salonika Congress

(February) Albanian revolt against Ottoman rule and perceived new privileges for Christians

(April) Salonika bombings by the Gemidžii

(May) Deaths of Svetkov in Mogila and Delčev in Banica

The MRO's Smilevo Congress

(August) Ilinden Uprising

1908   (June) Young Turk Revolution, or "Huriet"

1909   Counterrevolution by subgroup of Young Turks, rolling back progressive reforms that empowered Christians

1912   First Balkan War: Bulgaria, Greece, Serbia, and Montenegro against Turkey

1913   Second Balkan War: Bulgaria against her former allies

Treaty of London: Independence of Albania recognized

LOYAL UNTO DEATH

The Archival Imagination at Work

The body count just kept climbing. On New Year's Eve 1902, the British consul-general in Salonika, the largest city in Ottoman Turkey's restive European provinces, filed his latest update on violence in the troubled region around the region's second city, Monastir. Forty-three people were reported killed in the six-month period from April to October 1902—one every four days. He provided details on the grisly fate of two:

> On October 2 in the town of Krouchovo [*sic*] the girl Sophia Trencoff, who was the mistress of the police *mudir* [chief of police] and acted as his spy, and her mother were stabbed several times. The mother's eyes were torn out, and the daughter's tongue was cut out, her stomach ripped open and her intestines pulled out. No one doubts that this was the Committee's revenge. (FO 195/2133/937: Biliotti to O'Conor, 31 December 1902)

January 1903 began in similar vein. On January 7, a report came in from Uskub (modern Skopje) that a pregnant woman had been shot and wounded by a "Turk" who was demanding food from Christian villagers. She delivered the baby, which died soon after being born. Upon which, the report goes on,

> (t)he child's body which, it seems, had been dried, was brought to the Bulgarian agent at Üsküb, who sent it on to the Russian consul. The Russian Consul's *dragoman* [translator or fixer] carried the body to the Reforms Commission, and they sent it to the Vali who, my colleague tells me, immediately had it interred. (FO 195/2156/25: Biliotti to O'Conor, 6 January 1903)

From Monastir itself (modern Bitola), where reforms were underway to recruit Christians as gendarmes to protect against violence of this kind, the following response was reported in early February:

The only Christian, apparently, who braved the threats of the committee and sent in an application was a man of Lopotnitza [sic; Lopatica] some distance from Monastir and he was found three days later [January 31], floating in the river with his throat cut and a paper fastened to his coat, bearing the inscription "the fate of those who would serve the Turks." (FO 195/2156/130: Biliotti to Whitehead, 5 February 1903)

Four months later, the British vice consul in Monastir reported sixteen deaths in June—one every two days. Among them were the two men whose photograph appears here. In the British diplomatic records, their names are given as Nikola Bidin and his son Thomas (Toma); they are identified as Patriarchists and cattle dealers, murdered near their hometown of Kruševo on the road from Kičevo. The suspected perpetrators were two representatives of the Ottoman state: a tax entrepreneur whose father had recently been killed in a gun battle with an MRO band, and a gendarme (FO 195/2157/131: McGregor to Biliotti 8 July 1903).[1]

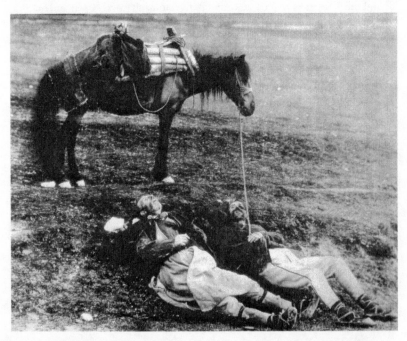

Figure 0.1. The bodies of Nikola and Toma Bidin(ov), killed outside Kruševo, June 6, 1903.

For a twenty-first-century reader, these incidents provide glimpses of a world that seems at once profoundly familiar and strikingly alien. In recent decades, reporting from Cambodia, El Salvador, Sierra Leone, and Bosnia has demonstrated, and sought to make sense of, the prevalence of dramatic violence in civil wars, whether waged along ethnic, tribal, or ideological grounds (see for example Richards 1996; Doubt 2000). It is common, albeit still shocking, that women and would-be peacemakers are victims, as they are in these two cases. So too, the idea that dead bodies can bear messages—whether to inform, intimidate, or embarrass different constituencies—is a phenomenon that crosses cultural and temporal lines, most recently described as "corpse-messaging" in the drug-driven conflict in Mexico but also reported from contemporary Afghanistan and colonial Algeria (Finnegan 2010; Perlmutter 2006/7; see also Lazreg 2008: 52–53).

What, then, makes Ottoman Macedonia different and noteworthy? First is that these events took place more than a century ago, and their targeted specificity has been largely forgotten. In the 1940s, Rebecca West famously wrote that "violence was, indeed, all I knew of the Balkans" (West 1941: 21) and also described the radical politicization of Balkan history by "Balkan-fanciers," in which sympathies for one or other of the peoples of the region shaped the way that the past was recounted (ibid.: 20). West captured perfectly the shortcomings of presentist perspectives—or what some scholars have termed "methodological nationalism"—on such violent acts. They may be aggregated into a picture of widespread and indiscriminate terror (the potential for which is somehow endemic to the region), or alternatively subjected to a double standard whereby violence by one's chosen people is either airbrushed out or justified, and violence by their enemy relentlessly publicized as provocative and/or unholy.

The seeds of these partial understandings of the past are already present in the diplomatic sources from the period. For in their reporting of regressive violence among locals, and their attempts first to identify perpetrators and victims in ethnonational terms and second to establish what British prime minister Balfour would in 1903, during the Ilinden Uprising, term the "balance of criminality" between different actors, these observers seldom reflected on the connection between incidents such as these and the larger political context of structural, state-sponsored violence.

In particular, in their painstaking—and at times prurient—cataloging of deaths, the consuls apparently missed reporting a less dramatic event with far more significant short- and longer-term consequences. On January 15, 1903, a group of delegates from "the committee" referred to in the double murder in Kruševo—the Secret Macedonian-Adrianople Revolutionary Organization (henceforth referred to as the MRO)—met in Thessaloniki (Perry 1988: 121–24).[2] Founded in 1893 under a different name, the group had established rules and regulations, gathered resources, and recruited members to the cause. By 1903 the organization boasted committees in villages and towns across Macedonia; its leaders were in contact with supporters and counterparts not just in Bulgaria—where many Macedonians studied and worked—but also in Russia, Switzerland, and France. With its stated goal of autonomy for Macedonia and a reputation and capacity for violence against internal and external enemies, it won support from villagers. Funds had been collected with the specific goal of acquiring arms with which to challenge Ottoman rule.

In the January 1903 meeting the eighteen delegates present resolved to escalate and transform the level of violence in the region. Despite opposition from several leading figures in the movement—who felt premature resort to widespread violence was doomed to failure and would worsen conditions further—a majority voted to launch an armed uprising against Ottoman rule, centered on the areas around Monastir and Adrianople (modern Edirne) (VMRO 1904). A statement by Damjan Gruev, one of the three men who would command the uprising, summed up the mood: "Better an end with horrors, than horrors without end" (Brailsford 1906: 116; MacDermott 1978: 348).

After several months of orchestrated preparation, the St. Elijah's Day or Ilinden Uprising of August 2, 1903, pitted as many as 20,000 armed insurgents against Ottoman forces that after reinforcements from Anatolia and the call-up of local reserves reached more than 200,000 (Perry 1988: 139; Dakin 1966: 103n).[3] The uprising did attract significant international attention to the plight of Macedonia—which was its goal for at least some of its planners—and even won admiration. In 1907, for example, one observer wrote that "no nation in the Balkan Peninsula had shown such a power of organization, such sacrificing spirit, and such fighting qualities as the Macedonians" (LeQueux 1907: 293). It was also followed by the implementation of reforms overseen by the European powers (Sowards 1989). For the organization, though, and the people it relied upon for support, the uprising was a disaster. In two and half months of sporadic fighting, approximately 1,000 insurgents were killed. Relief organizations put the civilian cost at more than 4,500 dead, with two hundred villages destroyed by Ottoman forces, in the fighting and afterwards. At least 3,000 rapes were reported, and more than 100,000 people were left homeless for the winter (Brailsford 1906: 166n).

The Ilinden Uprising and the tumultuous decade that followed—in which Ottoman Europe came to be divided between the nation-states of Albania, Serbia, Bulgaria, Montenegro and Greece—has dominated the writing of national history in the region. Yet the decade before the uprising holds its own fascination. From its inception, the MRO was at odds with the Ottoman government, neighboring states (Bulgaria, Greece, and Serbia) and their affiliated religious hierarchies, and a popular Albanian movement for statehood on overlapping territory—all of which had their own advocates in the international community. Although Ottoman authorities regularly recruited and rewarded informers, occasionally captured documents or intercepted arms shipments, and frequently arrested and tortured the individuals implicated for intelligence purposes, the organization had nevertheless not merely survived, but it had successfully transformed itself from a self-selected committee of six young urban professionals to a mass movement in which a significant proportion of the Slavic-speaking Christian population of the Ottoman administrative region, or *vilayet*, of Monastir directly participated.[4]

The attention to violence, and to the historical rights and wrongs of different national movements, has tended to obscure the magnitude of this achievement and the double puzzle it represents: First, how and why did so many members of a society generally perceived as composed of fatalistic peasants with profoundly limited intellectual and moral horizons, and in a context of widespread, oppressive violence, come to invest so much in a revolutionary movement over such a short time? And second, how did this organization equip, train, and mobilize such a significant armed force despite the efforts of better-resourced political actors, including the Ottoman Empire itself, neighboring states with their own expansionist agendas, and rival ethnically based national movements, to sabotage, co-opt, or undo its work? This book sets out to answer these questions and thereby contribute to understandings both of Macedonia's particular history and of civil war and insurgency more generally.

Uncovering the work of the organization, at the historical distance of more than a century, is a challenging task. This is due to both the specificities of

Macedonia—a territory and an idea with different meanings for different constituencies—as well as the distinctive, unruly, and contested history of the organization itself. After the 1903 uprising, recriminations and power struggles intensified. By the 1920s and 1930s, under the better-known name of the Internal Macedonian Revolutionary Organization (VMRO), it operated as a hybrid criminal/terrorist enterprise headquartered on modern Bulgarian territory, providing the assassin of King Alexander of Yugoslavia in Marseille in 1934. Even in its first decade, though, from its 1893 foundation to the Ilinden Uprising, it passed through several incarnations and changes of leadership and philosophy, at times aligning with or distinguishing itself from other movements that appealed to the same potential base of support (Kofos 1993: 25–28; Perry 1988: 215–16; Brailsford 1906: 171–72).

This organization operated in a world in which forms of violence persisted that were both commonplace and unpredictable in their causes and consequences. The murders of spies, traitors, or defectors that the committee sanctioned are perhaps intelligible to any audience familiar with the logic of punishment and deterrence in illegal organizations. So, too, the unlicensed resort to lethal force by and against the foot soldiers of semiprivatized empires—as reported here in the cases of an Albanian tax profiteer and a Christian gendarme—recurs in the historical record, most recently in incidents involving U.S. military contractors in Iraq.

Some specificities of this violence, though, remain unexamined in the consular accounts. In the Kruševo region alone, the blinding of the two cattle traders calls for further explanation, as does the parallel "hyperviolence" committed against two women by representatives of the revolutionary organization. While cutting out the tongue of the police chief's mistress has an obvious iconic meaning (she told secrets), and helps us intuit that the committee tore out her mother's eyes according to a similar logic of signaling (she spied), we are left with other questions. In a culture that demanded that dead bodies be treated with respect and where lethal violence against women violated numerous norms, who were the individuals who carried out these transgressive actions? What rules or principles guided them? Did they act willingly or under duress? How did they establish the emotional distance from their victims—whom they may well have known personally—that was surely necessary? What, in short, was the chain of decision making and order following by which the killings were carried out?

These questions highlight the second feature that makes early twentieth-century Macedonia a compelling case for closer study. As an early example of the use of terrorism by political activists opposing foreign rule, in a context of a truly diverse population, the province and its history combine elements of the commonsensical and the culturally specific, and therefore demand the use of different approaches. Social scientists concern themselves with regularities and patterns, with the goal of discerning the universal in the particular. A consequence is that in many of the social scientific disciplines, but especially economics and political science, priority is given to approaches that help us see past the messiness of lived reality and that offer rigorously tested, parsimonious explanations of underlying laws. In the humanities, by contrast, uniqueness and plenitude are more highly valued. Though many works of literature and associated scholarship contain or deliver apparent truth claims, they tend to do so through the medium of close scrutiny and rich exposition of human experience. In general, they recognize the temporal and cultural limits of the conclusions they present.

These fundamental characteristics underpin much of today's interdisciplinary miscommunication and intradisciplinary strife. Whereas the distinctions can be drawn in nonpejorative terms—invoking, for example, Isaiah Berlin's own invocation of Tolstoy and Archilochus, to divide philosophers between hedgehogs (who know one big thing) and foxes (who know many small things)—they frequently become rancorous, so that the "mindless reductionism" of political science is contrasted with the "sophistic complicationism" of anthropology. The debate is, of course, age-old in the domain of knowledge production, in which Thucydides, the scientist, sniped at Herodotus's anecdotalism; or Aristotle, the empiricist, challenged the scorched-earth idealism of Plato. Political science features similar tensions, in which ethnographic, idiographic, single case studies are generally marginalized, but where some within the discipline persist in making the argument for their utility (Schatz 2009).

The balance is more equal—and as a result, perhaps, the passion more fierce—in anthropology, which has offered a range of internal debates along these lines. One of the more recent and illuminating disputes along this grain pitted Marshall Sahlins against Gananath Obeyesekere over the place of the explorer Captain Cook in Hawai'ian cosmology and politics. Obeyesekere, not a specialist on the region, challenged the convention that Cook was read through a mythological framework predicting the return of the god Lono, arguing that this was surely a Western, colonial invention (Obeyesekere 1992). Sahlins responded to Obeyesekere's critique of his extended and intensive work on Hawai'ian history by calling the attack "pidgin anthropology" and "pseudohistory" (Sahlins 1995: 60, 62). In Sahlins' view, Obeyesekere claimed greater understanding of eighteenth-century Hawai'ians by virtue of a shared status as non-European "native," instead of attention to the relevant ethnography. The result, in Sahlins' terms, was a set of distortions that "have the quality of ad hoc fabrications based on a sort of generic primitivism" (ibid. 62).

In the chapters that follow, I revisit this argument, invoking Sahlins' term and applying it to dominant perspectives on late nineteenth- and early twentieth-century Ottoman Macedonia, which constitute a form of "pidgin social science." The relentless linkage of present and past in the historiography of early twentieth-century Macedonia—and in particular the near-exclusive concern with the presence or absence of "national consciousness" among its residents—deploys a theoretical vocabulary overdetermined by the course events have taken since, which has impeded a fuller understanding of the lived reality of that time and place. Early twentieth-century Macedonia's history has thus often been based on a sort of generic nationalism; my goal is to call into question the particular forms of presentism, disguised as universalism, that underpin this and to demonstrate the importance of historical sensitivity that evades the dangers of exoticism.

Anthropologists and historians pursue this goal by seeking to understand the worlds they describe, where possible, in "experience-near" terms, and thus explore the world as lived, through the exercise of imagination or empathy. Ottoman Macedonia, in these terms, is distant in time and space, but as a happy by-product of the politicization of the past in the intervening century, we can take the leap in two stages. Between 1948 and 1956, the new Yugoslav Macedonian government invited elderly men and women who had participated in the work of the organization in the Ilinden period to apply for pensions as veterans of the (proto-) national struggle. More than 3,500 did so in the expectation or hope that their activism would receive its due.

I have described the context for this pension scheme and the application process more fully elsewhere (Brown 2003: 130–52). Here I use them as a bridge to the Ilinden period. Fourteen of these personal accounts are presented in sequence in appendix 2. As a concrete example of a concise, data-rich, and well-organized biography, here is the account of his activity submitted by Nikola Zdraveski-Vince from Kruševo, "Tome Niklev" st. № 45, in 1951. The capitalization is preserved from the Macedonian original.

> I was born 1866 in Kruševo to parents: mother KOSTADINA and father ZDRAVE NAUMOSKI-VINCE both from Kruševo. By trade I was a tailor.
>
> In the movement for the liberation of the MACEDONIAN PEOPLE from the TURKISH OPPRESSION I participated from 1898.
>
> In 1900 I gave an OATH of loyalty to the ORGANIZATION, which was given to me by the teacher DAME NOČEV and then I became a member of the organiza-tion. As such I was given the task to recruit members and, as one was saying then, to convert them or to gather them into the ORGANIZATION.
>
> In 1901 in Kruševo, in the house of TAŠKO SURDUL I welcomed into the organization a group of 10 people. Also in the house of HALČU BERBEROT I wel-comed in the organization another group of 10 people. On the order of the COM-MAND of the organization I was sent in this same year to the village of KRUŠEANI to organize the villagers there as a members of the organization. Thus I went and in the inn of NIKOLE GJORGOSKI, by ceremonially inducting them into the orga-nization and christening them with the oath, I made a group of 10 people. Among them was BOGOJA MIRČEV-PATLIDŽAN from Kruševani, who is still alive now.
>
> Through 1901 and 1902, as a member with more experience in armed fighting, I trained our group in the use of weapons. I conducted these exercises with sticks.
>
> A month before the UPRISING I left for work in Bulgaria, but through Roma-nia and from Bulgaria I returned to Kruševo in 1906. Then I again I was elected to be HEAD of the ORGANIZATION in KRUŠEVO.
>
> In the organization I was PRESIDENT of TRIALS together with MILE ILČEV and STERJU BLAŽEV, both teachers, with whom we passed JUDGMENTS on members of the organization who had failed in their organizational obligations.
>
> For the above statements the following persons can testify:
>
> Georgiev Hristov Vasil, from Kruševo, now living in Bitola, 'Ohrid' st. №9; Bogoja Mirčev (Patlidžan) from the village of Kruševani, and I myself guarantee morally, materially and legally.
>
> KRUŠEVO 16.XI.1951
>
> Signed: Nikola Zdraveski-Vince

Zdraveski's pension biography, even in isolation, sheds light on aspects of the organization and its committees that passed unseen, or at least unreported, by the Western consuls. In less than a page, the recollections of an eighty-five-year-old man conjure the impression of an organization with its own terminology and hierarchy, and with the power of life and death over members who pledged their loyalty. Zdraveski's account also indicates the existence of training and a system of punitive internal justice for those who did not obey or conform. As such, it serves as a terse and evocative counterpoint to the consular report on the murder of Sophia Trencoff and her mother, alerting us to the fact that Trencoff was almost certainly killed by people she knew, on the orders of the organization—people like Zdraveski, bound to a cause.

Overall, the pension seekers use a consistent lexicon of insurgency, in which the oath is a central mechanism and where people defined as couriers, terrorists, receivers, *četniks*, secretaries, and treasurers all had specified duties. Together with the consular sources of the time, they provide a remarkably consistent and rich account of insurgent life in late nineteenth- and early twentieth-century Ottoman Macedonia, and the circuits of trust and terror through which the organization expanded its reach and came to constitute a state within a state. They also provide the opportunity to go beyond speculation on the existence or absence of ethnonational consciousness or identity by providing evidence on the MRO's social organization and mechanisms of loyalty.

In this book I draw on these historical sources to challenge the comfortable, but intellectually blinkered, presentism inherent in methodological nationalism. In chapter 1, I lay out this argument more fully by discussing the emergence of methodological nationalism in the Balkan context, as well as the historicity of the diverse archival sources out of which Macedonia's insurgent past can be reconstructed, and comparative perspectives from empirical and theoretical work on civil wars, insurgencies, the creation of solidarity, and the workings of everyday violence in a variety of disciplines. In that sense, chapter 1 lays claim to the "intellectual poaching license" claimed by Clyde Kluckhohn for anthropology (cited in Geertz 1983: 21) as I enlist literature from history, sociology, and political science.

Chapter 2 provides the socioeconomic context of the organization's growth and operating procedures, focusing especially on the phenomenon of *pečalba*, or labor migration, and the challenge it posed to Ottoman rule, and the preachings of the Orthodox Church, as well as to lingering ideas regarding Macedonia's supposed fatalistic and anomic peasantry. By altering the economic structure of Macedonia, as well as setting in place a human circuitry that connected Macedonian villages with each other and with the wider world, *pečalba* provided both the economic resources and the physical template for the organization's rise.

Chapter 3 examines the organization's use of oathing ceremonies as one mechanism for the maintenance of secrecy, obedience, and loyalty. The Ilinden dossier presents a diverse array of descriptions of oath taking and oath giving by participants in the revolutionary movement, in which metaphors of cursing outnumber those of christening, field commanders administer more oaths than do priests, private homes host more ceremonies than do churches, and women become members alongside men. The chapter argues that the imagery and practices of oathing serve to distinguish the organization from its church-based rivals for the loyalty and commitment of Macedonia's inhabitants. Drawing parallels with more fully documented cases of subversive oathing in Christian contexts—as practiced by the Carbonari secret societies, whiteboys, ribbon-men and the IRA in anti-imperial Ireland, and Mau Mau in colonial Kenya—the chapter identifies MRO oathing as a key vector of the insurgent imagination along which new configurations of power and solidarity were created.

Chapter 4 analyzes the MRO's practices of writing and record keeping, arguing that the organization undertook to make its personnel and practices legible both to bring into being its own institutional structure and also as part of its agenda of self-legitimization. The analysis focuses in particular on command and communication circuits created by written death sentences issued against spies and traitors. These decrees were generated by the organization's leadership and secretaries, conveyed by couriers, implemented by terrorists, and often left on the target's body where others could read them. Again drawing on comparative cases of writing in revolution, the chapter supplements conventional historical emphasis on the cultural ties of Macedonia's revolutionaries (who shared, for example, language and religion) with a detailed account of the terminology and new practices of the organization.

Chapter 5 focuses on the establishment and maintenance of the organization's "professional" armed wing, composed of bands or *četas* governed by explicit regulations and dependent on a broader, formalized network of civilian confederates, at the heart of which were *jataks*, or "receivers." The chapter examines the complex relationship between the organization and prior traditions of locally rooted, antigovernmental dissent in which these same terms had different meanings. The MRO simultaneously grew out of, drew upon, and defined itself in opposition to prior practices of "prerevolutionary" or "primitive" rebellion; the analysis here focuses on the radical transformation of ideologies of honor and the fundamental shift in flows of resources, effected by the work of the organization in the course of preparation for the Ilinden Uprising of 1903.

Chapter 6 analyzes the circuits through which members of the organization obtained and stockpiled thousands of rifles in preparation for the Ilinden Uprising of 1903, and the practical and symbolic effects of that effort on patterns of intercommunal violence in Macedonia. It focuses in particular on descriptions of purchasing rifles and ammunition from a purportedly threatening other, Albanians, to argue that the organization's emphasis on acquiring arms, even when undertaken in a spirit of self-defense, had important and far-reaching cultural consequences in reordering patterns of deadly retribution and escalation between different communities.

Finally, the conclusion puts the MRO and the violence of early twentieth-century Macedonia in comparative context, while demonstrating the importance for our understanding of close attention to the specificities that can be retrieved from partial sources.

To reiterate the central puzzle of the book: How did an organization grow, over ten short years, from a six-member founding committee in Thessaloniki in 1893 to a 20,000-strong armed uprising in 1903? I start with the commonsense hypothesis that it must have successfully tapped into, or mapped onto, existing dispositions to or mechanisms of collective action, while simultaneously generating new modalities of solidarity and obedience to direct that action toward a revolutionary agenda of autonomy and liberation. This much I share with those who would offer "nationalism"—or, more strictly, "ethnonationalism"—as the parsimonious answer. My hypothesis, based in part on analyses of insurgencies in other times and places, is that such parsimony obscures rather than illuminates the lived experience of protest in Ottoman Macedonia. In the spirit of a late work by Clifford Geertz, discussed specifically in chapter 1, I seek to replace "batting about vaguely at clouds and vapors" (1994: 4) with attention to the practices, roles, and material objects through which the organization created a new domain of Macedonian selfhood by managing complex, multiple loyalties rather than invoking a singular identity.

In parallel, and inspired in particular by the content of the life histories presented in appendix 2, I argue for the particular value of the archival imagination in making sense of early twentieth-century Macedonia in particular and the management of loyalties in insurgency and intercommunal violence more generally. The circuits traveled by things, people, and ideas—including anarchist publications, spoken oaths, written orders, rifles, and ammunition, but also labor migrants and the women they left behind, charcoal, peppers, and bread—provide the sinews of organization, discipline, and solidarity that, more than the clouds and vapors of nationalism or other ideological projects, make orchestrated human action possible and intelligible.

CHAPTER ONE

Terminal Loyalties and Unruly Archives:
On Thinking Past the Nation

"Why not Macedonia for Macedonians, as well as Bulgaria for Bulgarians and Servia for Servians?" (Gladstone 1897). This simple-seeming question, first posed by a former British prime minister with considerable knowledge of the Balkans, still remains controversial today. In its original formulation, it represented a continuation of Gladstone's long advocacy for the rights of diverse Christian subjects of the Ottoman Empire. In the 1850s, he was welcomed by the Greek population of the Ionian islands as a champion of their interests; in the 1870s, he deplored Ottoman atrocities in Bulgaria; and in the 1890s, he denounced the empire's treatment of Armenians. Yet whereas Greeks, Bulgarians, and Armenians—along with a number of other former Ottoman subject peoples in the Middle East—are now firmly identified with their own territorial nation-states, the precise status of Macedonians and their relationship with Macedonia has remained a source of contention.

Over the years, Gladstone's question has consistently been amended to include a definite article and turned into a slogan—Macedonia for *the* Macedonians—that continues to underpin scholarly research on the region's history and culture (Rossos 2008; Čepreganov 2008). But there is irony in this legacy. For by the time Gladstone posed his question on Macedonia—at a moment when Greece was preparing to go to war against Turkey on behalf of fellow Christians in Crete—he had already come to recognize that liberation from Ottoman rule was not a cure to all the region's ills. Indeed, he prefaced the question by stating that "next to the Ottoman Government nothing can be more deplorable and blameworthy than jealousies between Greek and Slav, and plans by the States already existing for appropriating other territory" and followed it with the prediction that unless these peoples stood together in common defense, they would assuredly be "devoured by others."

In some sense, then, Gladstone already provided one answer to his question. There would be no Macedonia for Macedonians, because existing, ambitious states would jockey for control of the Ottoman territory of Macedonia and usurp any aspirations its inhabitants might have. That was how history played out in 1912, when Greece, Serbia, and Bulgaria (as well as the tiny state of Montenegro) declared war on the Ottoman Empire and carved up the six *vilayets*, or provinces, that spanned the peninsula from the Sea of Marmara to the Adriatic coast of modern Albania. Gladstone's caveats also foretold how quarrels would undo the allies. Bulgaria, which had gained the smallest slice of territory from the first round of fighting, then launched a self-destructive attack against its former allies, sparking the Second Balkan War. When the lines of demarcation were drawn, the territory on which the MRO had aspired to create an autonomous Macedonia was divided along national frontiers that, apart from revision during each World War, have endured until today.

The Legacy of Ilinden: Methodological Nationalism

The defeat of the uprising in 1903 brought an end to the fragile unity of the organization. It also served as ground zero for a set of acrimonious debates about nation and national identity in the region, which took on renewed significance after the establishment of a Macedonian republic within the framework of federal Yugoslavia in 1944. Since that date, historians in Bulgaria, Greece, and the Republic of Macedonia (both before and after its declaration of sovereignty in 1991) have produced a substantial scholarship centered on the status of the uprising and the identity of those who took part. Notwithstanding dialogue and disagreement over historical theory and methodology within each national tradition, three dominant narratives have emerged, drawing on distinct bodies of archival material, to make sense of the question that the facts of the buildup to Ilinden, and the uprising itself, generate.[1]

The most straightforward accounts are those produced by successive generations of Bulgarian historians, who can draw on both state archives and those of Macedonian organizations, many of which had their headquarters in Sofia. They link Ilinden, in the Monastir region, with the Preobražene Uprising, in the *vilayet* of Adrianople, that began sixteen days later on August 19, 1903. Both, in this narrative, were aided by "progressive" forces in Bulgaria and led by Bulgarian military personnel who also provided the key leadership for the organization.[2] The Christian inhabitants of Macedonia who joined the uprising were motivated by shared Bulgarian ethnonational consciousness, which they also expressed by adherence to the Exarchist Church. Language and religious belonging—in social scientific terms, "primordial sentiments"—were the motivating factors of identity and subsequent participation. This view persisted after the division of Macedonia in 1912–13, as Bulgaria continued to abet local resistance to Greek and, especially, Serbian rule in the Monastir region, on the grounds that the majority of the inhabitants were Bulgarian.

Greek historiography draws on official Greek military, religious, and state archives, as well as the memoirs of self-identified Greek residents of the Monastir area, Greek officials, and military personnel who served in what Greeks refer to as the "Macedonian Struggle" (Kazazes 1904; Dakin 1966; Kofos 1993). Many of these are preserved by organizations established in Thessaloniki after the First World War, dedicated to preserving a record of the region's Greek heritage after it was occupied by Serbian forces. Where Bulgarian historiography elevates the significance of Ilinden by casting it as part of an orchestrated, larger uprising, Greek historians diminish it (Karakasidou 1997: 102). Skeptical of the depth or sincerity of local support, they suggest that those who took part were for the most part duped, bribed, or forcibly coerced into short-term participation, and deserted at the first opportunity. They acknowledge the existence of an organization, but deny it any genuine roots or support in Ottoman Macedonia: it was a tool of Bulgarian state interests and thus an external and illegitimate actor in a geographical region that, in this narrative, was a longstanding part of the Greek world (Mylonas 1947: 77–83). This view was operationalized by colonizing those parts of the Monastir *vilayet* that were incorporated into Greece after 1913 with refugees from Asia Minor (put in motion by the failure of Greece's war of aggression against Turkey in the 1920s), and by systematic, aggressive efforts to assimilate the Slavic-speaking population (Karakasidou 2000; Carabott 1997).

Before World War II, Serbian historiography likewise emphasized Ilinden's Bulgarian provenance and also sought to downplay its significance for the local population of the Bitola region, who were simultaneously subjected to a campaign of Serbian national assimilation. After the creation of the Socialist Federal Republic of Yugoslavia, though, and the recognition of a Macedonian republic and people (*narod*) within it, Ilinden was recast (Brown 2003). The late nineteenth and early twentieth century became a major focus for the work of the newly established Institute of National History in Macedonia's capital city, Skopje. Drawing primarily on archival materials and published accounts shared by Sofia during the brief entente between Bulgaria and

Yugoslavia (1946–48), Skopje's national historians presented Ilinden as an early expression of Macedonian commitment to national liberation, also infused by proto-Yugoslav ideals of brotherhood and unity. They focused attention on those leaders who had espoused socialist ideals and had reached out to Macedonia's Albanian, Turkish, and Vlah victims of Ottoman oppression and bourgeois (Greek) exploitation; those with obvious ties to Belgrade or Sofia (or both) were marginalized or cast as traitors (Brown 2003, 2004). Ilinden 1903 became part of a longer process of Macedonian national awakening, a precursor to the 1944 establishment (on the same date) of a Macedonian Republic quickly incorporated into Yugoslavia. This perspective survived the breakup of Yugoslavia, with the establishment of an autonomous, sovereign Republic of Macedonia represented as a third Ilinden (Brown 2000).

Divergent and seemingly incompatible though these narratives appear, they share a common frame of methodological nationalism (Wimmer and Glick-Schiller 2002; Chernilo 2007: 1–20). That is to say, in all three versions the nation-state occupies center stage as the agent of history, and all three assume that the establishment (or enlargement) of a nation-state must have been the ultimate goal of any organization that existed. For Bulgarian historians, again, the narrative is straightforward. The nation-state at the heart of Macedonia's history is Bulgaria. The activities of the organization and its supporters sought to unite ethnic Bulgarians within the boundaries briefly established in 1878, after the Russo–Turkish War, but then redrawn by the other great powers. Ilinden was an expression of the will of the Bulgarian-speaking majority of Macedonia's Christian population for freedom, and a united Bulgarian nation-state was the best provider and guarantor of that freedom.

Greek and Macedonian narratives share a central preoccupation with the primary significance of nations in history, but, in denying the straightforward Bulgarian version, are forced in different and directly adversarial directions. For Greek historians, focused on the region's Byzantine and Orthodox heritage and its inhabitants' supposedly underlying Greek national identity, the idea that the organization enjoyed authentic mass support, or sprang from indigenous activism, was simply unthinkable. So although acknowledging that it was an expression of Bulgarian nationalism, Greek narratives depict the organization as a façade maintained by an alien elite. While the MRO's leaders claimed their goal was to liberate fellow nationals, this Greek narrative asserts that they sought to advance Bulgarian state interests by fostering instability and violence in Macedonia at the expense of the territory's truly, deeply Greek population.

The same two ideas that are anathema to Greek historians—authentic mass support for the MRO and its roots in indigenous activism—are central to the post-Yugoslav Macedonian narrative. That puts Skopje's historians, obviously, at odds with their Athens- and Thessaloniki-based counterparts. At the same time, though, they also fiercely contest the annexation of the organization's story by Sofia and insist on the existence of a distinct Macedonian nation, and national consciousness, in the Ilinden period, which gave birth to and sustained the organization.

There is evidence in the historical record to support all three narratives. And all three have been articulated by diligent and conscientious historians, who are aware of the rival versions and seek to counter them. The effect of this heated debate, though, has been to focus the collective energy of scholars on a single point of contention: the national identity of Macedonia's Christian inhabitants, especially those who were members of the organization or participated in the Ilinden Uprising. In its simplest form, much of the historical research on early twentieth-century Macedonia and its residents has come to be organized around the question "Who were they?"

But while this appears to be a legitimate, open historical question, it disguises a strongly presentist, politicized orientation in the debate. For what it really asks is, "Of which subsequent nation-state were these people members-in-waiting?" That was already an urgent question for Western journalists and diplomats in the early 1900s; Greek, Serbian, and Bulgarian ideologues were happy to provide their own answers. And those answers still have consequences today, where the question is still asked regarding the Slavic-speaking Orthodox majority of the (Former Yugoslav) Republic of Macedonia (Poulton 1995; Pettifer 1999; Roudometof 2002). A hundred years later, the two established EU member-states of Greece and Bulgaria have continued to pursue policies toward their neighbor shaped by their different perspectives on the historical standing of the Macedonian nation, while domestic politics within the Republic of Macedonia have been profoundly affected by the dissonance between people's strong sense of national distinctiveness and the externally generated doubts cast on that distinctiveness. The struggle to establish a single, authoritative answer on the status of Macedonian national identity at the beginning of the century has profound existential consequences for the present.

Beyond Identity: Toward a History of Non-National Loyalties

Rather than focus on the presence or absence of national consciousness in the past, I seek here to move beyond unproductive methodological nationalism. Specifically, I argue that the Macedonian Revolutionary Organization's emergence and reception among the Christian population of Turkey in Europe reveals not the presence or absence of national *identity*, but rather a process of the creation, interaction, and conscious reordering of diverse *loyalties*. This formulation draws on a strand of social scientific theory that traces back to Edward Shils's classic article "Primordial, Personal, Sacred and Civil Ties" (Shils 1957). There, Shils lays out the argument that the work of making group solidarity is not only cultural but also social, involving multiplex ties, bonds, and attachments among persons as well as shared ideas and attitudes that orient individuals to abstract ideals. As an example from his own research, Shils stresses that relationships within primary groups—*bunde*—played a greater role than commitment to national ideology in motivating both German and Soviet soldiers during World War II.

Shils's insights were further developed by Clifford Geertz in the course of his now less fashionable work on the new nations in the 1960s. Geertz develops an argument that primordial sentiments or, in his gloss, "assumed givens" about common blood, race, religion, or language may weigh more heavily for ordinary people than calls from state elites to build solidarity out of shared self-interest (Geertz 1973: 255–310). Geertz's point here—that people in the "new states" of the postcolonial world could be pulled in opposite directions by the demands of state, nation, sect, tribe, region, or family—was subsequently reiterated, still more forcefully, by Walker Connor (1978). Often caricatured, along with Geertz, as expressing disguised racism (that in the last resort, after Bismarck, people "think with their blood"), Connor (again like Geertz) in fact states quite clearly an argument for attention to multicausal rather than monocausal explanations of behaviors grouped under "nationalism."

Both Geertz and Connor quote a key definition of nation by Harvard-based political scientist Rupert Emerson, as the "terminal community" or

> the largest community which, when the chips are down, effectively commands men's loyalty, overriding the claims both of lesser communities within

it, and those which cut across it or potentially enfold it within a still greater society." (Emerson 1960: 95; cited in Connor 1978: 37n)

Although, as Geertz comments, this definition at first glance seems only to shift ambiguity from the term "nation" to the term "loyalty" (1973: 257), the shift is in fact productive. For it offers, from convergent work in different disciplines from a half-century ago, an underexplored pathway by which to challenge some of the too easily assumed givens of scholarship on nationalism. Geertz himself, speaking in 1993, suggested that the discourse on nationalism felt more like "batting about vaguely at clouds and vapors than coming to grips with etched-in selves" (1994: 4) and suggested that reviving attention to primordial loyalties might redress the balance and encourage a return to the microsociological level at which anthropologists, as well as many historians, believe that important things happen.[3]

This book proposes a radical reassessment of early twentieth-century Macedonian history in this spirit. It draws in particular on an empirically rich vein of work on revolutionary activism by social historians, including classic and lesser-known work on eighteenth- and nineteenth-century working-class movements, and on mid-twentieth-century anticolonial struggles. In work on Mau Mau in Kenya, for example, John Lonsdale criticized the "Western transubstantiations that have squeezed African responses to colonial rule into the prefabricated, imported, moulds of nationhood or class formation" (Berman and Lonsdale 1992: 317). From evidence on insurgent India, Ranajit Guha offered the observation that the effect of Indian historians' focus on state and state builders has been "to exclude the insurgent as the subject of his own history" (Guha 1999: 4), while E. P. Thompson, in his classic *The Making of the English Working Class,* stated the problem that popular resistance or dissent is read

> in the light of subsequent preoccupations, and not as in fact it occurred. . . .
> Only the successful (in the sense of those whose aspirations anticipated subsequent evolution) are remembered. The blind alleys, the lost causes, and the losers themselves are forgotten. (Thompson 1966: 12)

Thompson and Guha, respectively, take issue here with presentist approaches to the past and the class-based overwriting of subaltern agency, while Lonsdale offers an anthropologically grounded critique of ethnocentrism. Though based in empirical work in Western Europe, South Asia, and East Africa, their perspectives are, I suggest, relevant to the Macedonian case.[4] It is only, after all, when one attaches normative value to a world ordered into ostensibly homogenous nation-states, each inhabited by citizens who recognized that state as "theirs," that the "nation-ness" (or lack of same) of Macedonia's late nineteenth- and early twentieth-century inhabitants becomes a salient question. The frame, in other words, that constructs the region and its natives as vessels either waiting to be filled, or already overflowing, with the substance of national sentiment (what we might, perhaps, call zeal), owes everything to the perspective or prejudice of the observer.

Not Simply National: Macedonia's Unwritten Histories

To focus only on the absence or presence of national zeal, and zealots, in Macedonia is to discount the profusion of social, cultural, economic, and political movements that flourished and competed there. To be sure, large parts of the territory were thinly populated and undergoverned: in the felicitous Greek term, much of Macedonia was *agrapha*—undocumented or unwritten. As such, in the spirit of James Scott's work, it was not legible to authorities, and at least some areas—especially hills and swamps—represented a refuge from the burdens imposed by acquisitive regimes (Scott 1998: 2010).

But Scott, as well as anthropologists and historians of other times and other places, also reminds us of the politics embedded in such state-centric tropes of emptiness. Anna Tsing has written of how the logic of expansive capitalism constructs the forests of Indonesia as "empty" where they are, in fact, full of social connections and cultural meaning for local communities (Tsing 2005). Writing of the roots of the "Mau Mau" movement against British rule in Kenya, Tabitha Kanogo stresses the mismatch between Kikuyu models of land rights and British authorities' readiness to categorize apparently unworked land as "undeveloped," and therefore expropriate it for sale to settlers (Kanogo 1987: 10–11, 59).

Though embedded in a very different economic system, late nineteenth-century Macedonia was similarly far from empty of affective and instrumental ties, or of institutions vying for influence. It was a still-evolving product of dynamic changes in landholding practices, educational opportunities, and religious affiliations. This was partly a product of modernization efforts within the Ottoman Empire, especially reflected in the Tanzimat reforms between 1839 and 1876. But outside forces were also having an impact, as the steady retreat of the empire's frontiers—from mainland Greece and Serbia beginning in the early part of the century, and Bosnia-Hercegovina and Bulgaria after the Russo–Turkish war of 1878—brought Muslim refugees from these former outposts into Macedonia. Emboldened by such indicators of imperial decay, the governments of the new Balkan states of Greece, Serbia, and Bulgaria sought to position themselves to gain further territory in the future. And beyond that, the other European powers made their own plans to carve out spheres of influence and shape the map of the future, through a variety of intricate and often inconsistent treaties and agreements.

These states were not stable actors, but were themselves works in progress. It was in the critical period between 1870 and 1913 that the modern nation-states of Bulgaria and Albania were conjured, Greece more than doubled in size from the kingdom created in 1832, and the autonomy of Serbia, Romania, and Montenegro was formalized. Cultural and legal developments accompanied these territorial changes. A key factor, for example, in the rise of Bulgarian nationalism was the establishment of the Exarchate in 1870. For more than a century before this, all Macedonia's Orthodox Christians had been under the spiritual jurisdiction of the Greek Patriarchate and therefore counted simply as members of the "Rum" millet. When the sultan officially recognized the Exarchate, which offered services in Church Slavonic rather than Greek, he created the grounds for direct competition for the souls—and revenues—of congregations across Ottoman Europe, especially those territories where a majority of the population spoke a Slavic dialect rather than Greek.

Wittingly or not, the sultan's decision considerably polarized relations among once-fellow Christians, for whom "Patriarchist/Greek" and "Exarchist/Bulgar" increasingly became mutually exclusive and antagonistic. Rival churches also sponsored schools, investing heavily in educational outreach conducted under the sign of modernization and linguistic standardization. In this regard, their strategy served that of the nation-states of Greece and Bulgaria, which were simultaneously mimicking the strategies adopted by other European nation-states within their own borders, of turning peasants into loyal citizens (Weber 1976). The intrafaith rivalries grew more bitter and deadly, even as the head of the Exarchate, Exarch Josif, asserted in 1903 that

Figure 1.1. Turkey in Europe and its neighbors in 1893.

"revolution will not rescue Macedonia, only evolution and education" (Hopkins 2009: 162).

Josif's "evolutionist" approach was not universally embraced in Bulgaria or Macedonia, where many students, teachers, and other young professionals mobilized in response to the Treaty of Berlin of July 1878. Superseding the Treaty of San Stefano that ended the Russo–Turkish war in March of the same year, the Treaty of Berlin established the Principality of Bulgaria while leaving a substantial area of so-called "Bulgarian lands," where the Exarchate and its schools operated, under Ottoman rule. The treaty also included a clause calling for Ottoman provinces, especially those inhabited by Christians, to be granted substantial autonomy. The sultan's refusal to enact this clause prompted revolutionary activism in many areas of the empire, including Armenia, Crete, and Macedonia (Stead 1896); the MRO's immediate goal when first formed was to insist on the implementation of this clause. This was a more limited interpretation of "Macedonia for Macedonians" than most who invoke the phrase, caught up in methodological nationalism, can envision. The organization's urgency, and constitutional focus, quickly put it at odds with the exarch's gradualist policy.

Economic transformation was also underway. New technologies of governance and commerce—especially the telegraph and the railroad—transformed the physical landscape, speeding up police and military communication and also changing the relative importance of market towns, as those that were situated off the tracks declined. Western industrial products became more readily and widely available, including cotton goods from England and silverware and pots and pans from Germany and Austria; their low prices undercut those of local handiwork, placing new pressure on the livelihood of artisans and further driving local residents to migrate to find better-paying work elsewhere. One visible marker of these circuits was the near-ubiquitous petroleum tin, which after its contents fueled industrial acceleration was recycled by local tinsmiths, put to use as seats in low-end cafes or hostelries or flattened out to serve in the construction of shantytown dwellings (Brown 2003: 65–66). Astute and progressive observers at the time emphasized the ways in which these imports drove underdevelopment: they saw Macedonia as akin to an island where the detritus of modernization washes up, or goes to die, and where conventional signs of progress became instead markers of backwardness and oppression (Brailsford 1906: 4, 178).

These far-reaching changes—political, cultural, social, and economic—prompted a range of orchestrated, purposeful responses from Macedonia's native population that do not fit the simple mold of national awakening. In the historically distinct cases of England, India and Kenya, scholars have documented the efforts of intellectuals and ordinary folk either to protect what was under attack, or to create a new and better world for themselves and their descendants. The dawn of the twentieth century was marked by multiple examples of anti-imperialist and anticapitalist movements around the world. These included the Boers in South Africa, and Bengali and Irish revolutionary forces in India and Ireland, respectively, all opponents of British imperial rule; the Moros in the Philippines, fighting first Spain and then the United States; a variety of anti-imperialist forces in Czarist Russia; a range of Christian-led movements in Armenia, Crete, and Macedonia against Ottoman rule; the Hereros in German West Africa; and the Boxers in European-dominated China.

We know most about these various conflicts from the documents of the colonizers. Military reports, consular correspondence, special inquiries, and the intelligence work of agents all constitute important sources, as does the output of journalists, scholars, travelers, and missionaries with experience in-country. The nature of this source material, however, has also fragmented inquiry into the period along separate, national lines. The Herero Uprising, for example, has been examined by German historians concerned with the recurrence of genocidal methods in the country's twentieth-century history (Hull 2005). Russian activism in the late nineteenth century gets read, obviously, as buildup to the revolution and subsequent establishment of Soviet rule, while the U.S. engagement in the Philippines is often analyzed as start point for U.S. imperialism in Latin America (Miller 1982).

Modalities of Protest in Europe and Beyond

The uprisings of the period, then, are often understood and distinguished through analysis of the ripostes that they prompted, and their consequences. In the case of Macedonia this has driven historiographies that emphasize the protonational character of the period's political activism. But other modalities also existed, sometimes overshadowed by the kind of nationally or rationally inflected presentism that Thompson, Guha, Lonsdale, and Sahlins warn us against. This was a period in which internationalist orientations persisted, especially in a variety of politically leftist circles whose members envisaged republican modes of citizenship, or embraced socialist, redistributive ideals in the face of capitalism's spread and growth. As one example, the Carbonari secret societies of southern Italy (and beyond) are often seen simply as precursors of bourgeois-led national liberation movements; yet some at least had supranational, more egalitarian goals (Galt 1994: 796).

Additionally, where some protesters sought solace and solidarity in common visions of an ideal future, others struggled to cling onto old ways in the face of the new. These were the "primitive rebels" documented by Eric Hobsbawm (1959), ranging from "Captain Swing" and the machine breakers of the English countryside (responding to new industrial conditions of production), to the robber-bandits of imperial Russia and Turkey (whose agenda was more narrowly antigovernmental). In both cases they have been cast as backward-looking and conservative, seeking to preserve former liberties and lifeways at the local level rather than collaborating with others to construct or envisage new alternatives. Again, though, like the Carbonari, they find themselves enlisted as the colorful heroes of national heritage. This has been especially the case in the Balkans, where Greek, Bulgarian, and Serbian folklore celebrates the cunning and defiance of the *klefts, hajduks, junaks,* and *vojvodas* who operated outside (or at least not fully within) the laws set during the centuries of Ottoman occupation (Koliopoulos 1987; Koljević 1980).

Elsewhere, the appropriation of such figures is contested by other currents of history. Nineteenth-century Russia is generally considered the birthplace of more radical anarchist ideas, which sought simply to confront and destroy an existing system of oppression. No new solidarity or social order was envisaged: in the Revolutionary Catechism of 1869, attributed to Bakunin and Nechaev, the revolutionary is identified as a "lost man" who has severed all ties with his fellow men and knows only the science of destruction. The catechism then charges the revolutionary to nonetheless "draw close to the people" and to ally himself with the brigands, with the ultimate goal "to regroup this world of brigands into an invincible and omni-destructive force" (Venturi 1966: 367).

Other forms of civic association too flourished on both sides of the Atlantic, of which the most famous (or infamous) are the Freemasons, but which also included the Oddfellows. In the national mythology of the United States, in which de Tocqueville's account of associational life looms large, such organizations constituted civil society and gave the country its particular democratic character; membership was often publicly proclaimed as a point of pride. Sometimes created with no broader goal than to deliver basic services to their members (burial, in particular, often being salient), such intermediary and voluntary organizations proliferated, and evidence suggests that they played a far more significant role in people's lives, and senses of self, than scholars of modern nation-states can readily appreciate (Skocpol 2003).

In conservative Europe, the status of such organizations was far more ambiguous and threatening, and they were more often construed by members and by authorities as the seedbeds of radicalism and nonconformity. In England, for example, in the aftermath of the French Revolution, Parliament passed laws against any and all secret organizations, including laws that imposed the death penalty for those swearing illegal oaths (Thompson 1966: 169). Yet people continued to join such organizations, and found new ones, throughout the following century. Thus forty years later, in 1831, a new Huddersfield Branch of the Old Mechanics was founded, and its first recorded purchase was a pistol, a bible, and ten yards of curtain material for the purpose of giving the oath to new members (ibid.: 511).

What all these cases point to is the creativity, imaginative capacity, and determination of a range of actors in nineteenth-century Europe and beyond who set out to preserve or remake the world by their efforts along channels that were not, necessarily, those of the industrial nation-state. Some looked forward, others "backward or heavenward" (Walton 1984: 200). Some rejected violence, others deployed it carefully against key enemies, others embraced mayhem. What all these movements had in common, though, was the challenge of building and maintaining of collective trust and the capacity for action with little in the way of economic or cultural resources. And despite the efforts of the authorities to deny it, they often achieved these goals. Thompson allows himself a moment of presentism in making this argument. Commenting on a mass demonstration in the Midlands, which prior scholars readily dismissed or downplayed as a mere reflex action by unruly workmen, he writes,

> Anyone who has conducted a raffle or organized a darts tournament knows
> that scores of men cannot be assembled at night, from several districts, at
> a given point; disguised and armed with muskets, hammers and hatchets;

formed into line; mustered by number; marched several miles to a successful attack, to the accompaniment of signal lights and rockets—and all with the organization of a spontaneous college "rag." (Thompson 1966: 576–77)

What the movements Thompson describes shared with their illegal or subversive counterparts elsewhere was a set of mechanisms of recruitment, retention, cohesion, and control. None could be taken for granted if an organization was to survive; each step demanded its own symbolic and practical apparatus in order to contend with the range of rival demands that other longer-established, or more powerful institutions placed on members. Kin obligations, religious sanctions, economic rewards, or state reprisals all threatened their existence. At the same time, all these forms of motivation offered templates on which such organizations selectively drew in their own practices designed to instill and enforce loyalty among members and to their shared cause—whatever that cause was.

The Unruly Archive: Comparative Perspectives in Historical Ethnography

How, though, to enter the world of illicit or historically marginalized actors to gather the empirical data to sustain interpretations that run against the grain? This is a problem for ethnographers and historians alike who seek to identify movements to establish "terminal community" in crowded, rivalrous contexts. In the immediate present, detailed accounts of the workings of insurgency in Iraq or the durability of support for the Taliban in Afghanistan remain elusive (though see Hashim 2006; Sinno 2008; Edwards 2002). Organizations (and their members) do not survive by being loose-lipped, especially in the presence of obvious outsiders. In her research into Mau Mau, even forty years after the fact, historian Caroline Elkins found potential informants still bound by the oaths of secrecy they had sworn, and therefore reluctant to divulge confidences (Elkins 2005: 27). Some early secret societies destroyed their own written records every year (Hobsbawm 1959: 160); others' records survive only in fragmented, captured form in official archives, which have their own vulnerabilities. All these remind us that "direct" archives of dissent and defiance are rare. More often, the form and content of these dispositions must be derived from narratives or archives constructed for a quite different purpose than providing a portal into the hearts and minds of the insurgents of the past.

In terms of method, I take inspiration from three broad strands in the use of narrative archival material to conduct historical ethnography. The foundational text is Natalie Zemon Davis's *Fiction in the Archives*. Davis's focus is pardon tales, submitted to a merciful king by sixteenth-century French citizens under sentence of death (Davis 1987). In her pathbreaking book, she focuses on narrative form rather than content. Her core argument is that the institution of the royal pardon had certain consistent and disciplining effects, and served the interest of the king in affirming both his mercy and his power, in the frames it demanded people place their stories in. She discovered a consistent pattern of contrition rather than the bragging, boastful terms in which a young man might narrate the kind of confrontation that often led to accidental killing, which thus showcased the letters' obligatory tone as "among the civilizing mechanisms of the early modern French state" (ibid. 57–58). She also notes differences in the ways different sets of stories resemble one another: while men's stories cluster along lines of occupation or estate, women's (of which there are substantially fewer) appear to emphasize their identities as wives or widows and are closely tied to domestic issues.

Davis was drawn to this particular source because, she argues, they gave a better sense of "relatively uninterrupted narrative from the lips of the lower orders" (ibid.: 5). Although no doubt often transcribed and perhaps reworked by scribes or lawyers trained in rhetoric, she sees nonetheless greater freedom of expression in these tales than in inquisition or other legal transcripts, another favored source of historians looking to capture the flavor of social life. Witnesses are interrupted or led, and more often than not the format is asking them to contribute detail to a master narrative orchestrated by a more powerful individual or institution. Such is the case in Le Roy Ladurie's *Montaillou* or Carlo Ginzburg's *Cheese and the Worms,*where authors reconstruct the dissident worldview of a community and an individual, respectively, from the transcripts of their investigations by church authorities (Ladurie 1979; Ginzburg 1980).

Davis's work has had a profound influence beyond her immediate object of study. In *Stalin's Outcasts,* which traces attempts by dispossessed Soviet citizens to rehabilitate themselves, historian Golfo Alexopoulos suggests an analogy between the ways in which the French king and the Soviet authorities constructed themselves as merciful. She sees, though, an important difference in the genres of sixteenth-century France and mid-twentieth-century

Soviet Russia. In the latter case, argues Alexopoulos, applicants drew on the form of the traditional lament, or *plach*, which served rhetorically to thrust moral responsibility onto the reader to act to improve the situation (Alexopoulos 2003: 115–22). Thus she interprets her case as one in which at least some individuals drew on existing cultures of narration to outflank Stalin's authority, rather than, as in Davis's case, necessarily adopting narrative modes demanded by the king.

Besides her debt to Davis's work, Alexopoulos's insight comes out of the recent explosion of opportunity created by the opening of Soviet archives to researchers. The leading figure in this development remains Sheila Fitzpatrick, who in a number of influential articles and books has mined the archives for different categories of sources to paint a vivid picture of, as she puts it in her 1999 book subtitle, ordinary life in extraordinary times. Where Alexopoulos focuses her attention on a set of appeals generated by disenfranchised individuals seeking reinstatement of citizen rights, Fitzpatrick documents a range of other kinds of citizen-regime interaction, among them the phenomenon of letter writing with a number of different purposes, including the expression of loyalty, attacks on leadership (mostly anonymous), and the denunciation of other citizens (Fitzpatrick 1994, 1999). Fitzpatrick has also used these sources as a basis for a comparative study of denunciation practices (Fitzpatrick and Gellately 1997). The picture created is of a society where fear and uncertainty dominate and where people frequently seek their own salvation by staging attacks on others, often neighbors or relatives.[5]

The third well-developed strand of multinational and interdisciplinary archival studies centers around the critical analysis of British colonial rule in India. In the United States, Bernard Cohn (1987, 1996) has documented the different ways in which the British administration produced knowledge of Indian society in their model of liberal imperialism, focusing in particular on the ethnographic impulse at work. His work inspired subsequent generations of South Asianists, including for example Nicholas Dirks (1993, 2002), who has reflected, after Cohn, on the disciplinary differences of historians and anthropologists drawing on the same kinds of data, with very different projects. Both have acknowledged the power and range of scholarship in India on colonial history, which produced the influential "subaltern school" pioneered by Ranajit Guha and brought into wider circulation in the United States by luminaries such as Partha Chatterjee and Giyatry Spivak, who have elaborated their own archival approaches (Guha 1999; Chatterjee 2002; Spivak 1985). All these scholars recognize that the archives record a contested process of attempts by the colonizer to "know" the colonized—attempts that, as Ranajit Guha has argued, "could never be neutral to the relation of dominance and subordination which bound them together" (in Cohn 1987: xix). The subaltern school builds on this consensus regarding the nature of British colonial archives to read them "against the grain"—in other words, by using a form of structuralist analysis to derive from these partial, consistently inflected sources the alternative history of indigenous resistance from the margins, as it were (Axel [ed.] 2002).

One particularly illuminating product of the subaltern school is Shahid Amin's account of a peasant riot in the town of Chauri Chaura in Uttar Pradesh in 1922. The rioters burned the police station and killed 23 policemen, to cries of "Victory to Mahatma Gandhi!" Their resort to violence was disowned by Gandhi himself and punished by the authorities, who brought charges against 225 defendants, initially sentenced 172 to death, and in July 1923 hanged 19 identified as ringleaders. Like Alexopoulos, Amin makes reference to Natalie Zemon Davis as "master practitioner" in the handling of narratives produced in encounters between lowly individuals and powerful authorities, yet shaped by oral traditions and sociocultural context (1992: 195). Where Davis focuses on "narrative performance" (1987: 196), though, Amin gives as his own concern "narrative detail"; he is concerned to fully utilize the different kinds of sources he has at his disposal, including the colonial court records, the nationalist historiography that brands the rioters as "rogues," and local oral histories that he himself collected. He describes how he weaves together the three strands of source material—the colonial/subaltern, the nationalist, and the oral historical, in the following succinct statement:

> Subaltern recollections of historical events—historic because they are on record as infractions of the law which did not go unnoticed or unpunished—are also remembrances of the role of the police and the judge. Novel and emphatic recollections of nationalist activity in the villages similarly yield significant clues about the ways of peasant activists. Therefore the fieldwork in this book is not intended to supersede the colonial and the nationalist archive. Rather, it is placed in a complex relationship of variation to the official record. (Amin 1995: 197)

Friction in the Archives (1): Consular and Journalistic Accounts

These three traditions—of exchanges between subjects and rulers in authoritarian, communist, and colonial states respectively—all inform this work of historical ethnography.[6] In particular, they provide guidance on how to marry together the data and perspectives from the two very distinct sets of sources that are at the heart of the book. The first is the consular record briefly introduced at the start of this chapter. Britain, France, Germany, Austria, and Russia all maintained consular offices across Ottoman Europe, including in Uskub, Salonika, and Monastir, the last of which was ground zero for the 1903 uprising.[7] Through the 1890s and 1900s they provided voluminous accounts of the battle for influence between the Exarchate and the Patriarchate, the activities of the different Balkan nations' "commercial agents," the uneven path of reform trod by the Ottoman authorities as they grappled with counterinsurgency methods while under international scrutiny, and, of course, the activities and aspirations of their great power rivals in the region.[8] They also charted the influx of war correspondents, humanitarian workers, and adventurers drawn to the violence of the region, many of whom produced their own accounts of their visits and observations to an area that fit closely with Carolyn Nordstrom's definition of a warscape (Nordstrom 1997: 37).

These sources lend themselves to the kinds of counterreading proposed by the subaltern school, but with an extra inflection. First, in the modality identified by Jane Cowan among League of Nations officials two decades later, they write in the role of supervisors, observers, or commentators of rulers as well as ruled in the region (Cowan 2007). They can be trawled for various kinds of racism and primitivism, directed both at the workings of the Ottoman state and at the practices of the various Christian, Jewish, and Muslim inhabitants of the region (Todorova 1997). But what gives them still greater interest is the diversity of perspectives—often at war with each other—that they represent. Within the British consular ranks, for example, it is clear that James McGregor, the young vice consul in Monastir between April 1903 and July 1904, often saw things differently from his superior, Sir Alfred Biliotti, stationed in Thessaloniki. Both demonstrate a commitment to on-the-ground empirical reporting, especially in correcting claims of mass murder. But where McGregor knew Bulgarian, cultivated sources close to the organization, and reported general support, Biliotti—a naturalized British subject who was born in Rhodes, spoke five languages and had worked his way up from the post of *dragoman*, or "fixer"—had stronger contacts and sympathies with the Patriarchist, Greek communities (Dakin 1966: 94, 98; Wyon 1904: 116). So where Biliotti reports the depredations of the committee in early 1903 and widespread "bitter resentment" toward the tax payments they levied, McGregor, reported (to Biliotti) less than two months later "the incontestable fact of the ready co-operation of the peasantry with the insurgents" (FO 195/2156/352: April 3, 1903, McGregor to Biliotti). Biliotti's recommendations, in general, counseled support for the status quo, while McGregor's reflected a sense of empathy for the insurgents.[9]

Consular officials also interacted with Western visitors in different ways that could reflect professional respect, shared sympathies, or the opposite. In 1904, McGregor stood up for *Daily Mail* journalist Reginald Wyon when the Ottoman government sought his expulsion, reporting that Wyon's coverage of Ottoman reprisals against local villagers was largely accurate. While both were critical of the increasing resort to violent methods, Wyon shared McGregor's broadly supportive stance toward the organization's goals. Biliotti, by contrast, was critical of journalists that he reported as alleging atrocities by Ottoman troops where none existed. His objections to journalists who acted as provocateurs were not, perhaps, solely due to his anti-insurgent stance. In 1898, British aristocrat Leopold Amery, Fellow of All Souls College, Oxford, future Conservative MP, and staunch advocate of imperial reform, had come to Skopje as a freelance reporter for the *Guardian*. In letters to his mother in February he reported outrage that a number of Bulgarians who tried to visit him were arrested and maltreated. In the course of his attempted intervention, an Ottoman policeman tried to physically drag him away, whereupon Amery clubbed him with an umbrella. Charged with assault, he "politely but firmly declined" (his words) to appear in Turkish court, and eventually the matter was settled to everyone's satisfaction (Amery, Barnes, and Nicholson 1980: 26). Amery records that the Bulgarians were happy with this direct challenge to Ottoman authority, while the Turks plotted to kill him. He also drew on the episode as an example of how stories get exaggerated through rumor, as reported in the same volume:

> The following autumn, travelling in the neighbouring Sanjak of Novibazar, he was [sic] greeted by the story of the previous winter's Macedonian insurrection, the climax of which was the saving of the insurgents from extermination

by an Englishman of gigantic stature—Amery was only five feet four inches tall—who armed only with a club, had routed two Turkish battalions. (ibid.: 27–28)

This episode reads differently in British consular correspondence. Although the vice consul in Salonika at the time shared an affiliation with Amery—they were both "Balliol men" who graduated from the same Oxford college—the report filed on the incident from the Salonika consulate paints Amery in a less flattering light than his own recollection. He comes across less as champion of the oppressed Christians and more as provocateur out to create a diplomatic row, in part by his attempt at subterfuge in not declaring his journalistic intent (he had described himself as a professor of geography and stenography) and, in the words of the consular record, "asking stupid questions like 'are you Serbian?' and 'Stop, let me take your photograph'" of Albanians between Skopje and Prizren (FO 195/2029/45: January 25, 1898).

This revealing account of Amery's exploits, along with consular commentary on the clashes between other journalists and Ottoman authorities, demonstrates the careful reading that these sources demand. Individual voices remain distinct, and they reveal the limits and scope of their knowledge. In this last case the consul, as resident, shows awareness of demographic and cultural realities (the sensitivity of ethnoreligious categories, and suspicion felt toward photographic equipment) that the tourist, be he ever so scholarly in his pretension, does not grasp.

What this episode also confirms is the need for caution in overvaluing contemporary, eyewitness accounts by travelers. At first glance, the abundance of "proxy-fieldworkers"—observers of life, customs, and conditions—appears to represent a considerable boon. They are accessible and diverse in their own right, ranging from the firsthand experience of band life by Miss Ellen Stone, a Boston missionary kidnapped for ransom in 1901, through the adventurer accounts of American and British men who tagged along with revolutionary bands and sometimes engaged in firefights with Ottoman troops, to the investigative work of humanitarian activists like H. N. Brailsford and Edith Durham, who participated in relief efforts (Stone 1902; Sonnichsen 1909; Smith 1908; Brailsford 1906; Durham 1905). The consuls round out this set, surely particularly valuable because their driving concern was the same as this inquiry—what was the MRO and how did it work?

For all that, though, power relations between authors and their objects of study profoundly shaped the data they could access and the conclusions they drew. Although freelance journalists like Albert Sonnichsen clearly acquired experience-near knowledge through their willingness to undergo the hardships of insurgent life, for the most part these various external observers never fully won the trust of Macedonian activists. Language barriers, as well as the restrictions put in place by the Ottoman authorities, made contact with a wider set of civilians difficult. Over time, Edith Durham established something close to ethnographic rapport with a number of Albanian clans in the region; others relied heavily on interpreters and based themselves in major cities. The enthusiasm they report encountering—characterized by the efforts of those Bulgarians to visit Amery in his hotel—owed much to the perception that they might be a resource for people facing desperate circumstances. Insofar as these are primary sources, then, they have their own frictions. And at times—as where, for example, Edith Durham appears to directly contradict H. N. Brailsford over stories of Christian women (his "chosen people") driven (literally) barking mad by their sufferings at the hands of Albanian irregular troops (hers)—the effect is to draw the reader's attention away from the realities of Macedonia to the prestige games of British intellectual life (Brailsford 1906: 37; Durham 1905: 132–33).

Friction in the Archives (2): The Ilinden Dossier Between Memory and History

The second set of materials blurs the category of "primary source" in a different way and poses a different set of challenges for archival methods. Among what John Davis (1994: 205) would call the "turdish aide-memoires" in the National Archives in Skopje—alongside account books of merchants, church records, and other primary sources from the Ilinden period—is the Ilinden Dossier, a set of approximately 3,500 pension applications dating from the early 1950s. These were submitted to the new Yugoslav Macedonian government by men and women in their sixties and older, in the expectation or hope that their activism in the Ilinden period would receive state recognition and yield them a pension.[10] For a majority, it did: statistical reports in the dossier indicate that by the end of 1954, a total of 2,154 pensions had already been given. When all the applications were archived in the 1960s, the 3,476 applications were divided between 41 boxes of alphabetized applications containing 3,218 files, and a further box, labeled as "not awarded," containing the remaining 258. Pension amounts ranged from 1,000 to 8,000 dinars per month; the modal amount was 3,500 dinars.

I have described the context for this pension scheme, and the application process, more fully elsewhere (Brown 2003: 130–52). In this book, my primary concern is with the period from 1893 to 1903, which they ostensibly describe, rather than the period from 1948 to 1954, which they simultaneously illuminate. The focus here, in particular, is on the content of the individual biographies that applicants were invited to submit, and that some did. These could range from a few lines to several pages: in some cases, responding to unfavorable decisions by the state commission, applicants submitted supplementary versions containing more detail. Including the concise, data-rich, and well-ordered biography by Nikola Zdraveski presented in the introduction, and fourteen other personal accounts included in an appendix, I draw here on a sample of 375, chosen with a focus on the area around Bitola, Prilep, and Kruševo in the modern Republic of Macedonia.[11] In aggregate, they provide a remarkably consistent and rich account of life in turn-of-the-century Macedonia. Most of the men identify themselves by profession, including tailors (like Zdraveski), masons, milk sellers, butchers, stock keepers, charcoal burners, sharecroppers, and fieldhands. This kind of emplotment, and the contrastive tendency for women to use marriages to provide a chronological frame, is in keeping with the trends noted by Natalie Zemon Davis. Many of the communities in which pension seekers lived had long traditions of migrant labor to urban centers in Asia Minor, Bulgaria, Greece, and Serbia, and community-level specialties revealed themselves. A high percentage of autobiographers from the villages of Capari and Gjavato, for example, earned their livelihood from producing charcoal, and many did so by traveling along one or more of several established circuits that linked their villages to Izmir in Anatolia, Katerini on the Greek border, and specific regions in Romania and Serbia.

Additionally, the narratives provide considerable data regarding people's experiences of the Macedonian Revolutionary Organization that orchestrated the Ilinden Uprising. Most referred to it simply as "the organization" and portrayed an entity that wielded power of life and death over its sworn members and boasted its own internal hierarchy, structure, and (possibly) culture. Former members, even a half-century later, defined themselves and other members as organizers, couriers, terrorists, receivers, *četniks,* secretaries, and treasurers, each with specified duties.

Obviously, then, the Ilinden Dossier offers the potential to serve as a rich source through which to enter the world of turn-of-the-century Macedonian activists. The three traditions in the analysis of narrative archival material, though, demonstrate the need to pay close attention to the context of production and the further ambiguities and tensions it may engender. In the first place, as noted above, the biographies in the dossier took their current, sworn form some fifty years after the events they ostensibly describe, which raises issues of "simple" error or misremembering. Second, its principal authors were, self-evidently, self-interested—their narrative accounts had an often explicit agenda of material reward, pointing to the possibility of deliberate deception. Third, it quickly becomes obvious, on reading, that the writers' experiences, or how they choose to represent them, were very diverse. Some had much to tell, some hardly anything; some were undoubtedly more selective than their more garrulous or inventive peers.

What also emerges from even a cursory reading, though, is the clear evidence here too of active friction among contributors to the dossier. Where some—like Zdraveski—included the names of living consociate as witnesses and were quickly approved for pensions with which they were satisfied, that experience was far from universal. For other applicants the documentary record contains multiple biographies, rejection letters, appeals, and third-party letters of affirmation of denunciation, signaling a more complex process of negotiation between individual and state.

Mate Boškoski, for example, also from Kruševo, reported much greater involvement than Zdraveski in his biography (provided in appendix 2)—including details of purchasing and storing rifles and ammunition and helping with preparations for the uprising itself. He received a lesser pension, and in his correspondence with the commission calls their decision making absurd (Record 5-B-27). Another applicant, Petar Kolarević, from the village of Svetomirci near Prilep, questioned the fairness of a generous award given to a prominent Ilinden veteran who had spent considerable time in North America since 1903 and now served on the commission to identify worthy recipients. Kolarević made the argument that the scheme should first benefit those who had stayed in the country to oppose the various anti-Macedonian regimes of the intervening period (Record 17-K-49). One set of appeals lodged in 1951, by seven villagers from Capari, in the Bitola region, claimed that negative verdicts against them had been engineered by an unscrupulous local committee. They demanded—and received—a review, which reached a favorable decision. From Gjavato, D. Petre Markovski addressed the commission in confrontational style, stating "I don't know why the other Ilindeners in my village have been given a larger pension than me" (Record 21-M-42).

All these styles of engagement between petitioner and authority point to a different relationship from that described in any of the three strands of archival methodology described above. There are clear signs that the communication people presumed was not limited to a distanced, respectful form of entreaty: instead, working in a state that had an ideology of equality as a "people's republic," various individuals record their determination to make the regime live up to its word. One man, Spiro Lazarov Stojanovski of Ramna, records an attempt to enlist his son-in-law to intercede directly with the Macedonian premier, Lazar Koliševski (Record 33-S-21). Another, Elena Grueva, who had been approved for a widow's pension under the similar Bulgarian scheme in 1943, wrote a complaint in 1947 in which she describes repeated visits to the Bitola office of the scheme to press her case (Record 8-G-39).[12] These are not cowed supplicants of a powerful state, but people with a sense of entitlement and willingness to stand up for themselves in their search for justice.

At the same time, the stories they told did not coalesce around an accepted master narrative, but instead, in their diversity, highlight that no such narrative had yet been set. What would emerge over the course of the Yugoslav–Macedonian period was a hybrid socialist-nationalist narrative of the Ilinden Uprising that put it in the tradition of the French Revolution and other progressive popular movements and that, more centrally, yoked it to the liberation movement of World War II, known as the Anti-Fascist Council for the National Liberation of Macedonia, or ASNOM (Veskoviḱ-Vangeli 1995). In this vein, Ilinden was cast as precursor to Yugoslav solidarity on class lines, and Macedonian history carefully distinguished from Bulgarian or Greek distortions.

The virtue of the Ilinden Dossier as a source is that it predates and defies such morally freighted categorical affiliations and distinctions. Few of these accounts reflect any such authorized version, because that version did not yet exist. ASNOM is barely mentioned. The antifascist struggle of the period from 1941 to 1945 is referenced by 13 out of the 375, mostly in the formulaic tag line of the period, "Death to fascism—freedom for the people!"

By contrast, many pension seekers emplotted their activism in 1903 as a concrete expression of their commitment to the ideal of an autonomous Macedonia, in line with the MRO's agenda. In the context of the late 1940s and early 1950s, though, such a stance was problematic for the Yugoslav Macedonian state. After 1948, when Stalin ejected Tito from the Comintern and brought an end to Yugoslav aspirations to create an expanded Macedonia, the commitment to "autonomous Macedonia," if understood as a larger geographical unit including parts of Greek and Bulgarian territory, had switched value. Until then, it had been a weapon serving Yugoslav interest; but after 1948, it represented a potential threat to the federal republic. This, then, was a further component of the frictions in the Ilinden Dossier—it pointed to the popularity among a segment of the population of ideas that were geopolitically dangerous. Biographies from natives of Greek Macedonia, in particular, now refugees in the Republic of Macedonia, were a reminder of the extent to which Ilinden had been organized on territory only later separated by borders which in the post–World War II period were clearly marked by the international community as inviolable.

Additionally, by stating their support for an organization that some called not TMORO or MRO, but VMRO, pensioners were again disrupting the preferred narrative of the new state. VMRO was by the 1920s associated with a criminal terrorist enterprise that operated out of western Bulgaria and had lost its former close ties with ordinary Macedonians. Its leader since 1924, Ivan (Vančo) Mihajlov, had openly collaborated with the German occupation, reportedly even flying in late in the war to consider an offer to play the same role of leader in Macedonia that Ante Pavelić of the Ustaša played in Croatia (U.S. Department of State 1954). Although Mihajlov refused the German offer, the name of VMRO still represented a form of right-wing, pro-Bulgarian nationalism that was profoundly threatening to the new authorities in Skopje.

All this background could be, and has been, taken as reason to discredit or marginalize the dossier as a historical source. To my knowledge it was not used systematically by Yugoslav-era Macedonian historians, who (as I understand it) found the narratives it contains too noisy, unruly, and partial. By contrast, these very qualities can be read as affirmations of the particularity and authenticity of the Ilinden Dossier's contents, both in political and evidentiary terms. Where many of the archival sources used by critical historians arose from contexts of adversarial or antagonistic relations between individual narrator and powerful authority—as, for example, in accounts that draw directly on court-room transcripts—the Ilinden Dossier is the record of an attempt by a state to enlist citizens as allies in an effort to recover "ground-level" truth. While the individual narratives do transformational and discriminatory work—identifying some individuals as rights-bearing persons under law, while denying those rights to others—in its aggregate effect the dossier is the legacy of a project to engineer loyalty by forging a relationship of mutual interest between a part of the population who enjoyed moral standing in their communities and the new government. Certainly financial incentives were offered. But the scheme also delivered symbolic rewards of validation.

The Ilinden Dossier thus records, represents, and demands different forms of archival imagination. Although at times the extended process of application, resolution, appeal, and complaint shows likenesses with the Soviet material, the process is marked by greater openness. Each submitted biography bears the names of two witnesses who confirm its contents, and people frequently declare knowledge of the awards received by others and use that knowledge to demand equitable treatment. Though there is evidence of anomie and distrust, the overall impression the dossier creates is of optimism and celebration. Although there is, obviously, an individualistic and self-interested aspect, a powerful sense emerges of a collective memory of past solidarity and struggle. It can be read as an archive of popular liberation, akin to the product of a large-scale oral history project in a democratic state. The very unruliness and uncertainties of the period of production, which made this source so unmanageable for Yugoslav-era Macedonian historians, enhance the value of the Ilinden Dossier as a key resource with which to recontextualize Gladstone's provocative question, engage with comparative and interdisciplinary perspectives on dissident thought and insurgent action, and think past the nation in making sense of early twentieth-century Macedonian political activism.

CHAPTER TWO

The Horizons of the "Peasant": Circuits of Labor and Insurgency

In the mid-nineteenth century, Karl Marx famously explained the inaction of France's peasants to act in their own interests by referring to the nation as "formed by simple addition of homologous magnitudes, much as potatoes in a sack form a sack of potatoes" (Marx 1963: 124). In the 1930s, R. H. Tawney pictured the prototypical fatalistic peasant as "standing permanently up to the neck in water, so that even a ripple might drown him" (cited in Scott 1976: vii), while Calvin Hoover wrote of Russian peasants' "reserve of Asiatic resignation to the inscrutable decrees of fate" (cited in Engerman 2003: 171). In their presumed passivity and conservatism, then, peasants have inspired memorable turns of phrase.

For many theorists and policy makers, especially in neighboring countries, the Ottoman Empire's Orthodox Christian peasantry—the stolid figures in the fields driving wooden plows pulled by water buffaloes, or occupying wattle huts in lowland villages close by malarial swamps—fit this stereotype. Slumped in what Edward Banfield, a scholar far from Marxian in outlook, would later dub "amoral familism" (Banfield 1958), paralyzed from forming any meaningful connections beyond the household, atomistic without being individualistic, the peasants of Ottoman Macedonia have been widely viewed as passive victims of fate, awaiting salvation from outside intervention, whether divine or European.

This view was shared by multiple constituencies at the time. Foreign diplomats, with their own imperial baggage and (at least in the case of the British) clear notions of class, bore witness to the "chronic destitution of the peasantry" (FO 195/2182/16: McGregor to Graves, January 4, 1904) and observed that many of the rural population enjoyed "no real security or feeling of confidence in the future" (FO 195/2156/74: Fontana to Biliotti, January 20, 1903). They concluded that improvement was unlikely and that the "frame of mind of the peasants in general can hardly be described as one of enthusiasm, indeed their intellectual level seems . . . too low to admit of such a feeling"

(195/2182/88: McGregor to Graves, February 10, 1904). Wretchedness was writ plain to see in the shantytowns at the edges of imperial cities, the inhabitants' perceived indifference to health and hygiene, stories of injustice and victimization, and the pathetic faith in foreign intervention. All are described in ways that resonate with accounts of beaten-down peasants in other times and other places, such as those offered of Russia's peasants during the Cold War (Engerman 2003).

Many of the journalists and humanitarian workers who visited the province reached similar conclusions, especially those who came in the immediate aftermath of the uprising, when Ottoman reprisals had left more than 70,000 civilians homeless and, together with the demands of the organization, had created severe food shortages. Borrowing a metaphor from his native London, Allen Upward dubbed the province the "East End of Europe" (Upward 1908), while Brailsford diagnosed "Eastern fatalism" and Edith Durham described "a sort of bovine stolidity, heavy, apathetic, interested chiefly in petty quarrels, and seeing that they got as much 'relief' as the people next door" (Brailsford 1906: 70–1; Durham 1905: 133).[1]

This impression of a backward, isolated, and supine people also appealed to the propagandists of the new states. Officials in both Greece and Bulgaria, rivals for control of the region, presented its rural Christian population as inert, incapable of autonomous action, and awaiting leadership from outside. In these nationalist narratives, although the peasantry knew who they were, deep down (Greeks or Bulgarians, respectively), they lacked the ability to speak for themselves, and these two nation-states were thus compelled to act on their behalf. Bulgarian authors emphasized the role of Bulgarian-educated elites in forming the organization and leading the Ilinden Uprising, while Greek sources stressed the lack of wider, indigenous Macedonian support for either.

A similar view of the limited horizons and capacities of Macedonia's rural population is also accepted and propagated in some of the most significant publications on late Ottoman Macedonia. Writing in the 1960s and drawing primarily on Greek-language sources, Douglas Dakin considered that the numbers of insurgents reported by Brailsford, relying on MRO sources, were laughably exaggerated (Dakin 1966: 99n). Duncan Perry, writing in the 1980s, treated Bulgarian and Macedonian claims regarding the scale of the uprising more seriously. He was nevertheless skeptical of accounts of widespread rural enthusiasm, basing that view on comparative reading on rural populations in Asia, Latin America, and the Middle East. From those sources in anthropology and political science, he was convinced of the "apathetic and quiescent state that normally characterizes their [peasants'] outlook" (Foster 1967: 8; cited in Perry 1988: 150) and applied it to late nineteenth-century Macedonia's rural population.

This broad consensus regarding rural mentality has profoundly shaped dominant understandings of the Ilinden Uprising. If peasants turned out to fight, most analysts conclude, they must have been coerced or duped by external agents—either in another country or from the urban centers of the empire itself. In an analysis that derives indirectly from the psychologically oriented methodological individualism of Samuel Huntington and Ted Gurr, Perry argues that young men from village origins, with expectations raised by schooling, came to the city in search of a better life, only to run up against barriers to further upward mobility. They were, then, driven into the arms of the revolutionary movement by their sense of relative deprivation; when they were mobilized, their horizons were those of the school system they had attended, in most cases Bulgarian (Perry 1988: 28–30; see Gurr 1970).

At the heart of Perry's model of motivation is a strong contrast between staid tradition and restless modernity, located in the rural hinterland and the cities and towns respectively. This division is then read into the minds of the people in each place: new urbanites are easily agitated, while peasants are disengaged and conservative, invested only in familial survival. The result of this interpretation is to deny the rural population of Macedonia any substantive agency, and any kind of positive energy. Instead, they become mere ciphers, manipulated by the urban leaders on whom Perry's analysis focuses. Movement to the city is given to instill a certain "modern consciousness" that breeds, depending on one's point of view, malcontents and troublemakers, or national converts.

Disaggregating Peasants: Alternative Perspectives

Perry's analysis is certainly parsimonious and neat. It also has the virtue of matching some archival sources: On May 12, 1903, for example, Sir Alfred Biliotti reported that "Mr. Schopoff, the Bulgarian agent, gives out the version that it is the vast number of young Bulgarians who finished 2–3 years schooling and thought it beneath them to return to work in the fields who make up the backbone of the Organization" (FO 195/ 2156/560: see also Brailsford 1906: 42). The Salonika High School, attended by several MRO luminaries including Boris Sarafov and Goce Delčev, was seen as a hotbed of revolutionary thought and activism (MacDermott 1978: 71). A number of individual participants' narratives in the Ilinden Dossier, including those of Lazar Svetiev and Angel Korobar included in appendix 2, assign considerable significance to their encounters with inspirational teachers or school classmates in Bitola, Veles, and other towns.

Neatness and parsimony, though, do not always manifest themselves in messy reality. Schopoff found a ready audience in Biliotti, who was consistently skeptical of the organization's broader support. But evidence mounted to challenge this view, until even Biliotti himself acknowledged that villagers were providing support to the organization's leaders and bands. As noted earlier, consular sources reveal different perspectives. McGregor referred to "ready co-operation of the peasantry with the insurgents" (FO 195/2156/352), whereas Biliotti saw the power of coercion at work. In either case, these professional realists came to recognize the steady spread into the countryside of a disciplined, secret movement, linked up by an effective postal service, resourced by taxes, voluntary contributions, and funds from kidnapping, and policed and protected by mobile armed bands. In the words of one later writer, "they knew that all that existed, but they were only able to see slow buffaloes and shuffling, plodding peasants" (Doolaard 1935: 104).

The verdict of the better-informed consuls and contemporary observers compel a reassessment of the view that Macedonian peasants—and perhaps others too—are best understood as what Perry termed a "conservative and frightened society" (1988: 151). The authority of that view can be challenged both in the cases from which it was derived and in its application to other parts of the world. Perry's work betrays the kind of cross-disciplinary time lag that often occurs; a majority of the works he cites on peasant mentality date from the 1960s. He does not acknowledge the fierce debates around peasant studies in the 1970s, where principles of methodological individualism—Perry's preferred mode—were already being challenged by examinations of collective sentiments. Two of the key protagonists in this debate were Samuel Popkin and James Scott, both working in Southeast Asia. Popkin argued for the application of commonsense models of rational choice derived from particular readings of Western economic theory. Scott, by contrast, took up the idea of the "moral community" discussed extensively by E. P. Thompson and other evidence-based scholarship on British agrarian and working-class life, and further explored in a range of anthropologically grounded studies elsewhere in the world (Popkin 1979; Scott 1976). Scott thus emphasized the significance of nonmaterial motivations that operated and were felt collectively and could not be rendered as the outcome of an aggregate of individual, self-interested calculations; as he put it in a recent, compelling interview, "how the hell can you explain millennial rebellions with a rational choice framework?" (Scott 2007: 361).[2] Perry includes both books in his references, but clearly—and problematically—accepts Popkin's more conservative position as representing the consensus on Southeast Asian peasantry.

Additionally, by his own testimony, Perry's list of comparative cases omits Africa, thereby excluding a rich seam of work on agrarian activism documented in a review article published just two years after his book (Isaacman 1990). Surveying this literature, Isaacman concluded that "(r)ural social movements are not just momentary aberrations, but are often part of a long oppositional history which over time took many shapes and forms, part of a larger engagement in the political world" (1990: 47; see also Ranger 1968). The Kenyan Mau Mau movement is just one example of the evolution of revolution over an extended time span that, by his choice of geographical parameters, Perry excluded from consideration.

A wealth of comparative material, then, exists to suggest that so-called "peasants," frequently lumped together as passive victims, might more accurately be split into different groupings, at least some of whom might be recast as passionate actors. This chapter draws on data from life stories in the Ilinden Dossier, as well as perspectives from elsewhere, to make this argument for Macedonia in the late nineteenth century. It focuses not so much on the roots of the revolutionary organization so many joined, but rather on the routes of prerevolutionary society, which reveal that the region was no backwater of static resignation, but part of a world in dynamic motion.

The Material Background: Circuits of Capital

One of the key institutions of life in rural Macedonia was the *chiftlik*, or large agricultural estate. Perry viewed this system of landholding as dominant and semifeudal; Turkish landlords were often absent figures, leaving day-to-day management to stewards and investing nothing in long-term improvement, so that the overall trend was worsening conditions for the largely Christian workforce. In 1900, *chiftliks* still occupied roughly half of the cultivated land of Macedonia; Perry's assessment was based on views of contemporary observers like Louis Leger, who calculated that of 811 villages in the Monastir *vilayet*, 169 were "feudal" and 106 "semi-feudal" (Leger 1904: 18).

But the story of neglect and stagnation was only one take on Macedonia's economy. In work on the Serres region of what is now Greek Macedonia, Anastasia Karakasidou adroitly summarizes how shifts in Ottoman legislation on landholding, foreign investment, and transportation infrastructure increasingly linked the region to the developing capitalist world economy (1997: 46–49). She notes in particular the modernization of the *chiftlik* system of agricultural production, thereby reinforcing the conclusions reached by Ottoman economic historians of the period. Where Karakasidou focuses on Greek landlords, Halil Inalcik and Fikret Adanir both document the existence of Turkish landowners who were similarly progressive, interested in land reclamation, and certainly not colonially exploitive (Inalcik 1991: 25; Adanir 1979: 17–34; Karpat 2002: 327–51).

They also point to the evidence showing the greater prevalence of sharecropping as a mode of work, rather than wage or—in extreme form—slave or serf labor. These distinctions in labor relations are laid out in specific detail by Trajan Stoianovich, who identified four modes of relationship between landowner and landworker;

> The chiftlik system was characterized . . . by the coexistence of four complementary modes of labor utilization in the cultivation of land: sharecropping or the division of crops between the providers of protection and/or capital (or of land and capital) and the providers of labor (or of land, capital and labor) either on a half-and-half basis (*izpolica, napolica*) or in other proportions; the leasing of land for a one-year term, with the lease contract to be paid in advance (*kesim*); the use of wage laborers (*momci, ratai*), generally young people from poor families who hired out their labor for six months or a year and were paid in money or in kind; and the use of day and seasonal laborers ([1976] 1992: 26).

Unlike the other *chiftlik* historians cited above, Stoianovich emphasized that these transformations in work relations enacted a system of progressive exploitation, which extracted the surplus labor of tenants through sharecropping. This shift toward market relations—albeit shaped by the conditions of inequality on which they were founded—went far beyond labor relations on *chiftliks*, especially when combined with the Tanzimat reforms, which allowed non-Muslims to own land, and the recognition of the Exarchate in 1870, which created a form of competition in the religious domain. Together, these reforms increased the fungibility of forms of capital that had previously operated in separate domains. In an earlier work, Stoianovich traced persuasively the ways in which Orthodox Christians had taken advantage of the position of "minority middleman" and developed trade networks across Ottoman territories, establishing family firms with ties to major European cities. The effect was the creation and concentration of capital in the hands of a newly constituted commercial elite, identified (by religion, culture, and language) as "Greeks." In keeping with the *Annales* style of history, Stoianovich then linked these economic and kin relations to the political domain, arguing that these networks then served as key vectors in ideas as well as goods. These merchants were the foot soldiers of Hellenic enlightenment and nationalism, as well as capitalist modernity, in the Balkans. After the reforms of the Tanzimat in the period from 1839 to 1876, they were well-placed to convert cash into real estate, becoming landowners and landlords themselves and thereby becoming employers of fellow Christians (Stoianovich 1960).

In a spirit similar to Stoianovich's analysis of merchant mobility, Carole Rogel analyzed the impact on Balkan nationalism of the travels of priests and monks (Rogel 1977). In their movement, in parallel fashion, they created extended communities of belief and persuasion that also had material consequences, as those communities contributed funds for the construction or expansion of churches and monasteries. The Christian monasteries on Mount Athos acquired land, property, and status in this period, in part as a product of the flow of gifts and other contributions along the channels that these spiritual middlemen conjured into being.

These bearers and creators of different kinds of cultural capital, as well as the finished goods of European provenance that increasingly made their way into the region, relied in turn on the transport guild of caravaneers, the *kiradžii,* whose timetables and routes played a key role in the emergence and relative significance of market towns like Guvezna, as described by Karakasidou. Additionally, growing affluence fueled demand for a range of artisans, especially stonemasons and other specialists in construction, whose labor was required to create buildings worthy of these new elites (Palairet 1997: 68).

Merchants, monks, muleteers, and masons, then, were all in motion across nineteenth-century Macedonia. If we were to imagine a speeded-up film of their activity, or a time-lapse sequence of photographs, we would see the enduring effects on the landscape of the towns their activities created. Large, multistory stone houses would sprout in market towns and also seemingly remote villages, as testimony to families' growing wealth, kinship, and patronage networks; churches and monasteries, similarly, would be constructed and elaborately furnished; inns and stores would appear around marketplaces that once, twice, or three times a week would teem with the people and products of the surrounding area.

In the province of Monastir, for example, besides the capital's growth, the low-lying agricultural town of Prilep grew from a population of around 13,000 in 1888 (Gounaris 1993: 254) to around 18,000 in 1897 (Palairet 1997: 342), as a market center for the surrounding villages. While residents of the countryside were mainly engaged in agriculture—Prilep was, and remains, known for its onions, tomatoes, peppers, and tobacco—permanent town residents were engaged in trades or *zanaeti* including tailoring, shoemaking, barbering, and other service industries. The more prestigious and organized of these trades had guild organizations, or *esnafi.*

Kruševo, by contrast, was a mountain town with a majority Vlah population, who were historically adherents of the Greek church. Kruševo was smaller than Prilep (around 11,000 inhabitants) and less accessible. Nonetheless it boasted its own regular market and its own commercial elite who, in 1844, banded together to purchase the land on which the town was built from its former owner, a Turkish bey. Large holdings of sheep and goats represented significant stocks of capital that after 1844 were partially converted into fine mansions as well as well-endowed churches.[3] Key products in the town's pastoral and trade-based economy were dried meat, cheese, tallow, and soap, and ample grazing for mules and horses supported a powerful local branch of the guild of *kiradžii*, who carried the town's products as far as Salonika, the region's largest city.

Prilep and Kruševo represented worlds removed from one another, separated vertically as well as horizontally. Such manifest visible differences between the two towns, and between either and their surrounding villages, caught the eye and the imagination of travelers, who were prone to make broad-brush generalizations regarding the contrasts between mountain and plains life, as well as between the busy bustle of the town marketplace and the dull monotony of the village (Garnett 1904: 247–51). Thinking about the region's development as if watching a time-lapse film, by contrast, makes apparent the importance of circuits of trade and communication and shows how intimately the lives of different urban and rural communities were tied together. As iterated patterns of movement across the landscape leave visible traces, we would see how precapitalist and capitalist modes of production rubbed up against each other. Differences in status and wealth were part of each community, wherever it was located. Poor families supplied labor for their rich counterparts, in the same towns or elsewhere; craft guilds served different clienteles; some professions—notably the *kiradžija*, after the arrival of the railways in Macedonia in the late nineteenth century, but also traditional coppersmiths, as imported tin was recycled for so many purposes—found their livelihood threatened by changes beyond their control.

What emerges from the Ilinden Dossier's biographies is a simultaneous sense of the diversity of lifeways within communities, and regularities across them. Mobility, in particular, was the norm rather than the exception, even among those who seem to fit best the economic profile of the ostensibly risk-reducing peasant. What the dossier also makes clear is the web of connections between seemingly disparate worlds, as their residents faced the opportunities and challenges of the new economic order in ways that created new circuits of solidarity among those whose livelihood was tied up with labor rather than with capital.

In the dossier as a whole, 66 percent of successful applicants identify themselves as coming from a village rather than a town. Among the 92 applicants in the sample of 375 who supplied information on their profession, 33 described themselves as farmers or agricultural laborers, while 25 gave a trade: Ilinden pensioners included tailors, masons, shoemakers, dyers, tanners, saddlemakers, butchers, and at least one comb maker. Others lacked such resources; a number of applicants from Prilep and its surrounding plains villages describe themselves or their parents working for beys (Turkish landowners) as *momci* (the plural form of *momok*), confirming Stoianovich's presentation of the six-month contract as the norm in these arrangements. They moved from place to place and employer to employer, signaling the existence of cash-based labor arrangements that offered little longer-term security.

This was the situation, for example, for the parents of pension applicant Ordan Apostoloski. Although when he was born in 1880 they lived in the city of Prilep, his father could not maintain his large family, so they moved to the village of Lagovo and worked on the *chiftlik* of the landowner, Bey Suleiman (Record 2-A-44). Another applicant, Kote Ognenov Gruevski, was born in 1878 in Suhodol, where his parents worked as *momci* for the Turkish bey. They later moved to nearby Utovo because, in his words, "we couldn't live as slaves" (Record 8-G-42). Others could not avoid it: Milan Ivanov Naumoski, of Prilep, born in 1876, worked as *momok*, or contract laborer, for various beys until 1903. Spiro Atanov(ski), of Selce, likewise worked as *momok* in the Turkish village of Drenovo (Records 24-N-61; 2-A-67). All these men were participants in the activities of the organization, as were the women Velika Hristova Dimitrova and Malinka Najdova Veljanovska, who in appendix 2 describe the desperate poverty of their early childhood.

Poverty was not restricted to the agricultural economy. Velika Nedanova Gjakerkoska, born on May 6, 1859, in Kruševo, started work at age nine and earned a living as her parents did, minding the stock of richer families (Record 11-Gj-1). Riste Georgievski, born in 1872 in Žurče in the Demir Hisar region, tended the village flocks when he was only seven, as did Milan Jančeski, of Dolno Divljaci, near Kruševo, and Stojan Jančevski, from Gabolavci, in the Bitola region (Records 7-G-47; 14-J-46; 14-J-45).

What all these families shared was severe economic hardship: among the biographies in the dossier these come closest to expressing the lived reality of Tawney's metaphor of living up to their necks in water. Particularly striking is that none of these applicants make reference to receiving any formal schooling at all; they all began work, under the immediate supervision of family, at a young age. It seems clear that these families could not afford to invest resources in their children's education or training. Although observers stress the initiatives of Greek, Serbian, Bulgarian, and Roumanist (Vlah) national or religious movements to subsidize education, families such as these could not afford to sacrifice the income of children's productive labor even for a year.

Another subset of the Ilinden pension biographies reveals an alternative pathway that demanded the investment of considerable family resources to prepare a child for future employment and, hopefully, financial security. Several speak of training for a trade, or *zanaet*. This practice, recorded by several petitioners, was clearly laid out in terms familiar from Western European systems of apprenticeship. A child would be sent to live and work with an established craftsman (*majstor*) to serve first as apprentice or *čirak,* then as journeyman or *kalfa,* with the ultimate objective of setting up in business himself as a *majstor,* either in partnership or solo.[4] Success stories include that of Nikola Drnev of Skopje (Record 10-D-52; see appendix 2). He had two sisters and one brother, and finished elementary school and one year of gymnasium before being apprenticed to a tailor at age twelve in 1890. After six years with two different *majstors* as a *čirak* and four years as a *kalfa* with a pair of brothers, he achieved *majstor* status in 1900 and set up business on his own. Nikola Neškov Kondarkoski, of Kruševo, born in 1855, went to Salonika after just one grade in the Greek language, where his father had him enrolled to learn the craft of embroidery. He returned at age eighteen to Kruševo, signed himself up as a *kalfa* to a *majstor* already there, and then later opened a shop of his own with his brother (Record 17-K-59). Milan Dimev Kajdžanoski, born in Prilep in 1880, was signed up to the tailoring trade by his father, so that he would be able to support himself and help his parents and other household members (Record 16-K-8).

In some cases, petitioners record that such investments failed. Mitre Ilieski, of Capari in the Bitola region, completed a primary education, this time in Bitola, and then completed the first year of gymnasium. His father then "gave" him to learn tailoring, and he learned for three years in the village, presumably with a local *majstor.* After this brief training, he reports, "I worked until 1901, but wasn't able to support the family" (Record 13-I-42). Gjorgji Mitrevski, of Ramna in the Bitola region, met with a setback even earlier. Born in 1876, he went to school between 1884 and 1888. But instead of taking the next step toward a professional qualification, he returned home to tend the family stock (Record 22-M-71). In his case, it seems that his family was unable or unwilling to finance an apprenticeship in trade and had to recall him and deploy his labor within the household economy until he was twenty, when he left to work in Constantinople.[5]

Circuits of Education and Opportunity: Students and Labor Migrants

These accounts indicate that rural families were not necessarily conservative but took risks to try and improve their lot—risks that often involved relocation. Aside from those members of the very poorest families who served as contract laborers or as stockherds, almost all the other pension applicants record being enrolled for one or more years of school. The outlier in this case is Angel Korobar. From an "old family" in Veles, he attended different years of high school in Thessaloniki and in Monastir, where he was involved in revolutionary circles. Forced to leave the country after his involvement in the bomb attacks of April 1903 in Thessaloniki, he then traveled to Geneva to study chemistry, where he continued playing an activist role in the cultural domain before returning to Veles via Sofia, Bulgaria (Record 17-K-61; see appendix 2).

Korobar's family, clearly, was far wealthier than most that supported the organization, and his freedom to travel was far greater. Nonetheless, what is also striking in the other accounts here is the physical mobility that they indicate. Although *momci* were constrained by their poverty, they could—as the Gruevskis did—trade financial security for a modicum of dignity. Trainees in a trade might, like Kondarkoski, travel to a different city as children to live there. These narratives bespeak not passive resignation or static lives, but rather willingness to adapt to changed circumstances through dynamic action.

This is particularly apparent in the pension applications from the village of Capari, which was centrally involved in the Ilinden Uprising. Together with the nearby villages of Smilevo (393 houses) and Gjavato (240 houses), Capari contributed a significant number of men to the uprising—reportedly, six hundred men from the three villages participated in Ilinden (Panaiotov 1983:

84). Smilevo was the seat of the high command during the Ilinden Uprising itself: Capari is just south of the highest peak in the region, Mount Pelister. Men from all three villages took part in some of the largest engagements of the uprising when Smilevo was attacked by substantial Ottoman forces, and several četas cooperated in a coordinated assault that allowed the surrounded high command to escape. To reflect this activism, the sample of 375 applications included oversampling from Capari (twenty-three cases), Gjavato (twenty-one cases), and Smilevo (eighteen cases), to explore whether biographies gave indications of the reasons for these communities' high profile in Ilinden.

Like a number of other villages in Macedonia, all three were known for particular professional specialties. Smilevo's residents included a large number of stonemasons, while large numbers of men from Capari and Gjavato engaged in the physically demanding and less lucrative career of kjumurdžija,—charcoal manufacturing and selling. This was an option with low capital outlay, which over half of the pension applicants from Capari mention specifically as their way of life. As well as practicing it in the immediate locality of the village—on the slopes of Pelister—a majority report traveling to work charcoal. As well as traveling west to the mountains between Lake Prespa and Lake Ohrid, as Naum Vrčkovski describes in appendix 2, a prime destination for this work was Katerini, in Greece. Smaller numbers also report working in the other neighboring countries of Serbia and Bulgaria, as well as in Romania, Austria, and Anatolia.

Figure 2.1 presents in tabular form the detailed narrative provided by Mitre P. Trajkovski, from Capari (36-T-72), demonstrating the seasonal nature of the migration as well as a range of destinations in Turkey in Europe, Asia Minor, Greece, and Austria-Hungary. What this also illustrates is the importance of social capital in making such work possible, as Trajkovski reports several instances where he was invited to work by a relative, as well as the broader usage of the category of momok or seasonal worker, described by Stoianovich in the context of the chiftlik. Finally, the table includes Trajkovski's report of the organization sending orders to the group of which he was a part in Katerini, and their swift compliance with instructions.

Circuits like those described so painstakingly by Trajkovski and laid out here in tabular form were a central component of the economic livelihood

Table 2.1. A *pečalbar* [migrant laborer's] work record. Compiled from the autobiography of Mitre P. Trajkovski, from the village of Capari. Typed. In Ilinden Dossier, Archive of Macedonia, Record 36-T-72.

Year	Age	Activity/event	Location
1878		Born, to a "middle" family.	Capari
1890	12	Finished 4 years school, began work at home.	Capari
1893	15	Traveled with (maternal) uncle to Izmir as charcoal worker, where he worked for 4 months.	Izmir
		Fell ill, returned home, staying for 8 months.	Capari
1894 (spring)		Contract charcoal worker (*momok*)	Kojazi, close to Solun
1894 (autumn)	16	Sat at home—6 months.	Capari
1895 (spring)		Went with (paternal) uncle as contract charcoal worker—6 month contract, 2 lira per month.	Brajčino (near Resen)
1895 (autumn)	17	With village group ("ours")—6 months.	Katerini (Greece)
1896 (spring)		Returned home.	Capari
1896 (winter)	18	Contract charcoal worker—6 month contract.	Katerini (Greece)
1897 (spring)		Returned home.	Capari
1897 (summer)		Charcoal worker—3 months.	Galicia, Austria
1897 (autumn)	19	Signed with (paternal) uncle to work charcoal.	Larissa, Greece

of Capari and a considerable number of other communities in Ottoman Macedonia. When mapped, alongside the various journeys and relocations described by other pension applicants, they make clear that Macedonia was a world in motion, both at the local and the larger scale. They challenge simple models of rural isolation or inertia.

At the same time, they provide concrete evidence that resistance to Ottoman rule was far more labor-intensive and economically integrated than national mythologies sometimes suggest. Writing of the idealized "hero-bandit," Dimitris Livanios notes that the mountain was his natural habitat

Table 2.1. *Continued*

Year	Age	Activity/event	Location
1898 (summer)		Returned home—then local work.	Ilino
1898 (autumn -Mitrovden)	20	Signed with uncle to work charcoal.	Katerini (Greece)
1899 (summer)		Returned home.	Capari
1899 (winter)	21	Signed for 6 months with Petre Krušjanov from Capari as contract charcoal worker.	Katerini (Greece)
1900 (summer)		Returned home.	Capari
1900 (autumn)	22	Went to cut charcoal: returned after one month, because conditions not suitable.	Vodena Buka, above Resen
1901 (autumn)	23	Signed up with Streta Trajkov as contract charcoal worker.	Katerini (Greece)
1902 (spring/summer)		Stayed home 5 months.	Capari
1902 (autumn)	24	Went with brothers to work charcoal. Ordered to buy weapons and await command to return to the Bitola region.	Katerini
1903 (spring)		Returned home with 60 other Capari men, all with newly purchased weapons. Met up with *četa* from the Voden (Edhessa) region.	Capari
1903 (summer)	25	In *četa* under *vojvoda* Gjorgi Sugarev, for one month.	Smilevo

(Livanios 2008: 191), and that he was often represented as free of ties to the rest of society. The mountain fastnesses around Capari would therefore seem a perfect refuge for young men who wished to identify themselves, for fellow villagers and for posterity, as opponents of Turkish rule. Instead, most of the Capari applicants for pensions emphasize at some length, when asked to narrate their revolutionary activism, their travel to work elsewhere. They present themselves as simultaneously economically constrained and socially embedded actors, rather than either free agents or desperate men driven to revolt.

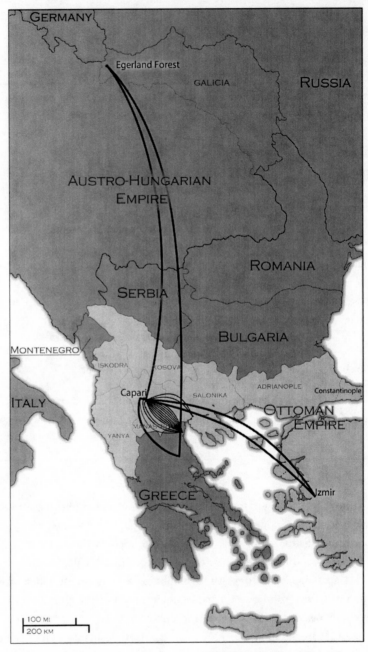

Figure 2.1. The long circuits of migrant labor: Mitre Trajkovski's travels.

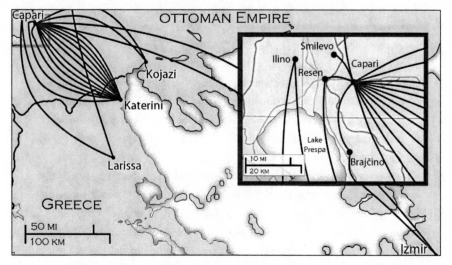

Figure 2.2. The dense traffic of migrant labor: Mitre Trajkovski's life in motion.

The Pečalba Reimagined: Flight as Fight

The fact that so many Ilinden applicants choose to represent their Ilinden activity in this way suggests that they saw a deep connection between the world of labor migration, or *pečalba,* and the world of revolution. Stoianovich himself hints at such a connection in his description of sharecropping teams, traveling from one employer to another:

> Peasant insurrection found especially strong support among sharecroppers who were seasonal artisans, members of military-like craft squads with their own designated leaders, exposed to non-peasant values and world views through their periodic contacts with one or more towns ([1976] 1992: 31).

In broader terms, the logic that Stoianovich suggests here is recognized by other analysts, who emphasize the central importance of *pečalba* for the region's development. One of the earliest to do so was the Serbian geographer Jovan Cvijić, who in 1922 wrote

> There is no factor in recent times that transformed the populations of the central areas [of Macedonia] like the *pečalba*. Lifestyle, work and habits of

mind all changed under the influence of ever newer waves of migration and contacts with new countries and new conditions. Those who prospered abroad returned to improve conditions in their villages and even in whole areas; novelties were introduced in businesses and handicrafts. They changed their household habits, their clothes and their food. The features created by the oppression of history were eradicated (1966: 459; cited in Schierup and Ålund 1987: 65–66).

Others have suggested that the idea of the *pečalba* is an enduring key component of Macedonian economic life, gaining more traction since its reinstatement by Tito's government in 1965 (Gounaris 1989; Halpern 1987; Schwartz 1996: 111; see also Panov 1968). It is a cross-Balkan phenomenon, known also as *gurbet* in Albanian and Turkish (Sugarman 1997: 13–14). Although *pečalba* is rarely used in the Ilinden Dossier, a substantial number of applicants refer to working in this way for some part of their lives, often starting from a very young age.

Jovan Kapinovski, also of Capari, enrolled in school at the age of eight in 1891, but completed only one year. At age nine, but strong for his age, he was taken by his father to work in Katerini over the winter (Record 16-K-24). They pursued this pattern of seasonal migration for the next ten years. Following August 1903, he returned again to Katerini, and then in 1907 went to the United States, where he remained until 1921.

From the nearby village of Ramna, Gogo Jovanovski, born in 1868, went as a *pečalbar* to Izmir at the age of fifteen, returning only ten years later (Record 14-J-55). As noted above, Gjorgji Mitrevski went to work in Constantinople at the age of twenty, in 1896. Stefan Kostovski went with his father to Constantinople to work in 1883, at the age of seventeen, returning only to get married in 1890. Spiro Stojanov Lazarovski, also of Ramna, was born in 1876 and went to Constantinople after attending school between the ages of eight and twelve and then working at home for three years. He gives no information concerning coworkers or family connections, but these examples suggest that Ramna had similar ties to the Constantinople area that Capari had to Katerini and Izmir (Records 22-M-71; 18-K-15; 34-S-21). The dominant trend in this village seems also to have extended to the nearby mixed village of Lera, where Jonče Naumovski, born in 1864, didn't finish school but went to work in Constantinople at age fourteen and stayed there twenty-five years. He indicates that this was a response to family poverty (Record 24-N-53).

Trajkovski's circuits, then, are hardly unique. These narrative accounts are consistent with the macro-level picture provided by Palairet's economic history of the Balkans, which documents how Ottoman territories and their populations were incorporated into the economies of the new nation-states, as well as the movement of people within the empire (Palairet 1997). Many of the specialties reported from the Ottoman period have now been lost, as have the seasonal pathways of motion that were created, often linked to different components of a pastoral economy that across the region, in Yugoslavia as well as Greece, virtually died under the assault of sedentarizing state policies in the 1950s and 1960s (Campbell 1964; Green 2005).

That ecological transformation, driven by national politics, is a big part of what makes the early twentieth century seem so alien. Cvijić's account stresses the temporary nature of *pečalba*, perhaps best translated as "sojourn" as it is used in scholarship on migration, to characterize the movements of "birds of passage" whose families remain behind and who continue to orient themselves, in social and economic terms, to their point of origin (Piore 1977). Such migration, then, was a feature of life before the founding of the Macedonian Revolutionary Organization. Later, the tradition of mobility fueled a willingness on the part of young Macedonians to travel further afield, to the United States, and it produced, for example, the English-language work of Stoyan Christowe, who presented this as an individual urge to self-betterment, very much in alignment with dominant U.S. foundation myths of the entrepreneurial immigrant (Christowe 1947, 1976). This movement accelerated in the years immediately following the 1903 Ilinden Uprising to such an extent that one author could write that "Macedonia, the land of sturdy and diligent workers, was no longer on the banks of the Vardar river, but in New York, in Granite City where one soon counted 35,000 Macedonians" (Risal 1917: 276).

Although an individual like Christowe might conceive of his journey as an escape from poverty, it served a different function at the systemic level. In the system of production as a whole, the *pečalba* played a part in the continuing underdevelopment of the region. Anton Blok summarizes such views with reference to Sicily's interior, noting that

it has been argued that backward areas like that of Sicily's interior are unlikely to be transformed by migrant labor to industrial regions, since it is the specific articulation of these structurally different zones to one another that precludes the development of new productive forms in the periphery. (Blok 1975: 20)

A similar model is claimed to have operated in Macedonia by Gounaris, who considers that it was primarily the invisible earnings of the *pečalbari* that maintained Macedonia's economic equilibrium at the time of the coming of the railways (Gounaris 1989, 1993; see also Schierup and Ålund 1987).

These views, though, do not account for the cultural impact that the *pečalba* had on the communities and individuals for whom it was an enduring way of life. It is in this respect that Stoianovich's work seems critical. As the above examples show, there were existing connections of labor movement in the mid-nineteenth century. Migration from the village of Ramna was clearly established as Asia Minor–bound, and Thessaloniki had already been a labor magnet for some time. But as the century drew to a close, cities outside the empire also attracted the *pečalbari*. In particular the capitals and other cities of the new Balkan states were also now absorbing casual labor from Macedonia as public works, funded by European loans, were undertaken. It appears that for the villagers of western Macedonia, the most important new center was Sofia, in part, it might be argued, because of the greater ease of communication but also perhaps a side effect of the new Bulgaria's strategy of engagement among the Slavic speakers of Macedonia.[6]

This strategy, and the various organizations that conducted it, were crucial factors in the transformation of the *pečalba* experience. For although *pečalba* was integrated into the lifeways of the village whence the migrant worker came, the experience also offered the chance to forge new loyalties and commitments that might in turn transform an individual's horizons. The concentration of young, male Macedonians without local family ties undoubtedly posed some threat to civil order in Sofia where they lived; additionally, it encouraged contacts between people of the same generation, on similar life trajectories but from distinct areas, who might otherwise never have met.

They met under conditions where they worked alongside one another, and it is this that Stoianovich seems to refer to when he speaks of "military-like craft squads with their own designated leaders" (1992: 31). The *pečalbar*, while working, exercised some of his own will and worked for himself. One can imagine the mechanisms by which the new ideas postulated by Cvijić could spread and take hold. Izmir, where many young men from Capari traveled, was where the first Bulgarian-language periodical, *Liuboslovie*, had been published in 1844. Like Salonika, it was a multiconfessional city in which proto-national activism thrived beyond the borders of any existing or even envisaged nation-state.

Further from the Ottoman Empire's center, in the bustle of construction in the new capital cities of southeastern Europe, aspirations could reach further. Migrants could, at least temporarily, stop wearing the legally mandated fez of the empire and think of themselves as something other than *rayah*—subjects of the empire. In reading rooms and cafes, they could read or openly discuss literature and ideas that were banned or restricted in the Ottoman hinterland.

Classy Migrants? Circuits of Transnational and Anti-imperial Activism

In this regard, *pečalbar* circuits bore a family resemblance to those of the fledgling intelligentsia and leadership of the MRO. At its founding in 1893 in Thessaloniki, the young men involved were very much influenced by their Bulgarian predecessors, notably Vasil Levski and Hristo Botev, in drawing up their statutes (Perry 1988: 39; Lange-Akhund 1998: 40; MacDermott 1978). A significant number of the key players in the history of the Macedonian movement—especially the two controversial figures Ivan Garvanov (who made the decision to launch the Ilinden Uprising) and Boris Sarafov, but also the better-regarded Goce Delčev, Damjan Gruev, and Pere Tošev—operated in the political and cultural space between the major cities of Sofia and Thessaloniki and spent portions of their careers employed by Bulgarian state or cultural organizations. Their ties and experiences, however, already went further. The first president of the 1893 organization, Hristo Tatarčev, had spent time in Zurich and Berlin during his medical training and writes in his memoir of the hope he took from the Swiss example, that a state without an army or aggressive police force could, through the rule of law, provide a home for many different elements and interests (Nikolov and Baševski 1995: 327; on the influence of Swiss ideals, see also Bérard 1904: 54).

Other prominent figures in the organization made further contacts with potential allies, funders, or teachers outside the Balkans, weaving the Macedonian Revolutionary Organization into a worldwide network of anti-imperial protest. Boris Sarafov traveled extensively, visiting Vienna, Paris, and Liège (where he met with the representative of a revolver factory) in fall 1901, and then made his way to Geneva to meet Simeon Radev, a supporter of the Macedonian movement and publisher of the journal *L'Effort*, who was then studying law at the University in Geneva (Nikolov and Baševski 1995: 156–58). Sarafov also found time to travel in Macedonia itself, but appeared to many at the time to savor more his role as self-appointed ambassador, public relations officer, and fund-raiser for the movement.

Goce Delčev reportedly traveled to Odessa in 1897 for practical reasons, to meet with Armenian counterparts. This was part of an initiative to exchange bomb-making skills and led to the formation of a bomb factory in the village of Sablur, near Kiustendil, headed by the Armenian bomb maker Krikor (Radin 1993: 79; Perry 1988: 168; Dadrian 1995: 51; MacDermott 1978: 171). The organization was almost certainly involved in the translation and distribution of a treatise on "the Use of Explosives and the Art of Destruction," published in Sofia, a copy of which fell into the hands of the authorities in June 1903 (FO 195/2157/27: Biliotti to O'Conor, June 27, 1903). This treatise opened by discussing Boer resistance to the English in the Transvaal and the importance of sabotage of rail lines in irregular warfare.[7] Bomb-making collaboration also extended to Russia, where members of various organizations in 1905 reportedly received the "secret" of "the Macedonian bomb" from Naum Tiufekčiev, the organization's munitions expert, and put it to work in the 1905 Russian Revolution (Geifman 1995: 201). It then traveled on to Bengal in 1908 (Heehs 1994; Laqueur 1977: 44).

Beyond Bulgaria, the closest ongoing ties were with Armenian organizations and brought different strands of influence together in circuits that ran through central Europe. The Hunchakian Revolutionary Party was established in Geneva by seven young professional Armenians in August 1887, drawing on the traditions of Narodna Volya, the Russian revolutionary movement. Even at its founding, the proposed use of guerrilla bands was reportedly "probably a result of Greek and Bulgarian revolutionary influence" (Nalbandian 1963: 113). Efforts were already under way to create federal ties between different Ottoman revolutionary organizations in Macedonia, Albania, Crete, and Armenia in 1891—that is, before the establishment of the MRO (ibid.: 119). The Armenian Dashnak party went on to cement its premier status among its peers for its successful bombing attack against the Ottoman Bank in Constantinople in 1896—considered by some as the first modern act of terrorism (Chaliand

1982: 30). Collaborative initiatives continued over the next decade, including a 1902 meeting, again in Geneva, to arrange more formal ties between the two movements (Hanioglu 2001: 14).

Russian and anarchist influences are also apparent in the memoirs of Pavel Šatev, one of the young activists involved in the Gemidžii, or "Boatmen," bombings in Salonika of April 1903. Among the readings he reports are *Underground Russia* (Stepniak 1885) and *Moribund Society and Anarchy* (Grave 1893). Minutes from an MRO committee meeting in 1902 indicate that funds were allocated to purchase anarchist publications from Simeon Radev in Geneva that Goce Delčev requested (Šatev 1994: 39; Kosev, Bozhinov, and Panaïotov 1979: 446).

Much of this reading and activism, of course, was likely unknown or invisible to the rank-and-file of the movement in Macedonia. But the Ilinden biography of Angel Korobar reveals that this kind of transnational engagement, and the involvement with revolutionaries from other traditions, was not limited to the organization's leadership. In Geneva after 1903, he reports being "most influenced by acquaintance with the students from Russia, mixing amicably with Poles, Armenians, Ukrainians and others" who were all, he reported, "working with great effort for the upcoming [Russian] revolution" (Record 17-K-61). He also reports that when he was a youth in Veles, local teachers shared revolutionary texts with him—an aspect of the organization's outreach reported also by Petruš Karev of Kruševo, who describes Vasil Glavinov bringing two trunks of "socialist books" to the Kruševo circle to "raise the spirits of the youth" (Record 17-K-51). Several years later, during his tour with a *četa*, Albert Sonnichsen came across a cache of leftist books and pamphlets in an organization supporter's house in Monastir, including works by Karl Kautsky and Marx (Sonnichsen 1909: 122).

Pečalba *As Weapon: The Ottoman Offensive*

Korobar's biography, as noted above, is certainly an outlier. For the most part, the pension requests make no explicit references to active discussions of revolution, or ideas of freedom and international solidarity. The *pečalba* is more often represented as being undertaken out of economic necessity than personal enlightenment: few of the requests explicitly link their periods of labor migration with any larger change in their own "social ideology." Secondary literature, too, on late Ottoman Macedonia has not systematically connected the organization and the institution of labor migration.

Here, though, the consular records of spring 1903—as the organization made its final, hasty preparations for the uprising—provide key data. They indicate that the authorities themselves had recognized linkages between the circuits of labor migration and the work of the organization and now took active steps to interdict them. A pivotal moment in the history of the movement was the Vinica Affair of November 1897, when Turkish forces investigating an armed robbery and murder uncovered stockpiled rifles and bombs (VMRO 1904: 9–10; Perry 1988: 76–77). That led to a large number of arrests and torture of suspected MRO members and supporters and the recognition that the organization posed a substantial threat.

Among the measures the Ottoman authorities took was to disrupt lines of communication, especially with Bulgaria. In 1898, before the post was left vacant for five years, the British vice consul in Monastir reported to his superior that a dozen Bulgarian villagers with "their papers in order, and with visas for Roumania and Bulgaria" had been prevented from leaving. He continued his report by saying, "(t)he reason given is that they were suspected of intending to join Bulgarian bands making raids into Turkey across the frontier" (FO 195/2029/284: Hampson to Blunt, March 28 1898).[8] Similar police action continued on an ad hoc basis over subsequent years as the low-grade harassment of migrants continued. In spring 1903, however, a far more draconian and comprehensive antimigration policy was implemented, and travel and residency permission for Macedonia's migrant laborers was rescinded, forcing them to return home in large numbers.

The operating logic of the authorities is not wholly clear. One explanation advanced at the time was that this was a form of economic warfare against Macedonia's population, who depended on remittances from migrant labor (Bérard 1904: 99). More plausible, though, given the increasing concerns over revolutionary action, is that the Ottoman government acted in response to their own February 1903 decision, adopted under international pressure, to issue a general amnesty to all political prisoners (Lange-Akhund 1998: 118). More than two thousand detainees from Macedonia were released, many of whom had been subjected to torture and some of whom might have been radicalized by the experience. Conscious that these individuals might blend in with the large numbers of migrants in Izmir, Constantinople, or Thessaloniki to unleash terrorist violence at the empire's heart, of the kind that their Armenian counterparts had launched in 1896, the Ottoman leadership chose instead to use a nondiscriminating approach, removing an entire population from the cities in order to quarantine these security threats in rural Macedonia.

In either case, the disruptive effect of Ottoman policy was quickly apparent to consuls in Skopje and Monastir, transit points for the returnees. By March 1903, "Macedonian Bulgarians" were being expelled en masse from Constantinople because of "some disturbance or another" (FO 195/2156/202: Biliotti to O'Conor). Describing the return of large numbers of *pečalbari* to Skopje in March 1903, Vice Consul Pissurica described their livelihoods as "carpenters, masons, milksellers etc." and reported that "as a rule . . . it is just about this time that they leave their villages for work in the capital [Constantinople] and elsewhere" (FO 195/2156/215: Biliotti to O'Conor, March 9, 1903).

Despite this large-scale effort, organization members carried out precisely the kind of high-visibility incident that the Ottoman authorities had feared. On April 28–29, 1903, the group known as the "Boatmen," or Gemidžii, completed dynamite attacks in Thessaloniki, disabling a French passenger ship and destroying a number of symbols of the Ottoman government including a branch of the Ottoman Bank and the city's gas distribution system

Figure 2.3. Shackled MRO detainees in transit, Salonika 1903.

(Moore 1906: 105–32). The group included Pavel Šatev and others with ties to transnational circuits of activism in Switzerland and beyond; as students and urban professionals, ironically, none had been impacted by the Ottoman dragnet.[9]

The Salonika attacks were followed by vigilante reprisals against Christians in Salonika by the Muslim population. In what was perceived at the time as a secondary outburst of Ottoman Muslim rage against Christian terrorists, violence subsequently broke out in Monastir (modern Bitola) on May 6, 1903, when according to consular sources, eleven Christians were killed after a dispute between a Bulgarian butcher and a Turkish ex-official (FO 195/2156/557: McGregor to Biliotti, May 7, 1903). Military reprisals against the organization were also stepped up. On the same day, the regular Turkish army attacked the village of Capari, where the villagers defended themselves successfully. On May 4, Goce Delčev was cornered and killed by Ottoman forces in Banica, and on May 20 the same fate befell another band in Mogila, led by the *vojvoda* Cvetkov. Boris Sarafov narrowly escaped the same fate in Smûrdeš, which later in May was pillaged and burned by Ottoman forces, who destroyed 160 houses and killed more than eighty inhabitants.

Additionally, the expulsion of migrants from the major urban centers of the empire accelerated. In mid-May, McGregor noted that Smûrdeš's young male population was "still abroad, as gardeners or masons" and would now return to ruined homes. He also observed that the forced return of workmen, whether Bulgarian or Albanian, "cannot fail to cause much distress, seeing that the majority of these men are carpenters and masons and are thus debarred from earning their livelihood in the usual way" (FO 195/2156/622: McGregor to Biliotti, May 20, 1903).

Whatever the immediate motivation, the Ottoman authorities surely hoped to degrade the organization's capacity for coherent, effective action. Their goal was to disperse a critical mass of known and potential operatives and cut off one potential source of funding—willing or coerced contributions from these migrants to the organization's treasury. In pursuing this policy, they acted as if guided by Marx's judgments on the stultifying, isolating effect of rural life. The logic of this counterinsurgency tactic presumed that in returning to the separate, native hearths, these urban sojourners would find orchestrated protest impossible and, with the pressure of making a living increased, divert their energies to feeding their families.

What transpired, though, demonstrates both the limits of such crude econ-omistic calculation and the limits of the Ottoman counterinsurgency intelli-gence network. The government's policy, as hinted in the description given by Mitre Trajkovski of his movements in fall 1902 and spring 1903, played directly into the hands of the MRO, which had simultaneously begun to issue orders to its supporters in Izmir and Constantinople, as well as Katerini, the town on the border with Greece, to return to their villages to prepare for the uprising. This decision is attested by Pissurica's account, already cited in part, where he reported that the primary reason these workmen had returned was not the Ottoman policy, but rather the "orders of the committee, which ordered them to return to their homes by the end of March" (FO 195/2156/215: Biliotti to O'Conor, March 9, 1903). Biliotti's letter of March 26, 1903, to O'Conor also indicated that a movement was expected in the next two weeks, and that laborers ordered to return home by the committees were obeying (FO 195/2156/277). It is also recorded in Naum Vrčkovski's recollection of an operative coming to mobilize all the charcoal workers then in the Resen region.

Overlapping Circuits: Pečalbars as Revolutionaries

Again, the consular record is confirmed in the memories recorded in the Ilin-den Dossier. Among the fullest statements of the way the organization had established such influence among these migrants that its orders could take precedence over Ottoman policy is the pension biography of Lazar Dimov Starčevski. Like Trajkovski, he lived his life along a circuit built on the produc-tion and sale of charcoal, which connected Capari with other locations inside and outside the Ottoman Empire. Starčevski's family was clearly wealthier than Trajkovski's, and he was able to attend school for eight years, after which he worked in a family-run store in Izmir for a year before returning to Capari to continue school. His mother's brother, a native of Srpci, was involved with the organization from 1898, and Lazar began work as a *kurier*. After returning to Izmir with his father in 1900, he describes the logistics by which the organi-zation communicated with its members there.

> There were people from Capari there, and people from Gjavato and workers from all over Macedonia. The teachers came—[Ivan] Garvanov and another

one from Kukuš [Kilkis], near Solun—and they took the address of our shop and said that letters would arrive and that I should distribute the letters to all the workers, and the letters were from home and said that people should go back for the uprising. With the arrival of those letters from the homes of the workers, all of them went back. (Record 31-S-11)

Todor Murdževski, of Gjavato, was one recipient of instructions to return, which he reported in his pension application (23-M-71). A similar process took place in Katerini, reported in more colorful terms by Risto Kolev Mučkevski of Capari, who indicates that some Ottoman authorities, at least, understood what was going on.

I went to Greece to work on the Greek–Bulgarian border. From there I returned home with 40 souls, after letters came instructing us to return in Capari immediately. This was before the uprising. As we were going, some Turkish *pasha* was waiting and said "Where are you going?" and they answered him that there was no chance to work there and we were going home. And he said "Why are you lying, when letters were written to return home?" (Record 23-M-70)

The reach of the organization, in this regard, is striking: the ability not just to issue orders within Macedonia, but to have pre-emptively set a system in place which brought people back home for a synchronized mass uprising.

What the Ilinden Dossier reveals, then, is a very different terrain for revolutionary activism than a set of isolated villages with little or no interconnection. Teachers and students, whether tracing roots to villages or towns, traveled to Switzerland, Russia, and beyond, and read still more widely. Workers habitually moved from their home villages to work for Turkish landlords, or to undertake specialized labor, trade, or paid service in towns and cities, within the empire and beyond its borders. They did so with kin or with fellow villagers and further expanded their social circles in so doing. People—mostly women—moved when they married, or were virtually or actually widowed, creating bilateral kin networks that could tie together different communities. Yet although people lived their lives along extended circuits, ideals of home were resilient: land and its ownership retained its hold on people's imaginations, evidenced by a theme of return and investment of resources earned elsewhere in house construction at home.

The enormous capacity of the organization was further demonstrated after Ilinden, when migration circuits extended to North America. Starčevski, for example, continued his mobile, multisited life after Ilinden, returning to Izmir between 1903 and 1905 and then traveling to North America in 1906, where he reports "there was a crisis and a shortage of work, and I lived with some Bulgarians and learned about the workers' movements." Others report continuing to work for the organization in the United States, including Dimko Ačkovski of Prilep, who collected funds, and Božin Trajkov Branov of Buf, who distributed propaganda (Records 2-A-69; 5-B-31). In correspondence to Macedonian villagers in 1905, a četa leader warned that they should comply with demands and not think for a moment they could escape to the United States, as "we also have men over there" (Yosmaoglu 2006: 62). And in an interview regarding labor law violations in 1908, when the U.S. immigration inspector asked an informant the political affiliation of the main suspect, he answered, "Being a Macedonian he is with the revolutionist party" and indicated that most of the immigrants were also members of the same party and, as such, owed him their loyalty (U.S. National Archives: File 51888/11, INS).

Whether at "home" in Macedonia, on pečalba elsewhere on Ottoman territory, Europe, or the United States, or in conversation with revolutionary circles in Geneva, MRO members and affiliates lived everyday and activist lives that were closely intertwined, or that overlapped. Ottoman personnel and British consuls recognized this only belatedly and partially. At the root of their lack of comprehension were stereotypes of peasant fatalism and atomism, combined with a methodological nationalism that presumed that national or protonational frontiers were the natural limits of imagination and action. These perceptions betrayed a misunderstanding of the dynamics of rural life and how successfully the organization had married together physical mobility and political mobilization, harnessing existing circuits of labor migration and communication to energize an insurgency that the authorities belatedly saw coming, but found themselves powerless to prevent.

CHAPTER THREE

The Oath and the Curse:
Subversions of Christianity

Between 1893 and 1903, the Macedonian Revolutionary Organization grew from a committee of six young men dedicated to an autonomous Macedonia to a virtual state within a state that mobilized and armed twenty thousand supporters in an anti-imperial uprising. In that process, traditions and practices of short- and longer-range mobility were one vector by which the organization's network grew. So too, though, was the appeal of a resonant, durable slogan that, like so much else, the MRO had in common with revolutionaries elsewhere. The flag that waved over the so-called, short-lived Republic of Kruševo in August 1903 bore the phrase *Sloboda ili Smrt*— "Liberty or Death." The phrase also inspired Armenian organizations with whom MRO leaders had extended contacts, including the Protectors of the Fatherland (Nalbandian 1963: 87). Bulgarian revolutionaries in the uprisings of 1876 carried flags with the same slogan, which was also at the heart of the nineteenth-century anti-Ottoman national movements in Greece and Crete. Before all these, of course, in a slightly different form—"Give me liberty or give me death!"—the pledge was made by the U.S. folk hero Patrick Henry in a speech in March 1775. It was also used in Latin America in revolutions of the early nineteenth century, and would become the national slogan of Uruguay.

The MRO placed considerable weight on the slogan, and it proved resilient. Multiple pension applicants in the late 1940s and early 1950s repeated the phrase in their biographies of the Ilinden period. So too did the movement's supporters and loyalists in the 1920s and 1930s, even as the organization came to be viewed as a terrorist and criminal enterprise. When long-time VMRO member and enforcer Vlado Černozemski shot and killed the king of Yugoslavia and the foreign minister of France in Marseille in 1934—an act that profoundly shifted the political alliances of southeastern Europe—police found on his left arm a tattoo with a skull and crossbones, the letters VMRO, and the initials S.I.S., for *Sloboda ili Smrt* (Broche 1977: 108).

Western commentators on the 1934 assassination drew attention to the "blood oath" sworn by the perpetrator and his Croatian coconspirators (Graham 1972: 144). Such observations, along with discussion of feuds, ancient hatreds, and intercommunal killing, have been part of a more general exoticization of the Balkans and its people and politics documented by historian Maria Todorova (1997). As Todorova notes, though, the region's stereotypes are themselves shifty and wavering. Černozemski's reported ruthlessness, and the more general stigmatization of mid-twentieth-century Macedonia as home to traditions of violence as well as social systems of clan, feud, and retributive justice that were mobilized in the service of political extremism, represents a significant departure from the late nineteenth-century images of stolid, passive, and resigned peasants.

This tendency—to treat slogans and sentiments of loyalty that potentially connect the Balkans to the world of nation-states and their heroes as instead markers of backwardness and primitivism—demands further re-examination in the direction opened by Todorova's compelling work. The dominant representation of Černozemski in particular—as bestial perpetrator of deadly violence—resonates with another case where contemporary observers were quick to demonize a movement for local self-government: Kenya's so-called "Mau Mau" revolt in the 1950s. In this East African case, a liberation movement that had its roots in long-standing grievances over access to land and that evolved specifically out of political activism through the institutional form of the 1920s Kikuyu Central Association (KCA), came to be represented as steeped in barbarism and evil (Majdalany 1962; Walton 1984: 126–127).

British commentators were especially fascinated and repelled by the oathing practices of Mau Mau, which were held to have particular power over ordinary Kenyans. A key component of the British counterinsurgency campaign—as well as reliance on "loyalist" Kikuyu "countergangs" who were familiar with Mau Mau's insurgent tactics—was "counteroathing" to undo the sinister and mysterious grip that Mau Mau held over its "superstitious" Kikuyu adherents (Kitson 1960; Branch 2009). This tactic was conceived by Louis Leakey, an anthropologist who grew up in Kenya and prided himself on his knowledge and understanding of Kikuyu customs. He and other British representatives saw Mau Mau oaths as a sophisticated and cunning distortion of traditional, positive tribal customs by the movement's leadership (Leakey 1952: 98–0000; 1954). One source went so far as to suggest that their particular power was a product of a form of degenerate anthropology. Jomo Kenyatta, the movement's spiritual head and a former student of Bronislaw Malinowski at the London School of Economics, reportedly mobilized knowledge of Middle Ages black magic that he had acquired during his studies in London (Corfield 1960: 169; see also Berman and Lonsdale 1991).

Recent scholarship on Mau Mau has called for greater attention to and understanding of the constructive functions—both practical and symbolic—served by oathing. Authors have also argued for recognition that Mau Mau was profoundly modernist in its aspirations and technologies of imperial opposition (Branch 2009; Peterson 2004; Smith 1998). Such works are part of the continuing response to decades of orientalist and primitivist writing on Africa: they offer compelling, empirically grounded critiques of stereotypical thinking about other times, places, and customs.

In this chapter I draw on the insights and methods of such works to examine MRO oathing practices. My ultimate agenda, though, is different. In the Macedonian case, I would argue, the problem is not an excess of exoticism, or of prurient Western curiosity, but rather a lack of close scrutiny or analysis. In contrast to the detailed, eyewitness accounts of the multiple levels of Mau Mau oathing, and discussions of the reappropriation of initiation techniques and the substitution of different material substances to transform meanings and enhance the efficacy of the ritual, sources on the MRO's oath ceremonies are fewer and thinner, and analysis is cursory. Whereas the Kikuyu and Mau Mau have both been objects of anthropological inquiry and speculation—for good and ill—the MRO and VMRO, and the historical trajectory between the waterfronts of Thessaloniki 1893 and Marseille 1934, have not. Instead, they are predominantly explained by a parsimonious history of frustrated nationalist energy.

This is the "pidgin social science" that was briefly introduced in the first chapter, which combines an emphasis on methodological individualism to understand motivations with a fetishization of the nation-state as the only thinkable vector of political action. In this overdetermined schema, the MRO's founders dreamed of statehood in the image of their neighbors; those dreams were denied, in part by those same neighbors who inspired them; later generations lost hope in their own dreams, and sought instead to bring down their neighbors. It is simple, neat, and wholly intelligible if one accepts—whether from ideological conviction or in the name of realism—the supremacy of

ethnonationalism. But in line with the approach taken in the previous chapter—which laid out the ways in which the political imagination of early twentieth-century students, self-styled nihilists, charcoal burners, masons, and
milk sellers diverged from that framework—this chapter argues that a variety
of Macedonians were already, in Arjun Appadurai's felicitous term, thinking
past the nation, and that much scholarly analysis has missed that fact (Appadurai 1993: 411).

In this analysis the oath provides a key focus for analysis of the making of
loyalty. As Mark Mazower writes, "revolutionary violence produced national
affiliations as well as being produced by them" (Mazower 2000: 99). Late nine-
teenth- and early twentieth-century Macedonian history was propelled by
group construction via politics, rather than politics as the work of preformed
groups in conflict; the communities seemingly straightforwardly indexed by
the terms "Greeks/Patriarchists," "Bulgars/Bulgarians/Exarchists," "Arnauts/
Albanians," or "Wallachians/Roumanists/Kutzo-Vlahs" were all works in
progress rather than preordained units. Consuls, travelers, and (especially)
expansionist states nonetheless fixated on them; the MRO did not, seeking
instead to foster a new form of polity that combined elements of the new
world and the old, in ways intended to resist the exclusive claims of states.
That novelty rendered the organization elusive for analysts then and now and
perhaps ultimately contributed to the failure of the project it launched. But
the very fluidities, improvisations, and innovations of the organization—the
social and cultural processes in which it was meshed and which defined it—
too readily disappear from the analysis when scholars themselves contribute
to the "magic of nationalism," the invocation of identity through blood, or language, or religion, or any other of Clifford Geertz's infamous "assumed givens"
(Geertz 1973: 259).

Power relations also disappear. They become visible again (it is one critique of Geertz's "assuming" and Benedict Anderson's "imagining" that these
terms conceal power) only when we pay attention to the micropractices of
deference, control, and incentive through which movements recruit and
retain members. When we take this perspective—in other words, if we challenge the teleologic whereby national movements gain support by harnessing
the national aspirations of nations-in-waiting—then any and all cases of popular mobilization demand close scrutiny. We know, from a variety of sources,
that the Macedonian Revolutionary Organization developed the capacity to

communicate internally, issue commands to members that were followed, and recruit and equip armed forces. But absent presumptions about protonational sentiment, it turns out that we have little or no idea precisely how.

In particular, although multiple sources mention that MRO members swore an oath of loyalty, none answer basic social scientific questions about it. What pathways did people follow to take the oath? How many people took it? Was it a matter of choice, or compulsion? How and why did it hold sway over them? And what happened to an oath and its swearers if and when their common purpose was thwarted? In this chapter, I set out to answer these questions, through a close examination of the data on MRO oathing and comparison with better-documented cases.

MRO *Oathing: The Evidence*

"I swear by God, my faith and honor that I will fight to the death for the freedom of the Bulgarians in Macedonia and the Adrianople region, that I will submit unconditionally to the leadership and will unprotestingly carry out its orders; that I will betray to no one, neither by word nor deed the secret to which I wed myself today and all that I shall see, hear and understand concerning the Cause from today on. If I break my oath, let me be killed by one of the comrades with the revolver or the dagger which here I kiss."

The oath is taken on the Gospels, a revolver, a dagger or any available weapon. The person taking the oath bows three times, kisses the above-mentioned objects which, after the oath has been pronounced, he kisses once again. The oath can be administered by any member, but priests are to be preferred. (Kosev, Božinov, and Panaïotov 1979: 422)

This version of the content of the oath, and minimal prescription on the way it should be taken, is provided in a Bulgarian collection of documents and reportedly dates to 1896. A recognizably similar version of the language of the oath was provided forty years later by Christ Anastasoff, an advocate for the organization with good access to members and written records (Anastasoff 1938: 44).

Outside observers during the Ilinden period, by contrast, appear to have known less about the oath.[1] Its first appearance in the British consular record comes in March 1902, and there are two further references to oathing in reports submitted during 1903. None give any hint that they knew the content, and each of the three flag different functions and contexts. In March 1902, a report from Monastir indicates that in Sistero, a village close to the modern Greek town of Kastoria, "A band installed itself at the house of the schoolteacher (female) and invited the inhabitants to take the 'catechism' to the ideas of the committee" (FO 195/2133/147: Pissurica to Biliotti, March 3, 1902). In June 1903, insurgents raided the village of Rakovo and kidnapped eight notables. They executed three and beat the other five until, by force, they undertook *under oath* to recognize the authority of the Exarchate (FO 195/2157/16: McGregor to Biliotti, June 23, 1903; my italics). And after the uprising in October 1903, McGregor reported from interviews with former insurgents now demobilized the following:

> In some instances the insurgents were accompanied by priests before whom the discharged men were required to renew their oath of allegiance, and every man to whom I have spoken is evidently determined to return to his band whenever he is summoned (FO 195/2157/731: McGregor to Graves, October 31, 1903).

The consuls here are describing three very different processes. Although the first report of an armed band "installing" itself in a teacher's house, and then "inviting" villagers to take the catechism, may reflect consular circumlocution or irony, the description seems to indicate a relatively open, noncoercive process aligned with an educational authority. Villagers, here, are "oathing in." In the second report, the description is of oaths thrust upon notables, where the literal alternative to swearing loyalty is death and where armed men extort statements of commitment to a religious organization, the Exarchate church. This is "oathing or else." In the third case, by contrast, an oath is taken (or retaken) as a reaffirmation of an existing sense of commitment to fellow members and is administered by a priest. This we might call "up-oathing."

These consular officials had their own biases or frames of understanding and relied on their own intelligence networks for their information. These three different accounts—generated within a period of eighteen months—show the same uncertain, shifting relationships between different bases of authority, and organizations, as other accounts do. In particular, they permit—and indeed encourage—a reader to conclude that the Macedonian

Revolutionary Organization depended heavily on the work of teachers and priests paid by the Bulgarian Exarchate, and is best seen as a simple extension of the Bulgarian national movement. The fact that the notables targeted in Rakovo included the Greek priest and other prominent representatives of the Patriarchate lends weight to this interpretation.

As a variety of authors have indicated, this certainly describes one wing of the fractured movement. Fikret Adanir, for example, distinguished "evolutionary" and "revolutionary" impulses in what he termed "Bulgarian" nationalism, the former of which represented conventional thinking along familiar nationalist lines and saw the movement's goal—of raising the consciousness of Bulgarians-in-waiting—as consistent with that of the Exarchate. The revolutionists, by contrast, saw this path as promising only a new set of exploitative external rulers over Macedonia's population, whatever their faith (Adanir 1979: 100–101). This distinction was also made by leaders at the time—most notably Gjorče Petrov, according to his own account of a heated exchange with the pro-evolutionary Bulgarian Exarch Josif in 1898 (Andonov 1985: 370–71).

If the authority granted to teachers and priests in these accounts of oathing reflects the evolutionary position, the revolutionists also appear elsewhere in the consular literature, challenging the authority of the Exarchate directly. One striking instance comes from early 1902, from Skopje, when a young socialist interrupted a Bulgarian church service to denounce the Exarchist metropolitan for his immorality. Reportedly, the metropolitan was unpopular "among the lower-class Bulgarians, in whose welfare he is said to take little or no interest" (FO 195/2133/6: Fontana to Biliotti). A month later, a Bulgarian Exarchist schoolteacher in the plains village of Mažudišta, Milan Tziorbeff, who had advised villagers not to pay the dues demanded by the Macedonian committee, was "literally cut up [sic] to pieces by four young Bulgarians from 18 to 20 years of age sent for the purpose from Perlepé [Prilep]" (FO 195/2133/127: Biliotti to O'Conor).

These indicators of friction between the goals of the organization and the Bulgarian state's proxies in Macedonia can, of course, be taken to confirm the fundamental confusion of the period. But they can also be read as evidence for the paramount significance of the oath as a boundary-making mechanism of a different order and scope from any of the devices employed by the different expansionist national movements. The oath demarcated a terminal community constituted not by primordial sentiment, but by self-assertion, which then

acquired its own force over its members. The last example is especially powerful in this regard. For regardless of the observer's silence (or ignorance) on the
precise motivations of the four young killers, it is surely likely that their own
oaths to the organization, "to unprotestingly carry out its orders"—as well as,
perhaps, a judgment by the organization that the teacher had broken his own
oath—were a factor in driving this act of murder and dismemberment.

Oathing from the Inside: the Ilinden Dossier

Evidence for this interpretation—of this particular murder and of the more
general centrality of the oath in the circuits of loyalty of revolutionary Macedonia—comes from the Ilinden Dossier. Out of the main sample of 375 applications, 82 make explicit reference to taking an oath, and two more (including Nikola Zdraveski, whose biography appeared in chapter 1) identify
themselves as oath administrators or oath givers. Though none are complete
in themselves, in aggregate the biographies provide useful corroborative
information about the terms of the oath, supplemented by information on
where oathing took place, the number of people involved in a ceremony, and
the identity of those officiating. They also make clear the power of the oath
for many of those who took it. Throughout, the noun form used most often
for the method of induction is *kletva,* with the verbal variant *zaklet sum*—I
was sworn in. As in many languages, the words for oath and curse are related:
in the case of these descriptions of joining the organization, too, individuals
thus acknowledge that they were cursing themselves should they fall short in
their commitment.

One particularly vivid description of the recruitment process, and a different set of fears that came with it, was provided by T. Vele Grujoski in a lively
and colloquial narrative form, which serves again as a reminder of the freedom
from constraint felt by many pension seekers when addressing the Yugoslav
authorities:

Todor from Poešovo, the regional *vojvoda* [band leader] who was a former
teacher, sought me out and said "Listen, Vele, to what I'm going to tell you.
Because you're a hardworking boy and I believe you'll pay attention, I'm
going to tell you something, but, you know what, you're to tell no-one, and
if you don't understand that, the higher-ups will kill us both. I belong to an

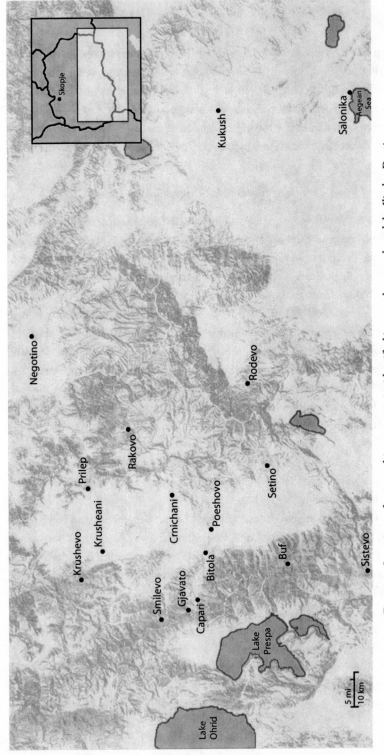

Figure 3.1. Locations of MRO oathing ceremonies identified in consular records and the Ilinden Dossier.

organization that does all it can for revolution, to free us from these beys who hold us in subjection and maltreat us." He gave me the oath in the church and told me "you're now a son of the organization, and you shall do whatever I tell you, for the freedom of Macedonia from the Turkish beasts, so that we might live as a people." (Record 8-G-32)

For all its colloquial turn of phrase, this recollection flags the two key commands embedded in the oath, also evident in the 1896 version. First, it is an oath of silence or secrecy; the organization, acting through its "chiefs," will punish with death any careless talk. And second, it is an oath of obedience, albeit couched in a familial idiom. After swearing, Vele was bound to follow orders and play whatever role he was instructed.

Secrecy is explicitly mentioned by only one other oath swearer, K. Riste Stamboliev of Smilevo, who was sworn in at age seventeen, and who recalls in his biography, "I was charged to keep the secrets of the organization and of the četi" (Record 32-S-54). Obedience, though, features more frequently in the memoirs: Božin Trajkov Branov, of Buf, reports being given the oath by two village leaders in 1900, to "work under the directions of the organization," while Nedelko Pop Nedelkov, of Kukush (modern Kilkis), pledged to "listen and obey loyally" (Records 5-B-31; 25-N-5).[2] Gjorgji Trifunov Adžipeev, of Rodevo in the Voden region, stated that "Goce Delčev came in person to our village and before him I gave my oath to serve the organization faithfully, from my heart," while Boris Gruev, who was based in Skopje but took the oath in Prilep, writes tersely, "The oath for allegiance that I would serve faithfully the revolutionary organization included the following sentence: If you foreswear this oath expect to be killed" (Records 3-A-75; 8-G-37).

Loyalty or faithfulness, as in these last three examples, are further recurrent ideas. The Macedonian term vernost is perhaps the single most-used word in connection with the oath, appearing in nineteen of the eighty-two accounts. Different writers recall swearing loyalty to different goals—to "the fight against tyranny" (Dimko Jošev Cvetanoski of Bitola, Record 39-C-18) or, like T. Vele Grujoski to "the liberation of Macedonia," cited by Kočo Daskalov of Smilevo, Risto Bojčevski of Crničani, and Mate Tomov Mitrušov of Kruševo (Records 9-D-27; 5-B-5; 23-M-17). Most frequent of all is invocation of the slogan of the uprising, that resonated over thirty years, to appear on an assassin's arm in Marseille, *Sloboda ili Smrt.* It is invoked by numerous applicants, including Ivan M. Božinov, Riste Zengoski, Hristo Mihajlov Ivanovski, Mate Tomov Mitrušev, and Dimko Jošev Cvetanoski, all of Bitola; Spiro Mitrev Pičalev of Gjavato, and K. Riste Stamboliev of Smilevo (Records 4-B-35; 12-Z-12; 13-I-23, 23-M-17; 39-C-18; 28-P-71; 32-S-54).

Loyalty, obedience, and commitment to sacrifice were thus explicitly declared. As ideals, of course, they were also simultaneously performatively buttressed in the act of taking the oath. If we presume the oath was the work of intelligent design—Damjan Gruev, in his memoirs, indicates that the MRO's founders envisaged an oath from the start (Gruev et al. 1927: 10–11)—then we can interpret this double articulation, in the words and in the deed of utterance, as intended to strengthen the ritualized quality of what was being done: to reference it simultaneously with the act of swearing itself.

Rituals confer "social status with special obligations" and often involve actions as well as words that incorporate the power of an oath into the initiate's body (La Fontaine 1986: 64). Initiations into organizations and those marking age transitions both exhibit the three stages observed by Van Gennep and later by Victor Turner: separation, the liminal phase, and integration. La Fontaine also draws directly on the work of Bronislaw Malinowski and Maurice Bloch, and indirectly on J. L. Austin's discussion of speech acts, to argue for the magical power of words; the effectiveness of verbal commitment, she says, paraphrasing Bloch, lies in its formalization by authority figures (La Fontaine 1985: 77). What is important, then, is not just the pledge but the acceptance of an external power over the individual to command future actions (ibid.). In all these cases from the Ilinden archive, the performative impact seems clear, in that an original formula is being recalled fifty years later, signaling acceptance of authority and personal commitment to the group and its ideals.[3]

What remains both frustrating and intriguing for the modern reader is the lack of specificity contained in the Ilinden archives about the materiality of the oath ceremonies. The 1896 oath, as well as Anastasoff's text, made internal reference to revolver and dagger as sacred objects on which the oath is sworn; modern historians of the movement follow this reading, including also the Bible (Perry 1988; Lange-Akhund 1998: 41). Only one of the accounts in the Ilinden pensions, however, explicitly matches this ideal. Nedelko Pop Nedelkov of Kukush (Kilkis) reports swearing the oath in 1900 before Pop

Stamat, at the altar of the church of St. Dimitar in Thessaloniki, on a dagger and revolver (25-N-5).[4] Two of the accounts in appendix 2—written by Donka Budžakoska of Kruševo and Lazar Hristov Svetiev of Bitola—make reference either to swearing on a cross, or making the sign of the cross, as part of the ritual they underwent (Records 5-B-2; 31-S-15).

In most cases, though, pension applicants make the most laconic of references to the act itself; none, for example, explicitly refer to kissing the dagger and revolver, as mentioned in the 1896 statute.[5] Relatively few specify the exact location where the oath was administered; several do name churches in cities or villages, but those numbers are matched by references to stores or cafés. Most report being sworn in in their places of permanent residence, though examples like Boris Gruev, who traveled from Skopje to Prilep to enroll and, more dramatically, several who report being sworn in or enrolled in Constantinople, at the very heart of the Ottoman Empire, provide further confirmation of the larger horizons of action described in the previous chapter.[6] The one detail that many do provide is the name of their oath givers, who include many more *vojvodas* and teachers than priests.

A New Faith: Recasting Religious Practice

Two pension applications from specialist oath givers provide further confirmation that the organization was not solely dependent on the symbolic or material resources of the church. Gligor Bojadžiev of Bitola and Nikola Zdraveski-Vince of Kruševo both describe themselves as working as recruiters in the period between 1900 and the Ilinden Uprising. Bojadžiev, who worked in his family dyeing/painting business, reports being tasked with selecting new members and administering the oath to them, which he did in his father's store (Record 4-B-54). Zdraveski's biography (see introduction, this volume) provides a more detailed account of his own oath taking and subsequent oath giving, in which he inducted thirty members in 1901. He describes three ceremonies: two in named houses in Kruševo, belonging to Tašku Surdul and Halču Berberot repectively, and one in an inn (*han*) belonging to Nikole Gjorgoski in the village of Krušeani. He uses a language of christening, which he qualifies by saying "as one said then." This contextualization of his use of the term "christening" signals an awareness, at least on his part, of the socialist, atheist orientation of the régime to which he was appealing in the late 1940s.

By extension, we might argue that the more general lack of reference to religious symbolism, or priests playing a central role, reflects similar sophistication—or self-interested cunning—among applicants. Certainly there is internal evidence elsewhere to suggest that applicants tailored their narratives to the public criteria for pension awards, using phrases like "with gun in hand" that were part of the scheme's announcement. The variation in the pension accounts, however, can also be read as confirmation either of the decentralized ethos that permeated the MRO, or of the almost inevitable divergence between the ideals and practices of a covert, illegal organization operating across considerable distances.

If we accept this interpretation, then the lack of references to religious symbolism in the Ilinden Dossier can be taken as evidence that the linkage to organized, authorized religion was anything but straightforward and close. Instead, those cases where religious text, location, or authority figures are involved suggest elements of inversion or subversion of the conventional order, rather than recognition and invocation of its power. Here again is a case where common sense may have contributed to a pidgin social science. The juxtaposition of dagger, revolver, and Bible has become iconic, for many historians of the movement, of its status as the armed wing of the Exarchate. But oathing over this particular combination of objects-made-sacred can also be read as profoundly transgressive or polluting. The revolutionary aims to which the new member pledged allegiance represented a challenge to the ideology of Orthodoxy, which preached endurance and forbearance; those priests who supported the organization, like Pop Stamat in Thessaloniki, were themselves out of step with church policy. If and when oath ceremonies were conducted in a church, the presence of a revolver at the altar plausibly marked a shocking act of profanation to the faithful.

In addition, Christians were forbidden to carry, possess, or display weapons in this period. Obviously some did, and it was part of organization policy to increase the numbers of weapons available to its members, as well as to train members in the use of those weapons. In line with counterinsurgency and peacekeeping approaches that were replayed by international forces in the Balkans and Iraq a century later, the Ottoman government sought to disarm the population by offering amnesty for turning in illicit weapons, though without tremendous success. The use of a revolver in the oathing ceremony, then, was both religiously and politically transgressive. It was also calculatedly impressive, in that it signaled concretely to oath takers the organization's capacity and willingness to defy the law.

As noted, Zdraveski felt obliged, in his pension application, to offer a quali-fication of his choice of the word "christening"—*pokrstuvanje*—for the oath ceremony. Relatively few pension applicants, writing in the late 1940s and early 1950s, used this term, borrowed from the language of Christian initia-tion. Far more employ the language noted earlier in T. Vele Grujoski's account of his recruitment and report that they were oathed—*zaklet sum*. Also com-mon is the phrase *se organizirav* ("I became part of the organization"). Again, the evidence of the Ilinden Dossier suggests that most applicants were acutely aware that they were joining an enterprise quite distinct from the church of which most of them were members.

Also striking in this regard is the organization's clear decision not to deploy a readily available terminology and social practice of trust and reciprocity between participants in Christian rituals of transition. Besides the authorizing presence of the priest, in Orthodox christening and marriage rituals a key role would be played by the *kum* (Slavic) or *koumbaros* (Greek): a term potentially translatable as "sponsor," "godfather," "or best man." The relationship between the new couple or a new child and their *kum* would ideally be lifelong, often creating (or continuing) bilateral relations that extended out to the families involved. *Kumstvo* relations are conventionally classified as a form of "fictive kinship" (Hammel 1968) involving material as well as affective ties that were generally considered equivalent to, or by some accounts more binding than, those of blood or marriage.

As such, the institution has at times been put to political use by powerful actors seeking to bolster their legitimacy. Serbian kings, and later Tito, played the role of *kum* to selected families, through a form of patronage (Bringa 2005: 154). But where Ilindeners use the language of christening, not one invokes *kumstvo* as an analogy for the relationship created by oathing. The organiza-tion did not harness this ready-made idiom of bilateral affinity, either between itself and the new recruit, or between oath taker and either oath giver or pro-poser/sponsor of their membership. In a counterfactual spirit, the nonpres-ence of this idiom can be taken as further evidence that through oathing, the organization was seeking to formalize an entirely new kind of association, in which members had a sense of horizontal solidarity with other members, together with unquestioning respect for the cause and obedience to orders than were issued through authorized channels.

Among the names of the swearers-in that Ilindeners often included in their biographies, teachers, *četa*-leaders, and individuals referred to as "organizers" far outnumbered priests. Additionally, besides the two accounts from specialist recruiters, many accounts indicate that the ritual was run by a team of three: in some cases, a *četa*-leader, a teacher, and a priest, but in others, figures whose authority derived entirely from the intensity of their activism within the organization. While the prominence granted to the number three—like the symbolism of the objects of swearing, or the reference to bowing three times—can again be traced back to a Christian, Trinitarian tradition, the frame thus created is given secular content, signaling the organization's emphasis on transformative action in this world, rather than salvation in the next.[7]

Finally, the organization's subversive agenda is also evident in the roles open to women. Christian services at the time were still segregated along gender lines, with women in a separate gallery; social life among the urban middle classes and the upwardly mobile was dominated by concerns over male threats to feminine honor, so that girls were sheltered, cloistered, and constrained. Accounts like that of Donka Budžakoska demonstrate a break with these class-bound practices. She gave the following account of joining the organization:

> At the beginning of 1901, I joined the ranks of the Regular [*sic*] Macedonian Revolutionary Organization, which was working for the liberation of the Macedonian people from Turkish oppression, and to which I made an oath, crossing myself, in the presence of Kosta Škodra, the teacher, Tirču Kare, the flag bearer (*bajraktar*), and Tome Nikle, all from Kruševo. Initially I was made a courier, to carry correspondence and weapons. (Record 5-B-52)

Rajna Nikolova Miloševska, also of Kruševo, attributes her active participation to the prior experience of her brother and uncle. In Bitola, Vasilka Mijakova Vangeleva took the oath from her own brother, Gjorgi Sugarev, and Vaska Konsuloska reported joining with the assistance of her brother Vangel Gjorčeski (Records 22-M-25; 22-M-13; 17-K-60). Other women stated that they joined "with their husbands." Although women are certainly a minority in the applications as a whole, such examples indicate a commitment to equality between the sexes quite distinct from the ideology of any church or nation at the time.

Terminal Loyalty: Friendship and Trust in MRO Recruitment

What they also demonstrate is behavior very different from that generally attributed to Macedonia's Christian inhabitants at the time. Travelers in the region frequently noted that families were often less unitary in political affiliation. Not knowing which of the competing organizations or national movements would emerge victorious, they often chose instead (in economistic language) to balance their portfolio or spread their bets by creating ties with different national movements. Brailsford, for example, notes cases where brothers grew up as affiliates (reportedly) of Romanian, Bulgarian, Serbian, and Greek propaganda (Brailsford 1906: 102–103). A similar pattern of what looks like a form of peasant rationality can be traced in the time of the Greek Civil War, when many of the same villages (including for example Buf, Rakovo, and Požar) so much in the forefront of Ilinden again found themselves at the meeting point of what Lewis Coser calls "greedy institutions"—nation-states and their armies, demanding total loyalty (Coser 1974). Families often had one son fighting with the partisans and the other with the regular army.[8] From the evidence of the Ilinden Dossier, the MRO mobilized kin relations more effectively than its nation-state rivals, as besides these women, other young men like Todor Borjar of Kruševo or Iljo S. Lokardev of Cetino, joined because blood relatives were already members (Records 5-B-14; 20-L-59).

Other memoirs indicate that friendships and professional connections were also factors in the paths of oath taking. Kosta Janakiev Dabiža, for example, of Kruševo, was persuaded by friends in Negotino to enroll in the komitet when he moved there. He reports that after expressing interest in joining,

> a few days later I was invited to meet by the leadership of the organization of the Negotino branch of the committee for the liberation of Macedonia, Gjore Slepiot and Igno Marčev. They informed me that I had been accepted, and that from that day I would work for the organization. (Record 9-D-01)

Similar processes are described by J. Mitre Karanfilovski, of Capari, who was initially approached by friends and then introduced to three men he refers to as "organizers," including the key Capari recruiter Simon Trajkov (16-K-32). Jovan Jurukovski, originally from Tresonče, a village in the Galičnik region, was recruited while on pečalba in Sliven, Bulgaria. After the initial approach was made by one teacher, Mihail Kantaržiev, he reports that two other teachers vouched for him with Goce Delčev, who then summoned him to a meeting in the Hotel Battenburg, which he describes as follows:

> He [Delčev] questioned me thoroughly and finally said: "[Peho] Jahorov recommends you highly and yesterday I also received a letter from [Petar] Vaskov, who reckons that you will be an asset in our work for Macedonia. We Macedonians have many enemies, and must combat them all, wherever they come from. In the first place the *vrhovisti* are our enemies. They are loyal servants of King Ferdinand, and even though they are Macedonians, do not work for Macedonia, but for him. So I will give you full powers, and write to the Bitola central committee. You should present yourself there, and you'll be assigned a *četa* of roughly twenty-five men, with which you'll begin work. (Record 15-J-54)[9]

In all these cases, an initial approach to a potential recruit was made by friends or acquaintances before a higher authority in the organization formally inducted the recruit. As with so much else about MRO's oathing, and other liberation movements that claim popular support, we can attribute both practical and symbolic functions to this sequence. First, it addresses the perennial paradox of a secret organization that seeks willing rather than coerced members: any attempt at recruitment is simultaneously a risk if people are ostensibly free to say no.[10] Second, the expansion through kinship or friendship circles emphasizes the horizontal solidarity of the organization, investing it with affective content and thereby infusing it with the reality of existing ties that operated beyond the horizons of church or state.

Oathing in Context: Comparative Perspectives

As noted earlier in this chapter, the specifics of MRO oathing practices have attracted little attention from most historians in or outside the region. The biographies in the Ilinden Dossier make very apparent that oathing took place, and this chapter has so far argued that the MRO's oathing practices were one mechanism that distinguished the organization from rival claimants on the loyalty of Macedonia's residents. To analyze the efficacy of the oath, though, demands attention to comparative materials. Prior initiatives in this regard tend to focus on proximate cases, in time and space and supposed genre of organization. The argument that Macedonian activism was primarily based on a Bulgarian template is served, in particular, by the view that the oath, and much more, were inspired or even directly copied from the famous Bulgarian revolutionary Hristo Botev. The oath is a recurrent theme in Bulgarian art, most famously portrayed in Svetlin Rusev's 1966 painting *Kletva*.

Once we engage with the complex realities of the Macedonian movement, though, some members of which explicitly aspired for something quite different from a nation-state, the range of comparative cases opens considerably, as do their striking similarities. The MRO's oathing then becomes a site on which to challenge certain enshrined antinomies, especially those that divide modern from premodern or traditional, west from east, or select and secret from mass and overt, in the analysis of the making of loyalties. One proximate

Figure 3.2. Kletva (Oath). Svetlin Rusev 1966. Used by
permission of the National Gallery of Art, Sofia, Bulgaria.

comparison, for example—where MRO practices had their own influence—would be the evolution of oathing practices of the Young Turkish organization of the early twentieth century. After initially using ad hoc methods of initiation, "oath committees" were formed and the process standardized: the candidate would be blindfolded and brought before the committee to hear the chairman deliver a speech. After repeating the oath, with one hand on a sacred book and the other or a dagger and revolver, the candidate would remove the blindfold to see four figures in red gowns—a piece of theater reportedly intended to add to the "secret and mystic" stature of the committee (Haniolgu 2001: 218).

Further apart in time and space, three literatures in particular stand out for the light they shed on the Macedonian case: the Carbonari of nineteenth-century Italy, the Irish "whiteboy" movements and the later IRA movement that drew on the same traditions, and Mau Mau in Kenya. All three posed different kinds of challenges to the religious—and specifically Christian—ideology shared by would-be recruits. Moving backward and forward in time and across national and continental frontiers in this way showcases the value of cross-regional and temporal comparisons of the type more common in anthropology than history.

The Carbonari: National Liberation, Crime, and Utopianism

The nature of Carbonari secret societies, which emerged in rural southern Italy in the early nineteenth century, has been well-documented, and yet remains ambiguous. While often seen primarily as precursors of and partici-pants in the bourgeois-led national liberation movement, they have also been tied to the emergence of organized crime networks, especially the Neapolitan Camorra and the more famous Sicilian Mafia. Yet some Carbonari, too, envis-aged as their goal Carboneria, an end state in which the whole world would be a republic, with an overarching law of equality (Galt 1994: 796). Such a vision has more in common with the various socialist utopian movements of the European nineteenth century, some of which later spread to the United States (Taylor 1982; Kanter 1972), than with doctrines of national liberation or the pragmatics of crime. The Italian case thus provides a precedent for the multiplicity of motives and orientations within a single movement.

"Great man" biographical approaches to history, of course, emphasize the fact that Mazzini, figurehead of the Italian national liberation movement and inspiration to similar movements in Austria, the Balkans, and beyond through his writings, was himself a member of the Carbonari until 1830. He expressed the view that Italy would be freed by "insurrection by guerrilla bands—the true method of warfare for all nations" (cited in Chandler 1975: 24–25). Still greater ambiguities of goal and function can be perceived in interpretations of Carbonari oathing. As with the MRO's rituals, the number three had particular significance, signaling reliance on Christian cosmology. Oathing occurred at midnight; initiates were led in and out of the chamber three times before being introduced, with three taps of a stick, to the three officials (Hobsbawm 1959: 154).

Other accounts stress that the oath featured three central material components: the axe, salt, and the cross. Writing in the 1960s, Arkon Daraul traced the different meanings entrusted to two levels of initiate via the same material content. In the first level of initiation, the recited text has it that the axe is the tool of the members' shared labor, the salt warns initiates to keep their hearts free of corruption, and the cross "foreshadows labors, persecution and death which threaten those that would be virtuous." At the higher level of initiation, though, the more revolutionary aspects of the same objects are revealed: "the cross is for the crucifixion of the tyrant who persecutes us, the axe is to behead him, and the salt to preserve his head as a reminder of our triumph" (Daraul 1961: 104–105). In this regard, Daraul identified a set of solidarity-making symbols at work that were then transformed into a far more radical message. The two sign systems operated in the same ritual space.

Focusing on the utopian components of the movement, anthropologist Anthony Galt emphasized the importance of an egalitarian antistructure, the desire for a return to "natural simplicity," and a form of aggressive antinationalism built on the idea that people should be "left free" to ply their trades (Galt 1994: 795). The symbolism of location, specifically the forest and the hut—in the final analysis, the work environment for a bulk of the original membership—work to emphasize the retreat from the world of "high" politics and the intrigues of elites (ibid.: 796).

Ireland: Whiteboys, Ribbon-men, the IRA, and the Evolution of Oathing

The Irish case provides an early modern and modern set of localist and anticolonial sentiments that would evolve into a more clearly nationalist agenda and organization. Long before the establishment of the Irish Republican Army (IRA), one of the best-known and more lasting twentieth-century national liberation organizations, Ireland was the site of "whiteboy" movements and "ribbon-man" organizations (Beames 1983; Pollard 1922). The earliest evidence of oath-bound secret societies in the country comes from the 1760s; historians have suggested that their emergence was inspired by exiles who had been in French military service and had encountered such ideas on the continent (Beames 1983: 33; see also Pollard 1922: 50). Organizations were formed along lines similar to those we have witnessed in the Macedonian case: a central committee was constituted and membership expanded only slowly, as existing members nominated or vouched for prospective recruits who had to exhibit good conduct and straight dealing and be members of "decent families" (Beames 1983: 63). Reputations from the everyday world, then, decisively shaped the contours of organizations established to try to transform it. Oaths emphasized loyalty, obedience, and secrecy; in a fuller account of the "Threshers" movement, the constitution also stipulates payment of dues to the organization and withholding or restricting the taxes paid to other, existing authorities, including the local church (ibid. 64; see also Pollard 1922: 36).

The early nineteenth century saw the creation of the so-called ribbon-men societies. Like the whiteboy movements, they were predominantly Catholic in membership and disavowed by the church. Members took oaths of loyalty to fellow members and perseverance in the organization's goals, which included land reform, political autonomy for Ireland, and (in some cases) the violent expulsion of Protestants. Membership and support remained robust through the 1820s; in 1833, the ribbon-men were held responsible for 196 murders across Ireland (Pollard 1922: 38).

This kind of localist, decentralized organization of rural Ireland against various dimensions of English rule was transformed in the 1850s when the Irish Revolutionary Brotherhood was launched, with support from emigrant circles in the United States. Drawing on these prior movements and sentiments, a new generation of leaders with explicit ties outside Ireland, especially in the United States and France, created a more coherent and disciplined organization (Pollard 1922: 46–55). Drawing on a broader pool of experience and knowledge—including, reportedly, the Carbonari lodges of France—they laid the groundwork for the further evolution of Irish resistance into the IRA. Analysis of the organization in the early twentieth century makes clear the enduring emphasis that the organization and its leaders placed on secrecy and loyalty (Hart 1998). What also emerged was a system of oathing that distinguished between different levels of commitment. Disregarding any oath, though, was lethal; the IRA targeted traitors ruthlessly and deployed stylized violence against them. The organization also established rules of conduct that had to be obeyed, again on pain of death. Counterinsurgency techniques by the English and their allies appeared pivotal in further escalating the severity of IRA codes of punishment.

Mau Mau: The Oath as Paradigm of Primitivism

The widespread Kikuyu revolt against British colonial rule that erupted into violence in the early 1950s is among the most exhaustively documented cases of how a once-selective and secret organization was able to mobilize a population generally perceived as backward or docile to participate in a major armed insurgency. The rich archival resources on Mau Mau are certainly a product of British imperial attention and unease, which generated a vast array of policy documents, court hearings and investigations, interrogations, and rolls of battle and military operations now ripe for subaltern rereadings against the grain, in the mode pioneered by historians of colonial India (Amin 1995; Guha 1999). Interest in Mau Mau has been further fueled by its iconic status in the literature on effective counterinsurgency, now under particular scrutiny by U.S. military practitioners.

What is especially striking is the particular attention paid to oathing practices, which were presented as having enormous, atavistic power to turn "peace-loving Kikuyu" into "murderous fanatics" (Leakey 1954: 43, 52). The existence of Mau Mau was uncovered—or, in the postcolonial critical literature, the phantom of Mau Mau was conjured—during a trial in Naivasha, where a Kikuyu man revealed that he had been enrolled as a member. When a Mau Mau gang subsequently butchered the Ruck family of white settlers—including their six-year-old son—the movement and its members were immediately pathologized. In this case, one of the killers was a former servant of the family, who days before had tenderly carried the young boy, Michael, home from a riding accident. How, British journalists, politicians and pundits asked, could a person's humanity be so swiftly and completely erased (Corfield 1960: 6; Elkins 2005: 42–43)?

British analysts quickly located the answer in the kinds of oathing practices described in the Naivasha case and other testimony. The Mau Mau oath was considered a debased adaptation and inversion of traditional Kikuyu oathing ceremonies overseen by elders, which had already been adopted by the Kikuku Central Association in the 1920s, in oaths sworn on the Bible and a handful of soil, pledging not to sell land to Europeans or Indians (Corfield 1960: 164; Leakey 1954: 77–85). Those oaths later added strictures on obedience and the requirement to pay dues to support Jomo Kenyatta, the association's leader.

According to Corfield, Kenyatta himself drew on his studies in London to further amend the oath and create a sequence of different levels of initiation (Elkins 2005: 25). Different levels of engagement, marked by different pledges or actions on behalf of the organization, were of course features of Carbonari practices, as well as those of the IRA. Inversions of tradition were an early stage in this development, including administering the oath by night instead of during the day, in secret rather than in public, and by force rather than with the full and willing participation of the oath swearer; this was, then, "oathing or else." Additionally, oathing was extended to women, traditionally not oath takers, but perceived in Kenya (as elsewhere) as primary purveyors of gossip and information and therefore representing a threat to Mau Mau's secrecy that oathing reduced. By the 1950s, though, such pragmatic and proactive reasons for oathing were barely considered, as participants and investigators reported that the levels of initiation were increasing as the organization sought to solidify its hold on its followers. Where once the "killing power" of the oath, per se, might have sufficed, the new variations reportedly employed increasingly polluting substances and practices—animal entrails, menstrual blood, semen, nakedness, cannibalism, necrophagia, and simulated copulation—to forge a community united by transgression of all that was holy or human.

This raising of the stakes, or "oathing-up," may have owed something to British policy, which fixated on the oath and introduced a campaign of counteroathing to undo it. There is no evidence that the variations reported late into the 1950s were the brainchild of Jomo Kenyatta, the movement's inspirational leader. By this time, pressurized by the militarized response of the British government (in which "countergangs" composed of Kikuyu, ex–Mau Mau members who had switched sides played a major role), Mau Mau's bands were operating more or less independently, deep in the forests. Cut off from

their urban compatriots and leaders, the surviving leaders received no guidance in how to preserve their forces and prevent attrition by desertion. The
addition of new and shocking elements to the oathing ceremony was con-
ceivably a response to these challenges, and the bestial, dehumanizing turn
could equally be taken as the product of communal desperation among these
holdouts.

An insider account of Mau Mau oathing that better reflects the movement's
policy and vision in its earlier incarnation comes from the work of Karari
Njama and Donald Barnett, which combines eyewitness recollection and
analysis. Njama provides a detailed account of his own experience of oath taking. He was a teacher in a colonial-run school and recalls his growing awareness that people around him were being inducted into the new organization,
while no approaches were being made to him. In his recollection, one of the
key moments when he realized the impact of Mau Mau membership on ordinary life was when he organized a house building in his home village by the
traditional method, brewing beer and inviting people over to drink beer and
work (Barnett and Njama 1966: 114). Although he considered himself popular
and accomplished, few people came to his event, whereas many in the community contributed to the house building of another man of lower standing.
Njama quickly concluded that this was the organization at work; his rival was
a member, and he also realized later that those few souls who had come to his
own house raising had done so because they assumed that he was already a
member.

It was shortly after this that Njama was, in fact, inducted into Mau Mau,
in a process he did not initiate. He was taken by a cousin to a third party's
house, on the culturally specific and socially embedded pretext that beer had
been brewed there; instead, he found himself, together with a number of other
unwitting guests, thrust into a well-orchestrated and elaborate ritual that left
him with little real option to decline. Indeed, he watched as one initial resister
was beaten and threatened with death until he agreed to take the oath. The ceremony included goatskin and goat intestines, the initiates licking each other's
blood off their fingers, repetition of actions seven times, and then swearing to
twenty-one declarations. Njama then recalls spending the night running over
in his mind the power of the oath he had just sworn, as it sank in that his life
was no longer his own and he had been "born again in a new society with a
new faith" (Barnett and Njama 1966: 117–21).[11]

Njama's insider perspective on the earlier stages of oathing—the so-called "unity oath" as the first level of initiation, which it is estimated was taken by as many as 70 or 80 percent of Kikuyu—is confirmed by a number of other sources, including the memoirs collected by Marshall Clough (Clough 1998). By appealing to the least-well-off, and also by integration with a form of economic and social boycotting or ostracism of the non-oathed, the Mau Mau movement set out to create new ties, offer access to social networks, and put in place mechanisms of reciprocal help. The oath was to generate a new meaning and a new solidarity for Kikuyu, mobilizing support by appealing to the sense of injustice sparked by years of colonial rule and exploitation.

Conclusion: Manufacturing Consent?

Creating sentiment is never straightforward. These three cases demonstrate that nonstate actors operating in different historical and cultural contexts turned to the use of oaths to recruit and retain members. They also show the necessary relationship between the oath and the practice or threat of violence, especially against oath refusers, active oathbreakers, or those who do not recognize the seriousness of what they have undertaken. The discussion of the three cases also illuminates the greater attention paid to tribal oathing in Kenya in the literature, which was held as more central in the power of Mau Mau than oathing among protesters or revolutionists in Italy, France, or Ireland. In particular, as Daniel Branch documents, the idea that oathing under duress is nonetheless efficacious appears to be tied up with enduring ideas about native superstition, which is at odds with ideals about modernity and individualism, and of free will, determinism, and selfhood (Branch 2009: 38).

One school of thought seeks to deconstruct such dualisms by importing the more rationalist explanations of human activity around the world, and (often) back in time as well. But I suggest that such an approach invites a kind of pidgin social science, in which unfamiliar cultural specificities are radically thinned in pursuit of a purported universalism that in fact is a thickening of our own cultural preconceptions. It may not be that Kikuyu oaths are peculiarly primitive; nonetheless, they (like those in nineteenth-century Italy or early-twentieth-century Ireland or Macedonia) may not all be fully explained as psychological mechanisms that conjure unity by altering militant lives

(Polk 2007: 112), or shape future action because the oath taker "gives over part of (his) individual conscience" (Sanford 1953: 40).

One response to the enduring psychologism that such claims represent is to highlight the ways in which accounts of cases conventionally viewed as disparate and incommensurable in fact demonstrate common social or structural features. This underpins, for example, the approach taken by James Scott in his debate with Samuel Popkin over the nature of peasant consciousness and behavior, discussed earlier. Where Popkin argued that peasants will reap the benefits of revolution whether they participate or not, and therefore operate as classical "free riders" and hang back from risky involvement, James Scott took up the idea of the "moral community" discussed extensively by E. P. Thompson and other evidence-based scholarship on British agrarian and working-class life to argue that other relational aspects of life—dignity, honor, justice—may short-circuit individual, self-interested calculations.

Oathing practices constitute a site that demands analysis of this kind. As Stathis Kalyvas puts it in a different context, the pursuit of individual motivations does not necessarily advance our understanding of insurgent mobilization (2006: 101). Oaths do not, as British commentators on Mau Mau insisted they did, work exclusively because of the individual oathers' belief in supernatural sanction. When Mau Mau swearers uttered the words "if I am disloyal, or reveal the organization's secrets, may this oath kill me" they were not, to reappropriate Evans-Pritchard's analysis of Nuer religion, mistaking the passage of air across their vocal cords for a dagger thrust to their heart, any more or less than the Carbonari, whiteboys, IRA, or MRO members who came before them in time would have done.[12] They were nevertheless, through their participation, affirming the efficacy of the ritual, for themselves, their fellow participants, and also for the organization itself. The oaths of these societies, in this regard, are all Austinian "speech-acts" of a particular kind; as such, they are first and foremost social.

The real proof of efficacy lay in later compliance. Hence both the ambiguity noted at the start of the chapter—the oath is a curse-in-waiting, its essence indistinguishable from its capillary effects in the world—and the escalation or acceleration in oathing, including cases where oath taking was not so much chosen as thrust upon new members, evident in both the MRO and the Mau Mau cases. In each, it is discovery and reaction by the imperial authorities that precipitates a dramatic change and, arguably, fractalization of oathing, both in terms of the spoken content, the material props, and the social scale of the ceremony. As the Ottoman counterterrorism and counterinsurgency ramped up in its use of direct violence and imprisonment between 1901 and 1903, just as the British did in Ireland in the early twentieth century and in Kenya after 1952, so the stakes increased for the insurgent organizations.

Oathing acquired new urgency as the priority shifted from secret keeping to preparing for direct, desperate action. It remained the core crossing point by which Macedonians—willingly or no, men or women, with friends, relatives and neighbors or alone, and in the presence of priests, or teachers, or military leaders—entered the "underground" that the organization had built for and through them. Insofar as "oathing-in" altered lives, it did so by thrusting knowledge upon the recruits, making them aware of this parallel, illegal world. It did not so much alter consciousness as generate risk, creating a set of combatants-in-waiting who could be viewed as predecessors to those on the "home front" of World War I and beyond, the population of a nation at war. This same kind of distinction within its ranks was reported of IRA organization in the 1920s (Barry 1956: 275–84), or of ETA mobilization in Spain (Horgan 2005: 99).

It was this effect of oathing that the British diplomats and Turkish authorities did not grasp and that underpinned the stubborn survival of the Macedonian Revolutionary Organization under Ottoman rule and beyond—all the way to Černozemski's murder of King Alexander in 1934. The Turkish military could through force of arms destroy individual četi, and they might, over time, successfully interdict the specialists in arms smuggling who operated among the pečalbari. But they never apparently targeted or succeeded in interrupting the MRO's oathing ceremonies. Through these recruitment efforts, the organization could count on networks of supporters whose lawbreaking was entirely invisible to the authorities but who were nevertheless, to appropriate a metaphor from economics, "vested," and from whom new četa members or other implementers of violence might come forward.

To be sure, the Macedonian Revolutionary Organization can be represented as one of the earliest and best-documented movements to harness terror; it can also be seen, in presentist mode, as a profound failure, in that the defeat of the uprising stymied the movement for several decades. But it was also one of the first insurgency movements to challenge the superior forces of an imperial power and survive, albeit in different form, to the next generation—whether one traces the continuity to Černozemski's deadly commitment or the rekindled activism that the Ilinden pension seeker Velika Hristova Dimitrova recalls from the early 1940s, in appendix 2.[13] The MRO endured, and attracted loyalty, not just by wedding its struggle to that of the Bulgarian Exarchate, nor simply by incrementally building on indigenous modes of the organization of resistance, but by transforming ideas that were enshrined in local practice into institutions of more extended significance.

The content and form of the oath, in this regard, are key sites for analyzing the particular mode of imagination that the MRO sought to conjure among its recruits. While the symbolism—Bible, dagger, revolver—evoked the concrete and the particular, the actual practices of oathing—in which marginalized Christians saw and laid their hands on forbidden artifacts, women earned a voice alongside men, and all oath takers uttered words they knew had been uttered by others before them and would be uttered again—encouraged a new and expanded vision of the collectivity to which they now belonged. Oaths, then, provide a key site for analysis, operating as a key vector of the imagination along which we can also trace new figurations of power, solidarity, and trust.

CHAPTER FOUR

The Archive and the Account Book:
Inscriptions of Terror

Whether simply borrowed from neighboring anti-Ottoman movements, inherited from revolutionary precedents, or developed organically along with other institutions typical of secret societies, the MRO oath expressed powerful sentiments and constituted a community. The scale and texture of that community evolved over time. In its first few years, the oath was administered to select, trusted individuals across the Macedonian countryside, especially teachers, shopkeepers, and urban professionals, who would then take on the responsibility of expanding the membership into their local circles of trust and acquaintance. It thus became a symbol of egalitarian solidarity, spreading in capillary fashion, cutting across existing divisions of wealth, generation, and gender. It was only as the 1903 uprising approached that the MRO began to expand its recruitment of new members exponentially through mass swearings-in to mobilize a critical mass of fighters to take the field.

In both phases, though, oathing alone could achieve nothing. What many of the stories of the Ilinden Dossier make clear is that oathing was almost invariably followed by the allocation of tasks and duties to the new swearer that made membership meaningful through practical action. The biographies in the dossier thus provide concrete answers to questions that methodological nationalism and pidgin social science tend to ignore. Although accounts focusing on the spread of nationalism may speak of the battle to win "hearts and minds," they more seldom address how exactly ideologies, national or otherwise, are communicated and enacted. This chapter explores how individuals brought together virtually in the symbolic moment of *communitas* represented by "oathing-in" proceeded to create relationships with others and demonstrate their commitment to the cause.[1]

The Archive in the Archive: Writing Remembered

Until the Vinica Affair of September 1897, the MRO had passed largely unrecognized by the Ottoman authorities. Given its short career before that, the

careful manner in which recruiting proceeded initially, and that the maintenance of armed *četas* was only institutionalized in 1896, membership was probably less than two thousand at that point, concentrated in towns and cities
where local committees were especially active.[2] Already, though, the organization had begun to plan for its expansion. Within a relatively short time from
its foundation by six young men who knew one another, the MRO put in place
tactics, techniques, and procedures to protect the identity of its senior members. An early device was the use of pseudonyms, which was made standard in
1896 (Perry 1988: 67); Goce Delčev took the heroic Greek name Ahil, Damjan Gruev took Marko (perhaps after the South Slavic fok hero Krale Marko),
while one of the Ilinden pensioners, Lazar Hristov Svetiev, reports that he had
the code name "Adam" and that only *vojvodas* and those who administered
oaths to new recruits knew his real identity (Record 31-S-15).

The Vinica Affair was launched by the Ottoman discovery of a weapons
cache—an unambiguous, easily legible sign of plans to use or threaten violence, even if the authorities did not yet know of what kind and against whom.
Later, though—both before and after the Ilinden Uprising of 1903—the biographies of the pension seekers point to other kinds of compromising traffic
that state scrutiny uncovered, including the existence of organization archives.
Dame Hristov Alžikočovski, of Prilep, records that he and a close associate,
Rampo Peškov, were arrested after a *četa* headed by Metodi Pačev was slaughtered in the village of Kadino; the *četa* archive was captured and the code
was broken (Record 2-A-72).[3] He also narrates a later incident when another
archive was captured by Ottoman authorities in the village of Toplica, Prilep region, and the entire leadership became outlaws. Sekula V. Jankuloski, of
Golemo Ilino, reports the Turkish authorities discovering his involvement in
the MRO when they killed a *četa's* secretary and thus captured the *četa* archive
in Slepče in 1904. Jankuloski was subsequently arrested (Record 14-J-32).

A variety of other pensioner biographies also attest to the importance
attached to archives of this kind and their own responsibility for them. Several
relate stories of being tasked with hiding or relocating archives when there was
danger they would be captured. Božin Stefanov Ilievski of Bitola, for example,
reports as one of his revolutionary activities keeping a *četa* archive in his house
during 1905. He was serving as a member of the Turkish gendarmerie at the
time, a dangerous double game where he took advantage of his position to
warn organization members if they were under suspicion, or to direct searches
away from neighborhoods where he knew of organization activities; in this

case, he knew Ottoman authorities were moving in on the archive holders, so he hid it in his home for a year as Ottoman authorities searched for it (Record 13-I-36).

During the Ilinden Uprising, when Kruševo was about to fall to the Ottoman counteroffensive, Donka Budžakoska reports that one of the *vojvodas,* Todor "the officer," brought a bag of books and materials from the organization and told her to hide it. She buried it in a rubbish heap and then told Kosta Škodra, the teacher, about it. He recovered it later (Box 5-B-52; see Brown 2003: 15–16, and appendix 2). Petruš Karev, brother of Nikola Karev, reported in his pension request that when the HQ of Kruševo closed down, the archive was entrusted to him, and fifteen months later he was instructed to bring the archive and documentation to Sofia (Box 16-K-51). The existence of archives is also documented in the correspondence of Nikola Kirov-Majski, a key intellectual figure from Kruševo. In a letter to Ljuben Lape, Todor Taleski, and Georgi Abadžiev, he records learning from his inquiries in Sofia that Damjan Gruev's whole archive was buried outside the village of Zašle (Kirov-Majski File, Macedonian National Archive, 1.976 2.101/172; letter dated Sofia, August 14, 1958).

Further evidence of the organization's commitment to record keeping comes from the existence of information specialists. Three pension seekers use the term *sekretar,* or secretary, to describe their own assigned role working with a particular *vojvoda* in a regional *četa,* while others apply the term to fellow members in the MRO.[4] All this strongly indicates that records were kept that were clearly transparent and compromising enough that their capture by Turkish forces could be catastrophic. According to Alžikočovski's and Jankuloski's accounts, these archives made it possible for the authorities to identify MRO members before they had taken any overt criminal action. The maintenance and protection of the archives of the organization, then, was always a major concern for all members, all of which strongly suggests that besides correspondence, regulations, and some kind of log of activities, the archives included lists of sworn-in adherents of the cause and possibly also records of tasks assigned to them.

As with the oath, historians of the MRO have invested little energy in interpreting the existence of archives. Duncan Perry, for example, passes over them in near-silence. Given his argument that much MRO activity was aimed at greater centralization of decision making (1988: 66), he would probably assign to the archive a straightforward functional role of making information available.[5] As well as membership details, the archive may also have included a record of financial contributions—always important to the organization, both to hold local leaders accountable for funds they had raised and to track those who were tardy or refused payment of dues demanded. The organization frequently issued receipts or bonds in return for contributions, and the issuing of such receipts seems likely to have been recorded in the archives (Moore 1906: 264, 268).[6] In at least two cases in the dossier, such receipts served to betray people to the authorities: Angel Korobar reports that a receipt for thirty napoleons, issued to his brothers by the Vrhovist organization of Sarafov, was intercepted by the authorities, and they were jailed. Lame Arnaudov, of Ohrid, reports being forced to flee when a receipt for money he had collected fell into Ottoman hands (Records 17-K-61; 2-A-52).

But the record-keeping practices of the organization can also be analyzed to reveal a cultural dimension. For even if membership records are practically necessary or instrumental, their form can also be symbolically or expressively significant. The fact that in the Macedonian Revolutionary Organization people recall the institution of an archive for local groups as well as permanent higher committees suggests an adoption, conscious or unconscious, of a bureaucratic form taken over from the state. The written document, after all, is a part of cultures imperial and colonial; Macedonians had contact with such artifacts in their contacts with the Ottoman bureaucracy. Such forms endowed legitimacy by giving the organization a certain aura of statehood for the people of Macedonia. The MRO's archives, then, can be argued to be one part of an iconography that people in Macedonia recognized as efficacious and powerful and a part of writing themselves into the future.

The information contained in the various documents generated and distributed by the MRO constructed virtual sinews for the organization as a whole. Bureaucracy is an important part of the modernist state's structure, permitting as it does the elevation of ties from the purely personal and providing a mode in which those ties can be imagined in more extensive ways. Macedonian leaders' efforts to provide their organization with this attribute suggest an agenda deeply concerned with creating and maintaining a collective project that could survive the loss of any particular individuals involved in it.

The act of writing, then—or more precisely, the iterated acts and circuits of record keeping—constituted a vital dimension of the MRO's instantiation of a "state within a state." The MRO embarked on the inherently risky project of making its personnel and practices legible as part of its agenda of self-legitimization. So, for example, when Albert Sonnichsen described the court hearings conducted in different villages by a četa in 1908, in which a "scribe" took notes, and referred to precedents established and written down during previous visits to the same village (1909: 171–74), we see a snapshot of a whole array of ongoing interactions between četas and local populations in which the organization vied for the status of incumbent regime. Their message in this process—which Sonnichsen described as "much like the progress of a circuit court"—was clear; we are here now to dispense justice, just as we have done before. And we are recording our verdicts and findings now, as we have in the past, to use when we dispense the same justice in the future.

Comparative Case Studies: Mau Mau Revisited

Again, the more extensive cycle of work on the Mau Mau insurgency in Kenya provides compelling evidence in support of a culturalist reading of this kind. Derek Petersen suggests that for Mau Mau supporters, the archive served as a status symbol for dispossessed people to document their involvement, as people otherwise without identity, in a project that was envisaged as yielding socioeconomic benefit. The Mau Mau rebellion, viewed in this light, was centrally concerned with land rights in the postcolonial state; Peterson argues that writing helped resolve questions of commitment among a people terrified that they would be forgotten in the march of the "modern" (Peterson 2004). Other scholars buttress this with further, concrete evidence. The Mau Mau leader Dedan Kimathi, for example, instructed fighters to retain records of property losses. By ensuring that fighters' personal sacrifices would be remembered, Mau Mau's record keeping created lineages of words in which fighters could invest sweat and blood (Smith 1998: 538).

In a second dimension, Mau Mau also used writing to imagine a new state that overturned British power. As Peterson puts it, "forest fighters used record books and identity cards to craft a sovereign polity in the forest" (Peterson 2004: 190); by co-opting markers of bureaucratic procedure, Mau Mau's educated leaders simultaneously provincialized the British (ibid.: 207). In parallel fashion, Smith states that writing (and reading) "facilitate social and spatial mobility, attributes associated with the colonial administration" (Smith 1998:

Figure 4.1. MRO leader Hristo Černopeev holding a conference with
a village local committee. Note the band's secretary at left, consulting notes.

526). Working independently with the same sources and a theoretical apparatus addressing symbolic appropriation, Peterson and Smith thus both suggest
that Mau Mau operated to become a "state within a state" by adopting and
appropriating rather than necessarily subverting the overt forms of colonial
domination.[7]

For Mau Mau, then, the archive operated alongside the oath to extend
and maintain the circuits of organizational loyalty. Although the context of
the MRO was anti-imperial rather than anticolonial per se, several aspects of
the archive's importance in Mau Mau seem consistent with the experience
of early twentieth-century Macedonia. Whereas the oath served as a primary
tool of moral solidarity, as members spoke themselves into a new unity, the
archives marked commonality only when in the hands of the organization's
enemies. By contrast, archives came into being as they were written, read, and
transported by different members of the MRO: In their turn, they brought into
being an internal and differentiated order among those members, defined by
interdependence. As the account noted above, those whose roles were most
obviously and intimately bound up with the production and maintenance of

the archives were the designated secretaries, who accompanied military leaders in the field, as this photograph from Sonnichsen's memoir records. But a focus on the social lives of the MRO's archives alongside its other writing projects and written products turns out to reveal much more about the organization than their content alone would indicate.

The Social Life of Insurgent Writing:
Secretaries, Couriers, and Words in Motion

The central place of schoolteachers, and to a lesser extent students, in the creation and ongoing leadership of the MRO is broadly agreed. The early activism of the 1890s encompassed literary and journalistic production including the journal *Loza*, denounced by Bulgarian leaders as separatist (Marinov 2009: 120–21). Later developments in this vein included Simeon Radev's *L'Effort* in Geneva, in which Boris Sarafov sank some of the returns from the Miss Stone kidnapping of 1901–1902, and *Of Macedonian Affairs*, the brilliant and polemical anti-Bulgarian and autonomist work of Krste Misirkov, first published in 1903 in Sofia (Misirkov 1974). Closer to home, within Ottoman Macedonia, reading and writing were more dangerous activities. Even Western journalists and travelers reported having their reading matter inspected; authorities were particularly sensitive to works of an anarchist or socialist orientation—the kind that Goce Delčev, Pavel Šatev, and others managed to smuggle in.

While early interchange between the founders of the MRO and their circle of acquaintances and future recruits was probably mostly unwritten, it remains notable that one of their first acts as a committee was to appoint Damjan Gruev as secretary and charge him with producing statutes for the organization. These were not published, but they did exist in multiple copies. Even though the document drew heavily on Bulgarian and other antecedents, this commitment speaks to an imagined future. So too do the procurement and circulation of instruction manuals and descriptions of operating procedures, which showed up on the bodies of MRO officials killed by Ottoman forces and are documented in the British consular reports (FO 195/2157/731: McGregor to Graves, October 31, 1903).

The foreign consuls were also aware of the circulation of letters and more specific instructions. These were intermittently uncovered by police action, with particular frequency in early 1903, when Ottoman security forces seem to have been on high alert. In January 1903, for example, Biliotti reported a letter seized on a schoolboy traveling from Resen to Bitola (FO 195/2156/130: Biliotti to Whitehead, January 26, 1903). In February 1903, he indicated (presumably on some authority) that "an inspector came from Sofia with letters from the Central Committee appointing him to the command of all the bands [in the Gevgheli region] but their chiefs refused to recognize him and he had to return (FO 195/2156/148: Biliotti to Whitehead, February 15, 1903). In March 1903, a written order from Sarafov to murder one of the consuls in Monastir was intercepted (FO 195/2156/238: Biliotti to Fontana & McGregor).

These clustered discoveries, together with the accounts of correspondence in the *pečalbar* circuits discussed in chapter 2, and cases like the exchange of letters between Sofia, Sliven, and Bitola described by Jovan Jurukovski in his biography, give a glimpse of the continuous, high-intensity generation and movement of written materials and instructions within the organization. Besides the secretaries who generated time-sensitive orders and maintained archives, a key role in its circulation was played by members of the organization that, in the Ilinden Dossier, described their role as that of courier (*kurier*). The term *kurier*, like *sekretar*, is clearly derived from a non-Slavic root. Almost 50 of the sample of the 375 explicitly use the term to describe themselves at some point in their association with the organization; others use it to refer to fellow members. Several indicate that this was their first title after swearing the oath, and indeed that it was generally the first level of activity expected from new members. Among their other tasks, which involved the transportation of munitions and food, and provision of escorts to *četas*, couriers carried letters. They thus met a functional need for an organization committed to indigenous action that therefore needed to communicate reliably and securely across considerable distances through an increasingly heavily policed area in order to synchronize and coordinate the efforts of local committees.

The risks of discovery escalated as the Ottoman authorities increasingly targeted the organization, especially its communication networks. The continuing crackdown promoted all kinds of ingenuity on the part of individuals and the organization. Operating in Salonika around 1900, for example, Nedelko Pop Nedelkov reported taking off his footwear, daubing his face with soot, and passing as a Rom (Gypsy) in order to carry messages within the city. He would carry on with the role, searching around for cigarette butts while he waited for an answer to be written, and then return (Record 25-N-5). Lazar Svetiev, who used the alias "Adam" in his correspondence, reported that although his letters were intercepted on several occasions, the Turks could not trace them back to him. In July 1903, though, he was trying to get a letter with the command to set fire to haystacks, thereby signaling the start of the uprising, out of Bitola to the countryside. Bitola was under close surveillance, and in his pension application he vividly relates a courier's quick thinking:

> The courier Sekule Kantar, from the village of Mogila, Bitola region, was standing at my side and I had to give him a letter, but at the time Bitola was under military blockade. At the market the Turkish officer was looking directly at us and we had to wait for him to go away in order to pass the letter. When the officer had left I gave the letter to Sekule and he left through the burned shop beside us, but then the Turkish officer came back and shouted after Sekule: "Wait, old man!" But Sekule replied, "Ah, let me meet you at the other side." At that instant Sekule threw the letter in a gutter filled with water and stepped on it and then continued to meet the officer. The officer took Sekule to the police garrison, and there they undressed him completely in order to find the letter, but couldn't find anything and so Sekule was released. (Record 31-S-15: see also appendix)

Couriers faced the risk of search throughout their journeys. Letters, of course, were easier to conceal than the food or munitions that were also frequently put in their hands to deliver. But conversely, the letters were often more urgent, and if decoded they could yield more incriminating data than, for example, a pair of shoes. And on the longer, iterated journeys between communities that many reported being part of their regular work, different kinds of ingenuity were called for. Rather than disguise or disposal, many opted for the cover of normality. Našku Nane, for example, handled correspondence between Prilep and Kruševo while plying his trade as a butcher, in which movement was commonplace. Because of that, he writes, "I could go to the villages without suspicion from the authorities, and I could thus make the connections necessary for courier work." As well as taking letters to a *vojvoda*, Iljo, in Prilep, he also conveyed rifles to named individuals in the nearby villages of Ostrilci and Žurče (Record 24-N-79).

The same principle that everyday business could provide a cover for illicit activities also emerges from the accounts of Dimo Hristov Dimoski, who, after domestic service in Kruševo and migrant labor in Belgrade, returned in 1901 to the village of Žvan to set up as a market gardener. He was quickly recruited and made responsible for carrying the regular MRO mail between Žvan and Belmevci, and he reported concealing letters, as well as arms and other materials, in the peppers he carried around to sell (Box 9-D-65). Lazar Dimov Aračeski exploited the rhythms imposed by kin-visiting obligations, carrying letters between his home village of Capari and Srpce, where an uncle lived (Record 2-A-48). Velika Gjakerkoska was charged with various trips between Sveti Mitrani and Kruševo and accomplished her work by leveraging the discipline of the regular Ottoman army. She reported that they would never search a woman the way that they did, for example, Sekule Kantar in Bitola, although he was already an "old man." And so, she reported, "(when) they sent us [Gjakerkoska and a friend, Cveta] to Kruševo to carry letters, and we didn't have any way to do it, we took off our socks and hid them under our feet" (Record 11-Gj-1).[8]

Such accounts show awareness on the part of the organization of the constraints under which Ottoman imperial authorities operated; according to consular sources, and also the journalism of Leon Trotsky, religious figures and women were not subject to search (Trotsky 1980: 127). The organization appeared to believe that that extended to low-caste or other apparently non-threatening figures—in Kantar's case an old man—who could blend into the urban landscape. And hence we read accounts of travel over a slightly wider radius, with men relying on soldiers' tendency to let regular routines go unexamined while women work the seams of cultural knowledge regarding Ottoman practice. In both regards, what we see are classic tactics of insurgent movements.

The courier, then, was the basic role played by the rank and file of the organization. They were the bulk of the membership described, in a Western-derived term that recurs across the Illinden Dossier, as *legalni* (legal) members. This is perhaps the single most important distinction among pension seekers themselves, all of whom claim involvement in the organization or the uprising. Where the *ilegalni* were the men in the hills, those formally identified by the authorities as threats to order, their number was never large. It did not need to be. Behind them was a much larger body of organization members still resident in their villages, going about their everyday business, but also serving a variety of vital functions. The fact that they existed was clearly known in the abstract to the authorities, and probably concretely, though without firm proof, by the troops on the ground. Some pension accounts recall vividly the anger and frustration expressed by Ottoman officers especially when they were forced to release men they had every reason to believe would resume the work of trying to kill them and overthrow the system they were employed to maintain.[9] This, perhaps, helps explain individual incidents in which the imperial army carried out lethal attacks on "innocent" villages such as Smûrdeš, which was destroyed in April 1903, to considerable outrage from Western journalists. Denounced as incidents of Ottoman "barbarity," they bear comparison to breakdowns of discipline within "civilized" armed forces operating in contexts of counterinsurgency. The My Lai massacre in Vietnam remains the iconic example of such breakdowns.[10]

Under normal circumstances, when the archives were protected and all members honored the oath of secrecy, *legalni* avoided individual identification and overt activism and thus were able to live out their lives in the open, while simultaneously constituting a network enrolled and invested in the organization's cause. The activities they conducted, although illegal in the sense that they made a contribution to the organization, were more often than not superimposed on activities that were habitual, the rigorous and consistent policing of which would have stretched imperial resources beyond their capacity.

For Macedonia was a space of perpetual, restless motion. In towns invested in pastoralist ecology, sheep and goats followed a seasonal round depending on pasture availability, and they would make their way down to market in Salonika, either on the hoof or as dried meat. Large groups of charcoal workers and construction workers, as well as more specialized craftsmen, would cross external or internal borders, following long-established patterns. Apprentices and schoolchildren might traverse substantial distances daily, weekly, or monthly, if education or training was not available in their home towns. And the enduring importance of kin ties out to several degrees of cousin, together with the Christian calendar of name and saint days, ensured a constant flow of people on visits for weddings, present or future, between nearby villages and towns. Such ritual obligations were maintained predominantly by women, who were also called on to play larger economic roles by the recurring absence of husbands on labor migration.

The result was a counterinsurgent's nightmare. The MRO's legal members were drawn from a far larger cross-section of the population than the young males who took the field in the Ilinden Uprising; they included older men who might be married with dependents, and a substantial number of resourceful and courageous women. Their biographies show their pride in the vital roles they played, and often defensiveness or querulousness in the face of the government's apparent ignorance or devaluation of their contributions. Thus when Stefan Stojanov Ilioski of Prilep, a tailor who repaired the clothes of četa members, reported that he always worked for the organization "*i ako bev legalen*"—"even if I was [just] a legal member"—the syntax betrays awareness that his importance might be misunderstood (Box 13-I-58). He perhaps also reacted to the explicit bias in the terms and conditions of the Ilinden pension scheme, which asked for examples where the claimant had participated with "gun in hand." In this regard, despite celebrating the notion of "people's war" through the pension scheme, the kinds of action that the Yugoslav Macedonian government explicitly valorized reflected a fixation on masculinist and nationally and territorially limited modes of resistance.[11]

The generation, maintenance, and circulation of archives and internal correspondence thus brought secretaries and couriers into close collaboration. For the most part the holders of these responsibilities had taken the oath of loyalty, obedience, and silence; their primary responsibilities were focused on organization building through record keeping and communication. Their efficiency was demonstrated by their work's being legible to others within the organization while remaining invisible to those outside. They provided logistical support and legitimizing force to those in the organization charged with carrying out precise, timely direct action against enemies. A number of those who reported their work as *sekretars* or *kuriers* specifically named *vojvodi* under whom they served. So for example Gjorgji Tomov Nikolovski reports that his designated role was to complete the circuit between "Koce," a četa leader, and Tome Niklev, one of the leaders of the organization in Kruševo (Record 25-N-62).

Such personal association is also confirmed in Jovan Jurukovski's account, which also reveals how significant the risks were for couriers. Jurukovski was the četa leader from Tresonče, near Galičnik, who was recruited by Goce Delčev in Bulgaria; he had a designated courier, Jovan Terziev Vrleski, under his direct command. In September 1904, another courier was captured with letters and other materials, and revealed Terziev's identity under torture. Turkish authorities then tortured Terziev until he agreed to take them to Selce, where the *četa* was stationed. Terziev honored his ultimate responsibility as a courier to protect what was entrusted to him. Jurukovski describes his last acts as follows:

> After a long period of torture he agreed to take them to Selce. But when they got close to the village, Jovan cried in a loud voice: "Run brothers! You are betrayed!" When the soldiers heard that they took out his eyes with hot irons and then killed him, after which a battle started. All the *četniks* managed to save themselves and escape. This took place around 2 o'clock in the morning. (Record 15-J-54)

Catalytic Power: Couriers, Terrorists, and Deadly Force

Alongside such enduring, stable, and sacred relationships with leaders and secretaries, though, couriers and the messages they carried were also instrumental in precipitating action that changed the status of other members. Besides their work in organization building, couriers were also vital mediators in the mechanisms of punishment and retribution upon which the MRO increasingly relied for its survival. For although the ritualization of the MRO's oathing practices was intended to enhance their impact and hold on the oath taker's imagination, there is no evidence that the organization or its leadership, centrally or spontaneously, sought to upgrade or intensify the experience of oathing, as Mau Mau's members, trapped in smaller pockets of the forest, did. Instead, the MRO enforced the secular sanctity of the oath by ensuring that tangible, real-world sanctions were quickly applied against those who refused it or who pledged faith and then reneged. Such measures further enhanced the organization's reputation as a perpetrator of swift and deadly justice—deterring would-be holdouts or double-dealers and also strengthening support among its followers—by also targeting representatives of the Turkish occupation who abused their power.

Those who meted out the organization's death penalty on traitors or enemies were assigned another title, again derived from a Western term, that appears in the Ilinden Dossier: *terorist*. Of the sample of 375 pension seekers, nine claim the title for themselves; two of those indicate that they were heads of terrorist groups. Tome Angelov Pop-Hristovski, of Prilep, speaks for a majority of these self-described terrorists when he reports his main roles as carrying out organization orders to eliminate "spies and traitors" (Record 29-P-59). Most of these victims were fellow Christians living in the same community as those designated to kill them. The small sample size here limits broader conclusions about the scale and scope of these terrorist cells and their activities, but it is striking that six of the nine who apply the term to themselves, including Pop-Hristovski, were from Prilep and operated out of that city.[12]

A majority also stress that they took up the role of terrorist in the years immediately after 1903. In his detailed account of a variety of roles that included organizer and terrorist, Dimitar Gligorov Bojadžiev of Bitola powerfully conveys the way a further form of organization-authorized writing was involved in these operations and constituted a key part of the terrorists' work. Writing in 1952, Bojadžiev recalled the following incident:

> In 1905 the struggles began between us and the Greeks, and the town and regional committee was formed to defend the population from violence and spies, and to prosecute spies and troublemakers. I was chosen as head of the town-area courts, and chief of terrorists. In the house of Frosa, who was in the organization, we drowned Dulger-Ali Teslaro, and took him [out] near Sveta Nedela and there we hanged him from a tree, and we put an account of his offense, with the stamp of the committee, around his neck, so that it would be known how we punished spies. (Record 4-B-54)

This use of writing after the fact—narrating the murder for a larger audience—recurs in a number of other cases from the period, including for example the would-be gendarme described in chapter 1 (FO 195/2156/130: Biliotti to Whitehead, February 5, 1903). Similar methods of punishment and deterrence were also adopted by other organizations operating in the region. Albert Sonnichsen, who like a handful of other journalists chose to "embed" with a četa on patrol in Macedonia, recounts an instance of a Greek government–sponsored band using similar methods of publicity for their actions. After the MRO četa left the village of Mesimir, close to Voden, Sonnichsen described the penalty exacted on their hosts:

The two who had been our guides were found the next evening in the forest with their throats slit, and on one was pinned a letter bearing the familiar crucifixial seal of the military arm of the [Patriarchist] church. Said the letter:

"Such is the fate of all those traitors who would betray their Church by serving the infidel brigand, Luka. Beware, you of the guilty hearts; when the brigand entered your houses last night, the eyes of the Holy Church was on him and the guilty ones." (Sonnichsen 1909: 74)

These efforts to articulate the agenda of the different organizations were intended for local audiences, and they blur the categories of communication described by Ranajit Guha (1999: 193–95). Guha contrasts typical forms of correspondence intended for potential allies as "insurgent peasant communications" (IPC) and for actual enemies as "anonymous threatening letters" (ATL). "Corpse-messaging" of this kind appears to be a hybrid form that sets out to impress would-be opponents or resisters and derives part of its persuasive power from the bodies themselves. A technique still in use by criminal organizations and insurgent movements who embrace terrorism (Finnegan 2010: 42–43), it had become sufficiently commonplace in early twentieth-century Macedonia to warrant a dedicated consular report (FO 195/2133/685: Biliotti to O'Conor, October 5, 1902).

In an even more dramatic fashion than written death warrants issued by the organization, these examples brought writing, reading, and action into close alignment. Two of the cases—the MRO execution carried out by Bojadžiev and the later Greek reprisal reported by Sonnichsen—feature use of an organization's seal, legitimizing the killing. Seals were vital then—as they are in so much bureaucratic paperwork today—in conveying authenticity and authority. In 1901, Ivan Garvanov came into sole possession of the seals and codes of the Central Committee of the MRO in Salonika after a series of arrests of his fellow members (Perry 1988: 97–98). Gjorče Petrov and Goce Delčev sent a circular to all local committees urging them to provide assistance only to četas or individuals possessing a "certificate" signed by the two of them, thereby seeking to "trump" Garvanov's bureaucratic power (Andonov-Poljanksi 1985: 384–85). Nonetheless, historians suggest that Garvanov's possession of the seals and codes gave him control of the organization and ultimately allowed him to orchestrate the timing of the uprising, against the opposition of Delčev and others (Katardžiev 1993: 41).

By affixing seals to letters, and letters to bodies, the MRO and its Greek rival passed judgment on perpetrators and issued a warning to their confederates, known or unknown. These cases represent attempts to draw a line under violent acts by narrating them to audiences in a way that makes clear that the violence is responsive and punitive, rather than pre-emptive. They ask to be seen as attempts to police and modify behavior, rather than to provoke further bloodshed.

Such attempts, of course, represented challenges to other utterances, written, spoken, or enacted. Some would undoubtedly dispute that Luka, whom the Greek assassins labeled an "infidel brigand," was godless, or at least any more godless than a movement that sanctioned such violence. Others—especially moderates, who might have welcomed the prospect of an internationally supervised police reform—would challenge the presumption that the Lopatica man who sought to join the gendarmerie was necessarily abandoning his own people to "serve the Turks." Such attempts to draw the lines of morally acceptable and unacceptable conduct by literally attaching definitions to dead bodies did not always achieve their apparent, external goals; instead, the rhetoric of terror, whether expressed in words or through increasingly shocking or painful methods of execution, escalated along with the tempo of killing. What writing made possible was a system of mutually assured retribution between rival insurgent movements struggling, and failing, to establish themselves as incumbent monopolists of violence.

Signaling to "outsiders"—that is, audiences with whom they did not already have channels of communication—was only part of the organization's agenda in ordering these executions. Of equal or greater importance was that each such assassination both affirmed the potency of the organization to command not just tacit support, but active obedience from its members. The use of writing, in particular, was central in this regard: it was part of a process of the organization's self-definition as modern, consistent, rule-bound, and therefore deserving of loyalty (in the best case) or, more minimally, fearful respect.

Money Matters: Blagajniks and the Circuits of Taxation

As alluded to earlier, couriers played a role in handling other forms of contraband—especially munitions but also food and clothing—as well as in ensuring safe passage for četas. The following chapter will address more fully the couriers' roles in managing other dimensions of communication and circulation, in which written instructions were less central. But there remains one circuit, involving written and paper artifacts, that was absolutely central to the organization's operations and yet where, by their own account, couriers played next to no role: the MRO's finances. Among all the descriptions of courier work in the Ilinden Dossier, not one explicitly mentions carrying hard currency or paper money from one location to another. A few pension seekers do claim for themselves a role in collecting money for the organization—including members who spent time in the United States, Izmir (Smyrna), and Athens, Greece.[13] As discussed earlier, finances were a continuous concern for the organization, and they prompted the actual and proposed kidnappings of wealthy locals as well as higher-profile foreigners like the American missionary Miss Ellen Stone, captured in 1901. The story of the ransom in her case highlights the logistical problems of moving money around the Macedonian landscape, where other forces—whether rival state-sponsored bands, predatory, semi-licit Albanian raiders, and the Ottoman military and police—posed the continuous threat of theft or discovery of MRO resources (Carpenter 2003; see also Sonnichsen 1908: 255–66; Stone 1902).

The consular archives also make clear that the organization levied funds from the local population. The Foreign Office records also allude to the collection of dues by the organization in the months before the Ilinden Uprising, most explicitly in a report from February 1903:

> Committee tax collectors traverse the country regularly, collecting the taxes levied by one of their numbers in each villages every fortnight or month, from every person without regard to sex or age—no longer one but two metalliques (1d) per week. These imposts [sic] are bitterly resented even by the Bulgarians, but they dare not object to them. . . . in order to make the extortion of money less objectionable, the tax collectors give the peasants receipts for the moneys paid, to be honoured when Macedonia is autonomous. (FO 195/2156/189: Biliotti to O'Conor, February 28, 1903)

Three months later, McGregor wrote from Monastir that:

> Blackmail continues to be levied, although apparently on a smaller scale, but I was recently shown a printed receipt for fifteen liras which bore the number

3000 odd and was stamped with the seal of the "Second Revolutionary Arrondissement"—that of Monastir. (FO 195/2156/61: McGregor to Biliotti, May 20, 1903)

Edith Durham, a critic of the organization, was also shown a receipt by an injured man in the hospital in Ohrid, who reported the leader of a band had "made him kill three oxen and turn 'četnik.' The note was for 5 pounds, but the man vowed his cattle had been worth 12 pounds" (Durham 1905: 202).

The organization, then, was also generating another set of written materials alongside the letters and instructions to its personnel. These included ransom notes and receipts, the primary function of which was to prompt and also document the flow of hard currency into its war chests. The instrumental end for most of this money, in turn, was to finance the purchase of munitions, especially rifles. The Ilinden Dossier contains numerous examples of members purchasing rifles either for their own use or in bulk. In both cases, as with the terrorists and executioners described above, they generally state explicitly that they did so on direct orders from the organization. Central MRO sources, reported by Perry (1988: 132–33), also indicate that regional commanders had a good sense of the total number of rifles that members in their region had acquired and stockpiled.[14]

This secondary evidence suggests that money and records of purchases were circulating along with all the other resources that the Ilinden archives describe; what is less clear, given the reticence on this matter among the pension applicants, is in what form, along what routes, and in whose hands. One answer lies in a further category of belonging that the sources use. Out of the sample of 375, three men—Nikola Neškov Kondarkoski of Kruševo, Cvetan Angelev Bogevski of Sveti Mitrani, and Sekula V. Jankuloski of Golemo Ilino—refer to themselves as occupying the post in the organization of *blagajnik* (treasurer), while a fourth—Lazar Svetiev of Bitola, who was in fact a regional *vojvoda*—reports being accused by the Ottoman authorities of being a *kasier*, or cashier (Records 17-K-59; 4-B-29; 14-J-32; see also 31-S-15).

In their biographies, Kondarkoski, Bogevski, and Jankuloski all claim long-term membership and senior-level participation in organization activities. Two—Bogeski and Jankuloski—had served earlier as *desetars*, leaders of the standard cell of ten members, before being tapped to serve as treasurers. Jankuloski had also participated in the execution of a spy and had been arrested and beaten by the Ottoman authorities before being released and taking on the new role. Kondarkoski, meanwhile, appears to have offered different credentials for the role: as a merchant and shopkeeper in Kruševo, he appears to have been tapped by the organization for this role because of his accounting experience in the "legal" world.

All three narratives thus indicate a wealth of experience both within the organization and at the interface between the secret world in which it operated and the wider world where it sought, ultimately, to make a difference. They also suggest that they managed written records of a different kind from those described in the domain of MRO's secretaries. The latter took primary responsibility for *internal* archives and correspondence, generating commands that drove action but that also created the structure of the organization in the very fact of their transmission. In a similar mode, loyalty, obedience, and secrecy came into being along the channels of communication that the courier network represented. The orders that passed through this network—the product of the work of the secretaries—had an effect on those that carried them, even though their contents remained unknown until they reached their final recipient. The effect of this writing on the world was most apparent in the case of authorizations of or orders for executions. As they traveled through the organization's circuitry, those written words simultaneously sealed the fate of an enemy of the organization, bound the executioner still more tightly to the organization, and through the public declarations frequently made at the time, signaled both of these accomplishments to wider audiences.

If secretaries, then, were the content providers at the heart of a system of message creation and distribution, the MRO's treasurers presided over a network far more closely interconnected with the world beyond the organization. Although dues were reportedly levied and paid by all members, requiring documentation, almost everyone involved was bound to the organization in more meaningful ways by the work they were asked to do—as oath giver, organizer, secretary, terrorist, courier, or treasurer, or in one of the roles in the *četa* system. Treasurers, then, were more oriented toward drawing material resources through the organization's circulatory system, rather than strengthening that system itself by generating written material that established and flowed along its channels.

As such, treasurers were ultimately more focused on preparations for a future event—the mass uprising or an expanded campaign of spectacular terrorism—than day-to-day functioning and human capacity building. Their objective was to ensure that the necessary weapons were available, either in organization stockpiles or in individual members' possession, for use within the time frame designated by the leadership. Because this vision of the organization's methods developed only at the very end of the 1890s, and also because the date of the uprising was set earlier than most of the regional commanders had recommended, the time in which treasurers played a key role was relatively short—one plausible explanation for the relatively low number of Ilinden pension seekers claiming the title for themselves.

Those that did were the stewards of the revolution rather than the managers of the movement. Where the *sekretars* trafficked in intangibles—loyalty, obedience, secrecy—the *blagajniks* were the overseers of transactions with very concrete outputs. Revenues each month, and additional rifles and cartridges procured, were the metrics of their success and also their probity. They certainly relied on some of the same personnel; tax collectors, who operated under orders from and in close coordination with cashiers, frequently included those designated as terrorists, who were brought into existence in that role by orders emanating from leaders, articulated by secretaries, and delivered by couriers. But once amassed, funds and accounting records were far less mobile; they were both too valuable to risk in the face of outside depredation and arguably too easily appropriated by couriers with less experience and investment in the movement.

Treasurers oversaw a different genre of writing from the secretaries: each role contributed to the making and maintenance of the MRO as a "state within a state." Their work constitutes the invisible dimensions of the uprising and the movement, revealed in the Ilinden Dossier fifty years later, but still far from completely mapped. Taken together with consular records and comparative cases, though, the biographies of MRO's foot soldiers and functionaries make it possible to discern the symbolic and pragmatic effects of these two different, but overlapping, circuits of trust and terror. Secretaries were the key guardians of the organization's growing, living history, as they generated and maintained archives that over time served to legitimate its claims to supersede the Ottoman authorities as protector of security and administrator of justice, as well as collector of taxes. Secretaries were also the primary generators of the written correspondence that both filled the archive and fueled the everyday work of the bulk of the organization's members, the couriers. Although the oath marked their formal induction to the MRO, it was through the delivery of messages that most members made their allegiance and reliability tangible. Secretaries thus also managed the organization's present, driving the traffic in messages that put couriers to work and that gave other members tasks, including the assassinations through which their status was transformed.

Treasurers, meanwhile, were charged with the task of building the MRO's future. They did so by overseeing the business of insurgency, drawing financial resources into the organization's coffers for the definite end of visibly and directly challenging the Ottoman Empire. In setting and administering taxes—transferring private or individual resources into a common treasury—and in taking responsibility for the funds thus collected, the treasurers too performed a range of inscriptive work, setting prices and generating receipts and ledgers of contributions expected and received. Both *sekretar* and *blagajnik* might appear as minor, bureaucratic roles in the organization as a whole. Both, though, were vital agents whose seemingly mundane work—for those willing and able to read it—conjured the MRO into being on a daily basis, built its institutional capacity, and demonstrated its unswerving commitment to autonomy to friend, foe, and bystander alike.

CHAPTER FIVE

The Četa and the Jatak:
Inversions of Tradition, Conversions of Capital

Between 1893 and 1903, the Macedonian Revolutionary Organization introduced a new lexicon of loyalty, obedience, and terror into Macedonia through
a set of interlocking practices and categories of commitment. The oath created a sense of horizontal comradeship among those who took the same oath,
knowing that others had taken it before and others would take it later. A variety
of writing practices, which generated archives, requests for information, death
sentences, and receipts, also created and maintained a set of interdependent
roles, through which a demographically diverse set of individuals contributed
in different ways to a project larger than themselves and their aspirations.
In the classical terms of social science, then, the organization could boast
mechanical solidarity and organic solidarity. It was by these means that the
organization's founders, and the circle of informed, future-oriented teachers,
students, merchants, and military officers they painstakingly recruited, grew
the movement beyond its "face-to-face" origins to constitute, in the minimal-
ist definition offered by Benedict Anderson, an imagined community.

Anderson's key insight, of course, was to insist that communities be distinguished "not by their falsity/genuineness, but by the style in which they
are imagined" (Anderson 1983: 6). In this regard, the MRO's project was to
reimagine a dispossessed and politically subjugated population as a sovereign
people. A key component of this project was the creation of military capacity as a means to achieve the popular goal of political autonomy. This was a
multistage operation: besides the material dimensions of acquiring sufficient
munitions to counter or deter attacks against the MRO's civilian supporters
by Ottoman army units and their irregular auxiliaries, or by the paramilitary
forces sent into Macedonia by neighboring states with their own territorial
designs on the region, the organization also faced challenges in the symbolic
domain. In an undergoverned imperial context where localized brigandage
and banditry had long-established cultural and social roots, the MRO sought
to harness and direct traditions of "social banditry" to win the local support

without which no insurgency can ultimately survive (Weinstein 2007). At the same time, the organization continuously struggled to counter the impression actively advanced by the sultan and the Greek Patriarchate that it was simply a more organized, larger-scale criminal enterprise along these lines. Finally, the organization also had to contend with the constant and often beguiling offers of assistance from Bulgaria and the Exarchate, which would have resolved many of their logistical problems but simultaneously undermined the principle of Macedonian autonomy at the heart of the struggle.

Legitimacy, then, was a key arena of concern for the organization, in its internal and external orientation. As indicated earlier, a key distinction that emerges from the memoirs of participants is the distinction between, and the relationship between, legal and illegal modes of activity. While many individual biographers refer to themselves as *legalni,* a minority refer to a one-time switch by which they became *ilegalni.* The distinction mirrors that made by many observers of Macedonia, as well as other territories under foreign rule, of two political and social worlds existing in the same physical space: the "slow buffaloes and shuffling, plodding peasants" were, for those with the sources and imagination to grasp it, also involved in the making and maintenance of a virtual underground republic (Doolard 1936: 104).[1] The circuitry described so far—of oath givers and oath takers, secretaries and couriers, treasurers, terrorists, and tax collectors—spoke, wrote, and financed this new world into being. It served simultaneously to draw a clear distinction between the work of the organization and the culture of brigandage. The work was covert and iterative, and it focused primarily on growing the organization itself rather than confronting its enemies. Where the written documents they produced and distributed had swift and decisive effects in the world—the instructions to terrorists who punished defectors being a prime example—they date for the most part from after the Vinica Affair of 1897, when the MRO's existence was uncovered by the Ottoman authorities. Until then, the movement had been visible only to its members and had been focused on recruitment and the creation of solidarity.

In its nonmilitant properties, the MRO bore some resemblance to other more recent popular movements, among then the parallel state constructed in the course of the 1990s by Kosova's Albanians in the face of Serbian apartheid-like rule. As a province within the Republic of Serbia, Kosova was home to an Albanian majority that consistently aspired to greater autonomy. This activism was manifest in the formation of numerous illicit organizations, many of which were uncovered by Yugoslav authorities in the late 1970s (Ramet 1995: 201–205). In 1981, inspired in part by protest movements in Poland, Kosovars staged widespread demonstrations against what they termed Serbian colonial rule, which prompted a severe crackdown, thousands of arrests, and the torture of those identified as leaders (Mertus 1999: 76–86). After a decade of increasing repression, Kosovars established their own underground republic. Patients sought treatment at makeshift hospitals and clinics staffed by doctors who were excluded from or chose not to work in the official state apparatus, while students pursued university studies through classes taught in improvised classrooms in garages, basements, or anywhere they could elude Serbian surveillance (Reineck 2000: 365–66; Udovički and Ridgeway 1997: 290–92). Critics call such systems "black" or "wild," emphasizing their lack of access to the full resources of a modern hospital and the fact that the degree earned is not authorized by any national government. The apparatus nonetheless won widespread support among Kosova's Albanians, who contributed financially to the enterprise through a 3 percent tax (Sullivan 2004: 76–77).

The 1990s movement, led by Ibrahim Rugova, was inspired by the nonviolent methodologies of Mahatma Gandhi and Martin Luther King. Its moral authority among Kosova's Albanians was finally superseded by the Kosova Liberation Army, whose leaders capitalized on widespread frustration that Serbian oppression continued—and indeed escalated—while the international community, whose support they had hoped to elicit, took no decisive action. Violence, argued the KLA, was necessary to bring about change.

The turn to direct, armed action, capitalizing on the foundations of solidarity laid by organizations created for other ends, can also be argued to characterize the Kenyan case discussed earlier, in which Mau Mau adopted and expanded on activism set in motion by the KCA. One can also see the same tensions at work in the Indian case, where anti-imperial movements included Bengali organizations that espoused violence in the same period that the MRO was operating; shared links to transnational activism (Heehs 1994); and later included direct attacks on imperial forces, like the case of Chauri Chaura documented by Shahid Amin (1995).

What these examples demonstrate is that there is no preordained path for how an anti-imperial movement will evolve. Biographically oriented historians point to the impact of particular charismatic leaders, where political scientists may emphasize recurring socioeconomic realities. Anthropologists and culturally oriented historians may point to the specific context of a situation. For example, Hobsbawm and others suggest that the *četas* of the Balkan revolutionary movements were significantly shaped by traditions of social banditry in the region; in Hobsbawm's words, "the village schoolmasters . . . copied the traditional pattern of *hajduk*-guerillas in their military structure" (Hobsbawm 1969: 91).

This chapter focuses on the transition from growing and maintaining the organization to carrying out military and paramilitary action. The first section documents how the armed wing of the MRO came into being, how it was organized and operated, and how it drew on existing traditions or armed anti-incumbent activism. The second section uses that data to explore how different interpretations of the military side of the organization have contributed to the broader historiography in ways that have overwritten the kinds of efforts that the organization and its members made to write themselves into history. Again, the analysis begins with the terms used by a range of sources to categorize different forms of engagement in the struggle, and it proceeds to reconstruct the logic and practice of the organization's military and paramilitary operations that reached a peak in the Ilinden Uprising of 1903.

Traditions of Resistance: Hajduks *and Their Brethren*

Chapter 4 examined how the terms *sekretar, kasier, kurier,* and *terorist,* all words imported into Macedonian usage from European languages, figured in the MRO's structure and practice. Ilinden veterans who claimed status as either secretary or cashier indicated that they had direct contact or experience with the MRO's armed wing. All male, they served in one or more bands, or *četi,* and reported directly to a band leader to whom they gave the title *vojvoda.*

The widespread use of the term *četa,* and the etymologically linked term *četnik* for a band member, provides an object lesson in the dangers of presentism and methodological nationalism in Balkan history. Since the bitter, internecine fighting of World War II, and even more so since the bloody breakup of Yugoslavia in the 1990s, "*četnik*" has come to denote Serb nationalist paramilitaries only. But in the late nineteenth and early twentieth centuries, the terms "*četa*" and "*četniks*" were used alongside a range of Slavic, Greek, and Turkish terms to describe armed groups (commonly termed "bands") and individuals (commonly termed "bandits") operating outside the jurisdiction of the Ottoman Empire and its successor states. These were the *klefts* or the *andartes* in Greece, and the various *uskoks, kachaks, celalis,* and, in particular, the *hajduks,* who play a central role in the national folklore of the region and who provide the raw material for now-classic studies on "prerevolutionary" or "primitive" rebellion.

Scholarly work on this topic was pioneered by Eric Hobsbawm, who coined the term "social bandit" to describe the outlaw of which Robin Hood is the English folk archetype, targeting the wealthy and powerful for his livelihood, treated as a hero by the peasantry with whom, at times, he shares his spoils (Hobsbawm 1959). In larger historical terms, Hobsbawm saw the figure as an intermediary step in the development of rural resistance and protest, a bridge between the purely mercenary activities of brigands and the revolutionary work of rural insurgents that may arise in modern agrarian systems. The social bandit, in Hobsbawm's view, is a specific form arising in certain stages of state development. He also distinguished, in *Bandits,* two other forms: the "primitive resistance" fighter he calls the *hajduk,* and the "terror-bringing avenger" (Hobsbawm 1969; see also Ranger 1968).

Hobsbawm's work, international and comparative in scope but drawing heavily on sources from the Ottoman Balkans, has inspired a significant body of subsequent literature that has considerably enhanced understandings of the realities of brigand life behind the romance. Anton Blok and other critics of Hobsbawm see all bandits, ultimately, as parasites who gravitate toward recruitment as enforcers by the powers that be; historically, they are seldom "bound" by anything but contingent ties to the peasantry that elevates them to the status of heroes (Blok 1975; see also O'Malley 1979).

Detailed studies of the Ottoman Empire appear to confirm Blok's view that many of these alleged rebels or social bandits are best read as symptoms of deep, systemic codependence and complicity between central authorities and peripheral power brokers. Karen Barkey, for example, in a study of Anatolian *celalis,* suggests ongoing accommodation between such groups and the states within which they operate (Barkey 1994: 230). Svetozar Koljević traces the history of outlaw figures in Serbian folk epic, drawing attention to their ambivalence, whereby they could cooperate with states and rulers as well as oppose them. Wendy Bracewell, documenting the Uskoks of Senj, suggests that these paramilitaries in the sixteenth century did find a state sponsor, as

Blok would have it, but they also emerge as ambiguous figures who some-times serve, even unwittingly, to protect peasants from depredation (Koljević 1980; Bracewell 1992).

In one extended case study of this kind, John Koliopoulos documents the basic social and cultural principles on which "Greek" brigand bands operated in the nineteenth-century imperial borderlands where "the already blurred line separating legality from lawlessness vanished completely." Cattle rus-tlers [klefts] or brigands [andartes] found employment as irregular auxiliaries [armatoles], local noblemen's retinues practiced extortion, and individuals found themselves occupying different roles at different times (Koliopoulos 1987: 317–18; see also Hobsbawm 1969: 89). Band life, reports Koliopoulos, was "neither independent from nor hostile towards the basic social compo-nents of the mountain world, [but instead was] an extension of those com-ponents, most notably of the pastoral association, which the law of the state aimed to sever but common interest held together" (Koliopoulos 1987: 258). Koliopoulos notes in particular the common cultural forms shared by pasto-ralist society and the brigand life, ranging from diet (heavily meat-based) to forms of fictive kinship (blood brotherhood, he notes, was a major feature of both, and so much associated with brigandage that the state took measures against it). There were basic forms of rank within bands, ranging from chief through lieutenants to common members, who were distinguished between regular brigands and novices. The designated roles included, for example, bajraktar, literally "flag-bearer," as a kind of lieutenant, and a secretary whose role was to deal with correspondence (ibid.: 261).

Rules of Engagement: The Brigands' Code

Koliopoulos also reports the existence of a "brigand code," which governed conduct and in which the elementary principles of social banditry can be traced (Koliopoulos 1987: 260–269). Social bandits, in their classic form, redistribute wealth and protect the weak. In so doing—or at least in cultivat-ing a reputation for so doing—they acted to assure their very survival. Any individual band was reliant on the goodwill of the local population: a dis-gruntled peasant host population could quickly make the life of a band unten-able. Thus apart from the brigand code's third commandment, which called for punitive measures against traitors, the bulk of the commandments had to do either with the mechanics of ransom, which was one of the core economic activities of the bands, or the management of relations with needed allies in this world or the next. The fourteenth commandment called on brigands to make offerings in churches to expiate the sins they might be committing—reminding us of the deep Christian religiosity in the region as a whole—while the last commandment ordered brigands to avoid women (ibid.: 265).

Like the Northern marches of Greece, Ottoman Macedonia was a peripheral zone, where a variety of political actors practiced the art of not being governed (Scott 2009) and jockeyed for influence and prestige. This was the world in which the MRO sought to carve out space to pursue its agenda.

A variety of sources buttress Hobsbawm's observation, noted above, that the organization and its leadership drew heavily on traditions such as those described by Koliopoulos. Certainly Koliopoulos's brigands and the MRO's members used several of the same words to describe key roles, including the "new" term *sekretar* and the decidedly archaic (and Turkish-derived) *bajraktar* (used in the Ilinden Dossier, for example, to refer to Tirču Kare in Kruševo). Sources from the time also highlighted the similar structure and function of oaths in the brigand and the revolutionary worlds. One account, for example, reports that a member of a bandit gang would swear "on gospels, cross or Koran—sometimes on sword or gun . . . to obey the chief in all things, and be faithful to his comrades to the death" (Garnett 1904: 204). Some of the violence that the MRO sanctioned did constitute vengeance against oppressive authorities, thereby fulfilling one traditional role of the social bandit. In the 1930s—when VMRO was active still in the region—different authors referred to the bands of their time as "lineal descendants of the *hajduks*," who had "kept alive the spirit of revolt, together with the national feeling, under Turkish rule" (Christowe 1935: 60; Edwards 1938: 66).

By the same logic, though, components of the brigand code appear also as lineal ancestors of later, formalized principles of insurgent and guerrilla warfare elsewhere in the world. The harsh treatment of traitors, for example, specified in the third commandment, anticipates not only the reported atrocities of the MRO and its Greek rivals, but also Che Guevara's discussion of the need for "inflexibility" toward those who provide information to the enemy (Guevara 2007: 20). Elsewhere in their classic texts of guerrilla warfare, both Che and Mao Zedong (in his "Three Rules and Eight Remarks") also provide specific instructions about treating civilians and their property with respect.

Both indicate the need for guerrillas to take every opportunity to display their moral superiority to their adversaries, which in Guevara's text includes a prohibition on alcohol when stationed in civilian communities (ibid.: 48), while Mao specifies that guerrillas should not "bathe in the presence of women" (Mao 1963: 92).

Other analysts, especially those working in the Marxist-informed Yugoslav Macedonian tradition, emphasized the revolutionary aspects of the MRO and its deliberate and conscious break with the past. From this perspective, apparent continuities mark the leadership's recognition of the need for the kinds of strategic essentialism that mark contemporary indigenous politics (Warren and Jackson 2002: 8). The apparent archaism or primitivism in choosing to employ terms like *vojvoda, bajraktar,* and *četa* as part of the movement's lexicon seems to represent, like Goce Delčev's choice of Ahil (Achilles) as his alias, efforts to anchor the MRO in local understandings and thereby win the support of villagers with their own mythologies of justice and heroism (Vasiliadis 1989: 79). Such practices, though, were embedded in an overall pattern of efforts to educate people inside and outside Macedonia that the organization was dedicated to a wholesale transformation of society.

Past as Prologue: The MRO's Tactics, Techniques, and Procedures

Such readings can have their own blinkers. Among others, Craig Calhoun has written persuasively of the shortcomings of the Marxian tradition that fails to acknowledge continuity between "the corporatism of the past and the socialist future" (Calhoun 1988: 131). Calhoun also points out that Hobsbawm himself, in the preface to the third edition of *Primitive Rebels,* acknowledges underestimating the importance of those he had previously termed "prepolitical" (ibid.: 144). Calhoun thus aligns himself with the perspectives offered by Ranajit Guha and James C. Scott, challenging the view that only the orchestrated and the self-consciously ideological are capable of genuine protest (Guha 1999; Scott 1985).

Nonetheless, categorical distinctions do appear justified from the empirical material. 1899 marked a break with the past, when the MRO's Central Committee issued a circular letter instructing local committees to establish a standing force of *četas* (MacDermott 1978: 198–99; Perry 1988: 155–61; Lange-Akhund 1998: 94–99). The decision followed the Cretan Uprising of 1896 and the Ottoman discovery of the organization in 1897, and also reflected acknowledgment of increasing Greek and Bulgarian state interest in Macedonia. Goce Delčev (who had studied at Sofia's military school) played a key role in creating the new *četa* system, the outlines of which are laid out in two documents captured by Ottoman forces during 1903 and reported in consular correspondence. "Instructions for the Macedonian Revolutionary Bands and the Affiliated Peasants" and "Regulations for Village Bands" (henceforth "Instructions" and "Regulations" respectively) are both included in appendix 1. What these sources make clear is the transformed circulation of material resources and the presumed relationship between bands and the wider population.

The MRO's "Instructions" and "Regulations" envisage a different operating environment than that of Koliopoulos's "Brigand Code," most strikingly in the contrast in the responsibility for the actions described. Where the code, and also Mao's and Guevara's handbooks, address themselves to the armed personnel in each case, the MRO's "Instructions"—found on the body of one of twelve members of an MRO *četa* killed on May 21, 1903, after they were surrounded in the village of Mogila—contain more explicit expectations of the populace than of bands.[2] The first item addresses the duties of couriers in particular, while the second and third call upon the village population to conduct what modern scholars would call "non-kinetic" operations against Ottoman forces: lodging complaints or requests for compensation with higher authorities or, where possible, foreign representatives.[3] The fourth item extends this kind of civilian paramilitary activity further by instructing supporters to eliminate spies or traitors, and then shift responsibility onto the occupying Ottoman forces.

Where the instructions do address bands, the content and form is very different from the brigand code. Besides outlining the precautions a band should take to protect against surprise attacks, the document lists the demands or burdens that the band should place on the civilian population: recruiting sentries, gathering information and monetary contributions, auditing the books of the local cashier, and assisting (or coercing) in the purchase and stockpiling of weapons. Overall, the message is that the *četa* and its members are more important than the villagers, and it is incumbent on the latter to protect the former (especially the *vojvoda*, who in turn "must always be surrounded by his men, just as a state surrounds and safeguards its capital city"). The instructions also attach considerable importance to the protection of information about material stockpiles, stressing that "no active member should reveal to another that he possesses arms: even less should he reveal to another the place where arms are hidden."

The second document, "Regulations," was captured in October 1903. It identifies two grades of *četa*, representing village and region, or *rayon*, respectively. It also makes reference to the "natural militia" composed of all armed villagers, which may be called out in times of emergency. The document also specifies the equipment required for each member of the *četa* and calls for the local *vojvoda* to conduct regular field exercises "in order that the members of the village band may be inured to fatigue."

These various injunctions, in their explicit language and their tacit assumptions, highlight two key components of the *četa* system instituted by the MRO after 1899. First, the organization's *četas* covered longer distances than their bandit predecessors and were not confined by the seasonal rhythms of the brigand life of earlier times. They were therefore more continuously in movement across territory with which they were not necessarily familiar; hence the detailed instructions for how villagers should use their own superior local knowledge to protect the *četa*. Second, the *četas* of the MRO were not ad hoc, local groups whose ranks could be readily filled from a pool of young men in the case of losses. In modern terms, again, they were conceived of as force multipliers, responsible for training and disciplining local populations rather than fighting Turks. They thus represented an investment on the part of the organization, and this "professionalization" is noted in several contemporary and secondary sources. MacDermott singles out Marko Lerinski, one of the *vojvodas* mentioned by pension applicants from Buf in the 1950s, as exemplary in this regard, and she dubs his unit the "Sandhurst of *četas*" (1978: 201; see also Perry 1988: 158).[4] A. D. H. Smith, who traveled with a band in 1907, spoke of the members as like the "ancient monastic orders of knighthood" (Smith 1908: 96). These are sources that are sympathetic to the MRO's cause; they represent the *četas* as close kin to Che Guevara's later ideal of the guerrilla as "a sort of guiding angel" (Guevara 2007: 31) or the A-teams of contemporary U.S. Special Forces in their multifunctional capacity (Simons 1997).

The parallel is instructive. For in each case, the primary goal of the personnel of these elite units is to prepare the broader population to take responsibility for their own futures. Although equipped for conflict with superior forces, and certainly able to intimidate and raid civilians, neither was the *četa*'s primary, everyday role or purpose. When the time came for the uprising, they would constitute the core of a larger armed movement; before then, they were not to precipitate violence. Hence the high value attached to the survival of individual members. MRO doctrine, in this regard, anticipated Che Guevara's argument that each guerrilla was a "soldier of high specialization" whose loss would be far more detrimental to the cause than that of a soldier in a regular army (Guevara 2007: 16).

The Band Economy Restructured: From Looting to Taxation

The MRO's doctrine, as well as practices reported in other sources, also reveals a further-reaching fundamental shift from existing patterns of anti-Ottoman resistance toward the kinds of revolutionary activism discussed by Guevara. As noted above, one key aspect of the social bandit's survival was the redistribution of spoils to civilian supporters. The *vojvoda* would take the largest cut of the profits but would likely use those funds to foster alliances and friendships. In this regard, the band economy shared common features with that of African hunter-gatherer societies, or Melanesian "big man" communities, as described in classic anthropological terms (Wiessner 1982; Sahlins 1963). Where material wealth—be it in the form of game, a large taro harvest, rustled cattle, or cash ransoms—cannot be easily or safely stored or transported, rational economic actors convert it into positive social relations that constitute less lootable, socially embedded forms of capital.

In the contexts described by Wiessner and Sahlins, the fruits of labor are redistributed to create or maintain relationships with either peers or followers. For a traditional Balkan *vojvoda*, though, operating in a context where Ottoman authorities constituted a continuous threat, the options were more varied. He might well, for example, extend largesse to local state authorities or functionaries, thereby providing them with a stake in his ongoing, profitable existence. He might, as the brigand code suggests, make offerings to saints to enlist their sponsorship. And with an (unheroic) eye to (banal) logistics, he might court some civilians—blacksmiths, merchants, or tanners, for example—more assiduously than others, to secure access to the perennial needs of irregular warfare: arms, food, and durable footwear. The effect, then, would be to create complex and ambivalent networks with a range of actors and thus embed the band in a set of multistranded relationships.

Although governed by the same basic material needs—food, clothing, shelter, munitions—the MRO *četas* ushered in a very different kind of economic system. Far from redistributing wealth to civilian allies or supporters, they oversaw the collection of taxes from those allies. They did not, prior to Ilinden, physically remove cash or gold from the villages they visited: the instructions for bands indicate that resources should be left with the local committees for their use. They did, however, audit accounts to make sure that those funds were expended only for goals approved by the organization, of which the most significant was the acquisition of rifles and ammunition. They also drew supplies for their own maintenance from local populations, usually offering receipts that were to serve as the kinds of "bonds of hope" described by Guevara fifty years later (Guevara 2007: 62).

The MRO's *četas*, then, represented a drain on local economies, rather than a boost to them: They imposed a war economy on local communities by which cash was continually redirected along specific channels and removed from local circulation. The economic flows in which brigands participated— significant sums from ransom, externally acquired, then pumped into the local economy—were reversed in the new *četa* system, which brought justice, protection, and the promise of future prosperity and freedom, but demanded cash payment for them.

This profound change was noted by some contemporary observers: Commenting on the second captured document, for example, McGregor, noted "its imperious claims on the population generally" (FO 195/2157/731: McGregor to Graves, October 31, 1903). Consistently, consular sources reported evidence that the population resented these impositions, collaborated with the organization only under duress, and betrayed it at the first opportunity they had (see for example Chotzidis et al. 1993: 66, on the betrayal of the band in Mogila). The Ilinden Dossier, though, suggests to the contrary that the "imperious claims" of the organization did gain purchase on a significant body of the population.

Sustaining the MRO's Armed Forces: The Jatak Redefined

As noted in the previous chapter, people who referred to themselves as *kuriers* played a key role in carrying and circulating messages through the organization's internal mail system. Couriers also played a vital role serving in sustaining MRO *četas*. Numerous biographers recall carrying food, clothing, or medicine from village homes out to *četas* in the field. Others report playing the roles described in the "Instructions" of maintaining security for *četas* and their personnel by serving as lookouts on their behalf, or escorting them between locations. Examples of couriers recalling these duties include Rajna Sugareva Barakova, from Bitola, who specifically recalled carrying shoes or boots—so central a part of insurgency—to the *četas,* as did Petar Naumov Damčeski and Velika Nadenova Gjakerkoska, both of Kruševo (Records 3-B-25; 9-D-17; 11-Gj-1).[5] Mile Jonov Gjorčeski, of the village of Dolni Divljaci, recalled working as a lookout man and reporting the movement of *askers*—Turkish forces—to *četas* (Record 11-Gj-24). Pere Mijev Tašeski of Godivle in the Kruševo region indicates receiving *četniks* in his village and escorting them to others, while Bogoja P. Bogoeski recalled being charged with escorting the *vojvoda* Petre Železarot and his *četa* on the first leg of their journey from Bitola to Mariovo (Records 35-T-41; 4-B-26). Petar A. Varnaliev, from Veles, recalled being ordered to escort two wounded *četniks* to Bulgaria. Together with a female member, Sofija Maneva, he took the two men, dressed in women's clothes, in a carriage to the village of Balvan, where they handed them off to other couriers (Record 6-V-5).[6]

As well as carrying correspondence and direct orders, then, *kuriers* such as these were part of the larger system that the MRO summoned into being, both creating the environment in which *četas* could circulate and contributing to their maintenance. They were again, though, the foot soldiers of the movement, following orders from others rather than taking on major autonomous responsibilities. They operated in conjunction with individuals who bore a different, indigenously rooted title: *jataks.* Just six of the 375 applicants in the sample explicitly describe themselves as *jataks,* suggesting that it represents a more elite, exclusive mode of membership and activism than *kurier,* comparable to the bureaucratized terms *sekretar, blagajnik,* and *terorist.* People used it to describe themselves in their biographies of the 1940s because they remembered being designated in this way by the statutes of the organization. Some also appear to suggest that it was a category-in-use for authorities seeking to suppress the organization. In either case, their narratives indicate that this role was central to the *četa* system.

Jatak—a Turkish-derived word generally translated "receiver"—has a longer local history than many of the West European–derived terms used by the MRO. It is discussed extensively by Dinko Tomasić in his 1948 study of the so-called "Dinaric" personality (Tomasić 1948: see Živković 2011: 79–86). Presaging Hobsbawm's observations regarding social bandits, Tomasić traces cooperation between the Balkan *hajduks* and elements of the local population. Essential to their operation were accomplices who did not take to the mountains, but stayed in the village or town (Tomasić 1948: 52). These *jataks* served as the eyes and ears of the bandits, provided them with accommodation and supplies when needed, and operated as fences to dispose of their booty. For these services they received financial compensation from the outlaws. The term appears in epic poetry from the region (Morison 1929); Svetozar Koljević reports the term appearing as early as 1818, and also that the importance of the role was recognized by the Turks, who would organize drives through rural villages to flush them out (Koljević 1980: 218–19). Foreign travelers in the early twentieth century also encountered the term, translating it as "concealer" or "henchman" (Stead 1909: 196; Vivian 1904: 259–61).

In Tomasić's narrative, the term had negative resonance in popular parlance. He cites a Montenegrin saying that "The *jatak* is worse than the thief" and "Whoever doesn't steal, but only hides what was stolen, eats for nothing." In several of the accounts cited above, there is the explicit or implicit suggestion that the *jatak's* relationship with the *hajduk* is shaped solely by financial self-interest and is not imbued with affective sentiment. As such, the *jatak-hajduk* relationship partakes of a range of other stereotypes that run through the region's history, including antinomies of city and country, money and blood, and profit and honor. As a literary figure the *jatak* has an unheroic or even antiheroic quality, providing continuous dramatic tension in that the relationship might always be subverted, and the *hajduk* betrayed to death, through bargaining.

The title of *jatak* carries very different weight in the Ilinden Dossier. Particularly striking is that it is used by women as well as men to describe themselves. Sevastija Naška Topuzova of Kruševo, for example, wrote that she was a legal member (*legalen člen*) from 1898–1905. She baked bread, cooked, washed, and patched clothes for visiting *četas*, always doing these things during the night— a further reminder of the risk that these activities could carry if observed by neighbors who could be Turkish state informers. She then describes herself as a *jatak,* reporting that she received *četas* in her house and also hosted meetings there. In this case, her *jatak* status was established by having *četniks* in her house, as opposed to only their clothing or equipment, or providing food for them (Record 36-T-25).

This key aspect of the *jatak's* role, involving direct contact with *četa* personnel in his or her own home, is confirmed in other references. Nenka Velkova

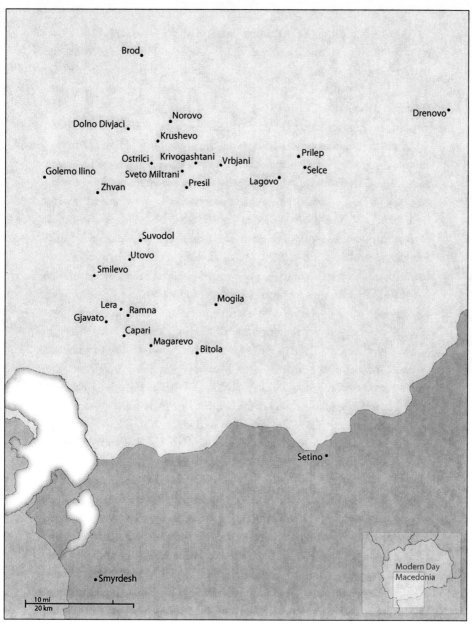

Figure 5.1. A sample of sites of significant *jatak* and *kurier* activity
described by Ilinden pension seekers.

Jošeska, born in Birino, near Kruševo, states that she took part in the movement for the liberation of the Macedonian people and that she received and
sent *četniks* and *vojvodas*; again, the actual personnel of the organization rather
than equipment. For this activity, she says, she was imprisoned as a *jatak*
(Record 15-J-43).

Men also report serving in this role. Vele Bogev Zdraveski of Krivogaštani
in the Prilep region records that he was in the organization from 1896 to 1903
and that he was a *jatak* who took *četas* from place to place (Record 12-Z-10).
Apostol Trajkovski of Capari was imprisoned as a *jatak* in 1918 by the Serbs
(Record 36-T-64). Temelko Anastasov Janevski, who grew up in the Veles
region but who, like counterparts in Capari and other villages, spent most
of his youth on the circuit of migrant labor, later served as *jatak* and then as
a fighter (*borec*) (Record 14-J-16). Stefan Koleski of Dolno Divjlaci, close to
Kruševo, worked abroad until 1901 and returned to work for the organization
until 1912; he was jailed as *jatak* in 1910 (Record 17-K-43).[7]

Although these references to the term are few in number, they again provide the grounds for reflecting on the distinctions that the MRO strove to
establish between itself and its rivals for civilian support. Unlike *sekretars* and
several *kuriers,* none of these self-styled *jataks* report a singular relationship
with a specific band or leader. Their responsibilities, as they describe them,
are larger and extend to any unit of the organization. Additionally, none make
any reference to any financial component to their relationship with the organization; they take it as given that the role they describe is a function of their
membership of and commitment to the organization.

Of the six cases, three—two men and one woman—report serving jail
time as identified *jataks* either under Ottoman or later Serbian rule. This
serves as reminder of the substantial risks of discovery that jataks bore, perhaps more than any other members of the organization. Whereas *kuriers* carried incriminating material such as letters, munitions, or other supplies, only
when in transit and "on duty," *jataks* put their places of residence at the disposal of the organization. In the context of village life, where household routines were largely visible to neighbors and deviations from normal practice
quickly attracted notice, a majority of residents would know the identity of
the MRO's *jataks.* Searches of their houses would likely reveal contraband, or at
least circumstantial evidence—extra sheets, male clothing, or surplus eating
utensils—that could all be taken as incriminating.

It is this last characteristic of the work of *jataks*—the enormous overlap between their day-to-day lives as ostensibly "legal" members of Ottoman society and their parallel careers as key functionaries in the organization, with regular personal contact with *ilegalni*—that warrants the conclusion that they played a similarly indispensable role to the others identified in earlier chapters. As secretaries generated and managed the circulation of orders and other written documents, and cashiers were responsible for financial records and accounting, *jataks* were at the heart of the system that sustained *četas* and safeguarded the weapons caches that the organization was assembling all across the region.

Although designated by a term drawn from traditions of local defiance of Ottoman rule, *jataks* occupied a pivotal and transformative role in the Macedonian revolutionary movement. The paramount importance of depots of arms and supplies in a larger-scale insurgency is discussed extensively in Che Guevara's account of guerrilla warfare. As the zone of operations extends and individual bands cover larger circuits in their efforts to educate, organize, protect, and police, lines of supply and communication become a critical battleground. As well as increasing the number of couriers required to convey orders and intelligence between static committees and units on the march, safe houses and way stations acquire greater importance (Guevara 2007: 64). In keeping with guerrilla practice across history, *četas* moved primarily at night and rested during the day. The locations of their places of refuge were treated as sensitive information and, in Guevara' terms again, restricted to "persons in whom the organization has the greatest confidence" (ibid.: 64). Far from their traditional image as profiteers, *jataks* were the MRO's trusted secret keepers.

Women's Work: Cultural Awareness and Cultural Constraints

As noted in earlier chapters, the MRO was revolutionary in the extent to which women were treated as coequals in the movement for autonomy. They took the oath alongside men and in a few notable cases fought in the Ilinden Uprising, as reported, for example, in Vaska Konsuloska's biography (17-K-60). The iconography used on the seal of at least one local chapter of the organization flagged their presence in its ranks, depicting a handshake between a woman and a man. But it was in their roles as *kuriers* and, in particular, *jataks* that women were most prominent. The life history submitted by Velika Nedanova

Gjakerkoska of Kruševo as part of her pension application offers a detailed account of the multiple ways women could contribute, ways that were virtually unthinkable for men.

Gjakerkoska was born May 6, 1859, in Kruševo: Her early life, related in her biography, was a tale of considerable hardship. Born into a poor family, she started work at the age of nine and earned a living as her parents Kote Spasevski and Kalina Spasevska did, minding the stock of richer families. Because her own family could not support her, she was first married at sixteen in the village Zabjani, where her husband worked for a Turkish landlord. In the six-month pattern of *momok* labor, described in chapter 2, he then moved to Lažani, and then again to Vlaško. There he died, and Gjakerkoska returned to live with her family in Kruševo for three years before marrying again, to Stefan Tintoski in Sveti Mitrani. She lived there for twelve years before her husband and son Blaže were killed "at the plough" by "Turks." After her third marriage, to Nedan Gjakerkoski, in the village of Sveti Mitrani, her life did not get easier. Her story continues as follows (Record 11-Gj-1):

After some time the Turks came and took my husband Nedan and asked him to reveal the *komitet* (committee) and sought weapons from him; but he said nothing, because he was in that organization. They beat him and he was laid up in bed for six months. I wrapped him in woollen blankets and bathed him. I crumbled his food into small pieces and fed him like a little baby, because he couldn't eat. He was very badly beaten.

After he got better he went to the *komitet* [band] and I worked to await them and send them on, and seek them at night. Afterwards the command came for Nedan to repair the *komitet*'s weapons. He couldn't go, because he was under surveillance by the Turks, so they sent me together with Cveta Miceska to take the weapons to be repaired at the Karevs' house. Then the weapons were taken by Petruš, Gjorgi and Nikola Karev, and they fixed them. They also gave us *komitet* clothing to take back to the village of Sveti Mitrani, and we were scared to take it and didn't know how. So we undressed and put it on under our clothes, and thus brought it to Sveti Mitrani and gave it to Nedan and Mirče Toteski.

The second time they sent us to Kruševo, we didn't have any way to do it, so we took off our socks and hid them under our feet. From Sveti Mitrani we took two donkeys and two mules we had, in order to bring from the Karevs' boots for the *komitet*. Afterwards I took hay and put the *komitet*'s boots in it. And with Cveta I took them to Sveti Mitrani and gave them to Nedan and Mirče Toteski, and they took them to the committee's *četa* and handed them over to Blaže Birinčeto and Pitu Guli. Afterwards, Pitu Guli's revolver broke, and he gave it to me and Cveta, and we took it to the Karevs to be fixed. She's now dead.

The *komitet* came into the village and I washed their clothes and that night dried them in my house over the fire, and my husband went out early with the clothes for them. I personally worked with the *komitet*, as my biography shows, and I was connected through my husband with the Karevs in Kruševo.

Although Gjakerkoska does not refer to herself directly as *jatak*, the variety of the contributions she describes matches closely the work of that category. Additionally, they show again the ways in which the MRO—or its more cunning operatives—harnessed the cultural constraints on police and military action against insurgencies and revolutions. As noted in chapter 4, the regular Ottoman military were known for their respect toward women. In his role as war correspondent, Leon Trotsky reported,

As a rule, the Turks don't touch churches, priests or women. Two officials of our [Russian] former consulate in Skopje told me an interesting thing. When our government was arming the *komitadjis* in Old Serbia, the revolvers and cartridges that passed through the consulate were handed to priests and women— and nearly all of them reached their destination. The Turks don't search women or priests—not, of course, the Albanian *kochaks* [sic] or the Ottomanized Serbs (they're the worst of the lot) but the real Ottomans, the Turks themselves: they undoubtedly possess some elements of chivalry. (Trotsky 1980: 127)

Depositions given to consuls by local people distinguished Turkish soldiers from irregulars for the correctness of their behavior (FO 195/2157/551).[8] The same point about professional restraint was made, more than fifty years later, by Che Guevara, who noted that whatever the situation, women are subject to less rough handling by state authorities. Gjakerkoska's concealment of weapons and letters around her person constitute some of the "thousand tricks" that Guevara indicates women master and that facilitate their work as couriers (Guevara 2007: 70). Other examples akin to those described by Gjakerkoska are provided by Rajna Nikolova Miloešeska of Prilep, who was nicknamed

"Komitetka." She described her awareness that because she was a woman, the Turks could not search her; she carried cartridge belts under her clothing, gunpowder in water jugs, and rifles under loads of loaves being taken to the bakery (Record 22-M-25).

Gjakerkoska's other reported actions—nursing her husband, and cooking and mending clothing—similarly anticipate Guevara's discussion of the contributions women can make by carrying out "habitual tasks of peacetime" to advance the revolution's goals.[9] His point is straightforward: Whatever the romance of insurgent or brigand life in the hills, logistical realities intrude. And however progressive a movement may appear, the gendered division of labor in everyday life asserts itself also in the work of revolution.

The Economics of Revolt: Ilinden and the Conversion of Jatak Energy

It is only by attention to the role of the *jatak*, though, and the redirection of the flow of resources that it is possible to discern the distinctive shape of the MRO's armed activism in the lead-up to the Ilinden Uprising. Women like Gjakerkoska, Miloŝeska, and Konsulska—and many others whose names have not been recorded—were indispensable to the *četa* system created by Delčev and other leaders committed to the principle that Macedonians should determine their own future and pay their way. In particular, it was the circuits that the MRO's *jataks* and *kuriers* established and maintained that made possible the formation and movement of bands led by charismatic young men like the *vojvoda* Cvetkov, who died in Mogila in 1903, or Jovan Jurukovski, who lived to narrate his activism through the Ilinden Dossier, and whose story is included in appendix 2. And those same circuits, as well as the economics at their heart, make it possible to distinguish the MRO's *četas* from others operating at the same time. In 1902, for example, several *četas* led by Bulgarian army officers, with General Cončev at their head, mounted an incursion from Bulgaria into Macedonia and sought to establish a "liberated territory" around the area of Gorna-Dzumija in the eastern part of the region. Representing Sofia-oriented, Vrhovist elements and drawing on the resources of the Bulgarian government, they posed as representing "Macedonian" interests. But denied access to the MRO's network of guides and safe houses, they were unable to maintain themselves in-country and were quickly forced to withdraw to Bulgaria. Elsewhere in Macedonia, bands operated that drew primarily on traditions of outlaw banditry and brigandage. Although they often made common ground with the MRO—as in the case of the *vojvoda* Apostol, for example, who operated in the plains between Salonika and Voden (Edhessa)—they relied on the kinds of personalized politics of survival practiced by their *hajduk* forebears. Apostol reportedly was offered a substantial sum by an Ottoman official to simply "retire"; although he did not take it, the offer was a throwback to ways of doing business that preceded the organization's commitment to liberation and autonomy (Sonnichsen 1909: 36).

The MRO's specific and distinctive history is often distorted, pulled between these two modes of armed violence. The Bulgarian military pedigree of leaders like Delčev, Sarafov and Cvetkov, as well as numerous others, is taken as evidence that the organization's efforts, just like Končev's ill-fated incursion, were simply an extension of Bulgarian foreign policy. Conversely, those that deny the movement any wider coherence or cohesion take Apostol's band as archetypal. Both views serve contemporary methodological nationalism, which seeks yes-or-no answers. In this frame, the MRO's efforts to manage violence are translated into either new (Bulgarian) nationalism, or traditional (prenational) habits of resistance.

In literature from the period under discussion, though, the confrontation of "traditional" and "modern" takes a slightly different, and more illuminating, form. In a 1914 novel of revolution, *Pawns of Liberty*, the authors stage a debate between "brigandage and revolution," which more closely reflects the tensions of the time. The heroine of the story, Adalena, confronts a brigand, Vasko, who is trying to persuade her to reveal the location of a stockpile of gold. She wants to preserve it to engineer a mass uprising across the whole of Macedonia, while he wants to use it to strike an immediate blow. They trade critiques of one another's position. So Adalena says:

> You keep Macedonia in a ferment. You stir up the Turks here, they send an army to subdue you; by the time the troops arrive, you are far away, stirring up trouble in another district. . . . You sing and dance atop your crags, but plowing men and women down in the valleys have to pay the piper. And you glory in it, in this sort of costly unrest, which kills, while it brings them no nearer freedom to-day than they were five hundred years ago? Your brigandage exhausts the Bulgar peasantry; it touches the Turks as little as they touch you. (Tsanoff and Tsanoff 1914: 314–15)

Vasko, the brigand, responds with equal vehemence:

> I am weary to death of your principles! Principles and by-laws and *ustavi*
> (constitutions) you elaborate, rules and regulations, and you forget the daily
> sufferings of live men and women. For the sake of a bloodless principle, you
> would hand me over to the first Turkish *zaptieh* [gendarme]. (ibid.: 317)

Central to the staging is the source of the dispute: the resources built up
by the organization to which Adalena belongs, in the name of the common
good. The authors highlight the core dilemma the MRO faced. The demands
of its growing infrastructure, combined with the continuing surveillance and
increasing intervention of the Ottoman authorities, necessitated creating
covert stockpiles of equipment and other resources. Where the treasurers
oversaw the financial transactions involved, *jataks* were frequently the primary coordinators of the equally vital in-kind contributors. They coordinated
or provided the resources that were, in the final analysis, beyond price in the
MRO's state of war against the Ottoman authorities: a secure night's sleep, safe
passage from one village to the next, a range of goods that money could not
necessarily buy. It was this support network that particularly impressed Europeans who came to support the organization and who saw its robustness as
evidence that "somewhere beneath the awkward reserve of the [Macedonian]
Bulgarian character there lies a fund of loyalty and steadfast faith more reliable
than any picturesque or feudal chivalry" (Brailsford 1906: 169).

Nonetheless, the situation placed demands on all the organization's members and supporters, as they were asked to make increasing sacrifices in the
present. The bonds they were issued, after all, carried no redemption date.
Macedonia's rural inhabitants were the ostensible long-term beneficiaries of
this revolutionary work and were therefore invited and sometimes coerced to
invest on good faith alone. Brailsford's admiring observations notwithstanding, the continued death roll of tax withholders, dissenters, and traitors is evidence that some people remained unconvinced. Their numbers, and the level
of violence, were always at risk of increasing as long as the only evidence of
organization activity was the cycle of visits of the *četas* and the requests for
further contribution, in cash or in kind, to the cause.

The pressures that the Tsanoffs here encapsulate in fiction were also manifest on the ground, reaching their peak in late 1902, after General Končev's

incursion from Bulgaria. Most MRO activists, especially those who heeded the circular sent around by Gjorče Petrov and Goce Delčev, had refused to cooperate with Končev's *četas*, and in some cases fought against them. This reflected the degree to which different factions within the organization disagreed on the prospects for, and ideal timing of, a popular uprising. In the end, after considerable internal frictions, the leadership called for a general uprising on August 2, 1903—in some sense ceding to the "brigand" argument, framed differently by Damjan Gruev, who at the Smilevo Congress where the date was set reportedly said, "better an end with horrors, than horrors without end" (MacDermott 1978: 348).

The confusion between the two fundamentally opposed courses of action continued to play itself out in the conduct of the MRO's forces during the uprising. It was most apparent at the micro-level in Kruševo, where two local leaders, Pitu Guli and Nikola Karev, fell into a high-profile dispute. Guli was a localist and a literalist whose persona, preserved in folklore, is that of the brigand-turned-revolutionist. One of his more famous utterances was a standard bandit statement of the cutting of familial ties, in which he claimed that the mountain was his mother, his rifle his wife, and his bullets his children (Brown 2003: 196). Reportedly, he declared that he had not participated in an uprising, and liberated Kruševo, in order to run away. He prevented excesses against the local townspeople, from whom the insurgents requisitioned money and other material. For Guli, the time for "principles" and for collecting resources from the civilian population for the future was past; like the fictional Vasko, it was time to expend stored resources in a direct confrontation with the hated enemy.

By contrast, Nikola Karev appears as the more calculating, long-term planner; the uprising was a move in a longer strategy, and once Ottoman troops descended on the town, the objective was for the valuable, trained *četas* to escape. Through their survival under arms and ability to retaliate, he argued, they would continue to pose a deterrent against Ottoman atrocities (Dimevski 1971: 204). It followed, too, that any money they left behind would be plundered in any case, so better for it to be carried into the mountains in return for pledges. Karev tried to minimize attacks on the Muslim population and prevent insurgents and their supporters from indiscriminate looting. His philosophy remained one of husbanding resources of all kinds, including Muslim villagers' goodwill, which he elicited through a letter urging them not to strike against their fellow underclass members. This pragmatic initiative was clearly at odds with the more dramatic line represented by Pitu Guli. Structurally, though, it represented the networked orientation of the MRO, which recognized and relied on the ongoing symbiotic relationship between *jataks* and *četas*.

Nikola Karev escaped from Kruševo before it was encircled. Pitu Guli fought and died at Mečkin Kamen, defending the town of Kruševo against overwhelming odds.[10] His last stand has come to occupy the same iconic status in Macedonia's national history as sites like Thermopylae, Kosovo field, Masada, or the Alamo have in others'. Such engagements are material defeats and spiritual victories; they are also icons of an insurgent strategy gone awry. The Ilinden Uprising—the focus of the pension scheme and elevated, in a masculinist idiom of resistance, to occupy center stage in subsequent national appropriation of the movement—marked a decisive turning point for the organization. By the time the uprising was finished, a significant number of the organization's best-trained and most committed members were dead or had been forced to flee into exile. The regional *četas* fulfilled their duties, mustering their village counterparts and calling out the militia to engage Ottoman forces. The organization's *jataks* orchestrated the provisioning and supplying of the armed forces in the field. It was, in terms of the flows of resources documented in this and the previous two chapters, a massive expenditure of the stored human and material capital that the organization had amassed. The uprising thus represented a different kind of rationale, a kind of conspicuous effort to impress audiences in Macedonia and beyond. It reflected, then, a brand of the seemingly reckless romanticism of the traditional *hajduk*, who in the words of the epic, cares not for the odds, but responds to the call of reputation and honor.

As such, Ilinden can be read as a reversal of a particular kind of economic logic familiar in anthropology, in which actors seek to convert capital between different domains. Before Ilinden, the organization had capitalized on traditions of resistance and protest but had turned them into a more ambitious, progressive purpose of major political change from within. A key, unsung role was played by *jataks*, people going about their everyday life, but in so doing creating the logistical infrastructure of a nation-in-arms, with military specialists as its most visible marker. They had constituted the heart of a formal and informal system of taxation, whereby the cost of creating and sustaining this military force was shared widely across society, with the anticipation that its benefits would be similarly shared. It was antiromantic and relentlessly pragmatic; resources that formerly circulated as part of agonistic prestige games were sequestered, to be expended only on public goods.

This incremental project came under multiple pressures, including externally supported rival forces and indigenous enthusiasm for the supposed honor of issuing a more direct challenge to the oppressor. The MRO's own casualties in the period before Ilinden perhaps contributed to the organization's change of heart in early 1903, both because some of the most radical opponents of a premature uprising were either jailed or killed, and because some sought to act in a spirit of vengeance before they lost more men. Many of the MRO's surviving leaders in 1903 likely knew, from Ottoman conduct of recent years, that Christian civilians would face lethal reprisals, as they had after the Salonika bombings of April 1903, and perhaps calculated that the loss of life would yield its own political payoff. In opting for an uprising, though, they ultimately reversed and undid much of the work of the previous five years, which had incrementally built wider circuits of generalized trust within the organization. When romantic heroes die, they opt out of the credit system that they have often relied on up to that point. In this case, the organization left its contributors holding worthless bonds and its *jataks* vulnerable to betrayal or direct assault. The short-term symbiosis between *četa* and *jatak* was severely compromised by the Ilinden Uprising, which in this analysis marked a reassertion of the primacy of the romantic hero and a remarginalization of the practical *jatak* on which his very life—and any prospects for achieving any broader progressive goals—depended.

CHAPTER SIX

Guns for Sale: Feud, Trade, and Solidarity in the Arming of the MRO

In the first two decades of its existence, the Macedonian Revolutionary Organization posed challenges to both the irredentist nationalism of Bulgaria and the status quo of Christian subjection to the Ottoman state, in which the Greek Orthodox Church served as willing handmaiden. The evidence of the Ilinden Dossier and the consular archives makes it clear that the MRO's campaign to win and maintain popular loyalty for its distinctive mission of political autonomy deployed the threat and practice of violence by terrorists (especially against those identified as spies or traitors) and by četas (in deterring violence against MRO supporters and preparing the population for the uprising). That campaign also sought to foster trust and establish legitimacy through the accompanying machinery of communication, control, and logistical support.

Much of the work of the organization, then, directly targeted the Orthodox Christian inhabitants of Macedonia who were its primary constituents. But even among these ostensible beneficiaries of the organization's success, the MRO triggered a range of reactions, from total commitment through partial, tepid, or wavering support and stubborn neutrality to bitter resistance. Additionally, the MRO operated in a context where it had also to navigate relationships with at least two other constituencies: the international audience of potential intervenors, also split between sympathizers, bystanders, and adversaries; and representatives of Ottoman governmental and economic misrule, who could include landowners, tax collectors, field guards, and gendarmes.

The organization's interactions with these different constituencies took different forms. The violent and confrontational are the best known: executions of spies, dynamite attacks on European-owned enterprises, kidnappings, and the assassination of Ottoman state representatives who abused their authority were all forms of terrorism and signaled both organizational capacity and seriousness of purpose to these different audiences. The organization also exhibited other state-like characteristics, such as engaging in crypto-governance by dispensing justice and levying taxes in its outreach across rural Macedonia, or conducting proto-diplomacy in its regular dispatch of spokesmen to the capitals of Europe and its introduction of regular press releases for consuls and journalists during the uprising (Wyon 1904: 144).

Few would dispute the MRO's state-making ambitions; what remains unknown, despite the best efforts of several generations of Balkan historians, is the exact national ideology and precise long-term aspirations of its members. This is not for want of trying: The correspondence and memoirs of the leadership, in particular, have been extensively scrutinized for evidence that they and the broader Slavic-speaking Christian population of Ottoman Macedonia were really, truly, deeply Bulgarian. Or Greek. Or Macedonian. This reflects recognition of the undoubted importance of culture and ideas in the making of history, specifically in the ways that people come to imagine themselves as part of a larger community, most of the members of which they will never meet. But while the question of how, when, and why the different peoples of the Balkans "got" the religion of ethnonationalism is an important historical question, combing over the evidence for unambiguous and incontrovertible statements of intent one way or the other has generated more heat than light.

What the sources from insurgent Macedonia remind us—as much of the best literature on the region concludes—is that meanings and messages do not float free, but are themselves anchored in material matters. They also indicate, in crude quantitative terms, that nation per se was not the most important issue with which the MRO's members grappled. In the sample of 375 pension requests from the Ilinden Dossier, there are indeed multiple references to liberation for Macedonia and (to a lesser degree) the Macedonian people— the simplest and most accessible formulation of the organization's intention, each appearing more than one hundred times. But more than liberty or death, or autonomy for Macedonia and its residents, the petitioners wrote about the practicalities of accomplishing these goals. Specifically, they talked about the MRO's pursuit of the hardware of killing and self-defense, referring more than 270 times to rifles, weapons, arms, guns, ammunition, bullets, revolvers, cartridges, and munitions. Similarly, British and other European diplomatic representatives seeking to determine the organization's capacity to challenge Ottoman rule wrote more about the number of guns it had stockpiled than about its ultimate intentions or underlying ideology.

This final chapter follows this emphasis in the sources, examining the concrete ways in which the MRO and its members obtained arms in preparation for the Ilinden Uprising, and the social and cultural contexts and consequences of that process. In one of the few reflections in the existing literature on this dimension of Macedonia's insurgency, prominent Macedonian historian Ivan Katardžiev offered the following terse analysis:

> Weapons had magical power in the revolutionary mobilization of the village masses. They were a tangible proof of the possibility that the goals of the organization would be realized, and provided a sense of security in the eyes of a disempowered population. For these reasons, their acquisition absorbed the entire attention of the organization. (Katardžiev 1993: 26)

I seek here to expand on and refine Katardžiev's key insight, and also explore in greater detail the different pathways that the organization took to acquire arms. By drawing on the discussions of arms smuggling in the Ilinden Dossier, as well as broader anthropological literature on the social lives and cultural meanings of prized objects, this chapter seeks to map the physical and symbolic circuits created by the MRO's campaign to arm the Christian villagers of Macedonia, and the impact of that campaign on patterns of deadly violence that served to consolidate the strength of ethnic, religious, and national divisions. It draws on comparative material, paying particular attention to the generally underexamined relationship between the MRO and the large Muslim Albanian population of Macedonia at the time, to argue that besides learning from worldwide insurgencies, European revolutionaries, and previous intervention-driven liberation movements in the Balkans, the MRO modeled aspects of its management of violence on the allegedly primitive blood feud system of its immediate neighbors.

Guns in Transit: The MRO in the Global Arms Bazaar

In July 1903 the French vice consul in Skopje reported on the results of Turkish efforts to disarm the Christian population. As noted earlier in the discussion of the symbolic significance of the revolver in MRO oathing ceremonies, Christians were technically forbidden from owning or carrying guns; in 1903, Ottoman authorities sought to enforce that law through continued aggressive counterinsurgency methods of intelligence gathering and raids, combined with the tactical provision of amnesty for people who turned in guns voluntarily. The French consular report covered May and June 1903 and indicated that in this period the authorities took possession of 1,886 rifles, 227 revolvers, and 54,336 cartridges (Volume 35: July–August 15, 1903: 89: Max Choublin). Ever since the Vinica Affair of 1897, the Ottoman authorities had stepped up their efforts to interdict the organization's supply routes, arrest its operatives, and discover its arms caches. While the net haul was impressive—it included 369 kilograms of dynamite and 183 "bombs" (of which 130, described as "round bombs," were probably hand grenades, on the design of which the MRO had collaborated with Armenian bomb makers)—the sheer number and diversity of weapons showed that the MRO's channels of finance and transportation were still in full operation in the summer of 1903.

This picture was confirmed in other consular sources, which contain both revelatory incidents and attempts to present the bigger picture. Writing from Monastir earlier in 1903, vice consul James McGregor reported an explosion at a Christian-owned shop in the city's horse market. When police investigated, they found five hundred cartridges together with tools for filling them (FO 195/2156/363: April 4, 1903: McGregor to Biliotti). Small groups of men transporting rifles continued to be intercepted and arrested on the roads, even after the Ilinden Uprising, and when Ottoman gendarmes or field guards were found dead, their purses and other personal items were still on their bodies, but their rifles and ammunition had been taken by their killers (FO 195/2157/194: McGregor to Graves, July 27, 1903). In his April report, McGregor reported "the general impression is that a well disciplined organization exists which already possesses at least 40,000 rifles in the three vilayets and also a considerable supply of ammunition." Even after the uprising, when another amnesty was issued, McGregor estimated that most of the three thousand rifles handed in were "old and worthless" and represented less than 10 percent of total still held by the organization (FO 195/2157/672: McGregor to Graves, October 19, 1903).

What was particularly revealing in Choublin's report was his breakdown of the rifles by original provenance or manufacturer, as follows: 1,416 "old Russian"; 120 Gras; 92 Martinis; 41 Mannlichers; 18 "Turk" [sic]; and 25 Snyders [sic]. Choublin's report thus confirmed both the buying power and also the range and reach of the organization and its members. For these rifles, discovered in the hands of "peasants" who had no right to own them, included weapons manufactured in Russia, France, Austria, and the United States, and in military use in Bulgaria, Greece, and the Ottoman Empire itself. While this distribution was assuredly not a random or representative sample of the MRO's entire armory, it nonetheless provides a frame with which to read the accounts of weapon procurement from the Ilinden Dossier and other sources, and to illuminate the three primary circuits by which rifles reached the MRO.

The Bulgarian Military Connection:
Sarafov, Sofia, and the Miss Stone Ransom

Choublin's haul of "old Russian" rifles was almost certainly composed of a mixture of Berdan and Krnka rifles. These were both breech-loading, single-shot designs from the late 1860s and had been standard issue in the Russian Imperial Army when new. After the Russo–Turkish War of 1876–78 and the subsequent establishment of the Bulgarian principality, Russia served as the major arms supplier to its new client state, sending significant quantities of the already obsolete Krnka to the Balkans, followed by larger numbers of the Berdan when it was adopted by the Bulgarian Army. The Berdan was in use until 1890, when it was replaced by the Mannlicher, a magazine rifle that allowed a more rapid rate of fire.

The older Russian rifles and the Mannlichers, then, almost certainly reached Skopje from Bulgaria. The sheer numbers of the first category suggest that they did so in bulk that is, in one or more shipments negotiated by the MRO's leaders with representatives or agents close to the Bulgarian military. Most sources concur that Boris Sarafov played a key role (see for example Perry 1988: 167). One of the three leaders of the Ilinden Uprising, Sarafov was also a former Bulgarian military officer and retained strong ties with younger officers in the army. In his memoir, he reports that he drew on funds from the Miss Stone kidnapping, as well as his own contacts throughout Europe, to arrange the purchase of rifles from Bulgaria (Nikolov and Baševski 1995: 146, 153).

In the Ilinden Dossier, Iljo Lokardev of Setino wrote that he met personally with Sarafov late in 1901 and that subsequently he and his father traveled to Bulgaria to transport 350 rifles to their region (Record 20-L-59). A number of other individuals indicate that četas were routinely equipped in

Bulgaria, which served as "safe haven" for the organization for much of this period.[1]

This supply chain had benefits for both parties but potential drawbacks for the MRO. The clear benefit for the Bulgarian military was that they could dispose of obsolete weaponry by this means. Whether or not there was unscrupulous dealing is not clear. Consular sources suggest that Sarafov believed he was acquiring significant numbers of modern repeating rifles for the organization, which would certainly have created a tactical advantage for the MRO's četas against any of their likely military or paramilitary opponents in the region. Choublin's report and other contemporary sources make clear, though, that repeating Mannlichers and Mausers composed only a tiny proportion of the organization's weapons and were mostly in the hands of established leaders.[2]

Access to rifles and ammunition in bulk carried advantages for the organization as well. Especially after Vinica, many leaders felt they needed to assemble the forces for an armed insurgency as quickly as possible; shipments on the scale reported by Lokardiev served that goal. Additionally, standardization in weapon type would simplify training and repairs—especially if, as was frequently the case, present and former Bulgarian military personnel were directly involved in providing leadership and support.

These same benefits, though, were transformed into drawbacks as the relationship between the MRO and its Bulgarian counterparts cooled. A major issue in the worsening relationship was the clash between Sofia's desire for centralization and control, and the MRO's insistence on autonomy and local decision making. Involvement on the supply side of the MRO's arms acquisition gave Bulgaria a powerful bargaining tool in this set of linked disputes. Bulgaria could simply shut down supply or, even more destructively, it could take payment and then reveal to Ottoman authorities the date and time the organization's couriers would be crossing the border with their purchases. Equipping the organization's četas with Bulgarian-issued rifles, whether old or new, had symbolic effects as well as practical, insofar as it contributed to the impression that the MRO was simply an extension of Bulgarian state policy, thereby reducing its broad appeal.[3] These factors conspired with the escalation of tensions between the MRO's Macedonian-based leadership and their Bulgarian-oriented counterparts, leading to direct armed confrontation during the summer of 1902, when MRO četas fought against General Končev's incursion from Bulgaria.

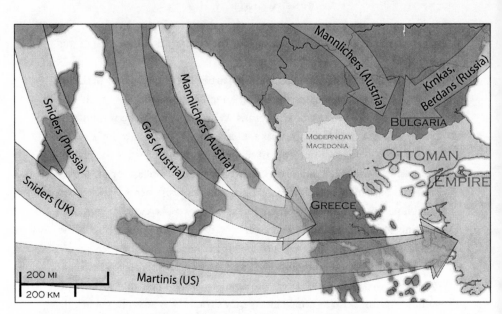

Figure 6.1. Guns in transit: from state to state.

Figure 6.2. Guns in transit: into the hands of the MRO.

The Greek Connection: Guns and Charcoal

The organization had already, though, opened other channels to acquire arms. After the Bulgarian weapons, the next largest number of rifles in the Skopje haul was the 120 Gras rifles. These were, again, single-shot breech-loading rifles, in this case designed in France in the 1860s. The Gras rifle was adopted in 1874 as the standard weapon of the Greek army, which purchased most of its supplies from Austrian manufacturers, working under license. These rifles, then, most likely found their way to Skopje from Greece, where the army began replacing the Gras with the Mannlicher as its standard infantry weapon in 1894, thereby making the older rifles available for purchase.

Macedonia's migrant workers, the *pečalbars*, fanned out across the region each spring, pushed by the oppressive conditions of life and limited economic opportunities in their home villages, and drawn by the promise of better wages elsewhere. Circuits were established over many years, with fathers guiding sons, and uncles guiding nephews on particular paths of migration, which they in turn may have learned from earlier generations. The charcoal burners of Capari and Gjavato traveled repeatedly to Izmir, in Asia Minor, and also to the environs of Katerini, which then lay on the Ottoman side of Greece's northern border, around Mount Olympus.

A quarter of the forty-four pension applicants from these two villages, which together with Smilevo supplied more than five hundred insurgents during Ilinden, explicitly report buying rifles for themselves in Katerini, at the command of the organization. According to Jovan Kapinovski, the order was delivered by Nase Bečvarov of Capari in spring 1903—along with the order to return home, discussed in Chapter 2 (Record 16-K-24). Others indicate that they were involved in moving rifles up from Greece and its borders over a longer period. Jane G. Vrjkovski, for example, wrote in his application that already in 1902 "in the very charcoal there had always to be one or two rifles, which I carried to Capari and gave to Simon Trajkov, who was a teacher in the village and had worked from before for the uprising" (Record 6-V-70).

These were most likely Gras rifles, reportedly sold by enterprising Greek and Jewish merchants (Turquie-Macédoine Volume 33 (1903): Harvey to Delcassé, April 24, 1903: p. 52). Ilinden participants from Kruševo make reference to Greek rifles: Šapardan, in an unpublished memoir, recalls obtaining significant numbers through Magarevo—a Vlah village—while Mate Petrov

Boškovski states that Kruševo's armory in the uprising contained four hundred of them (Šapardan n.d.; Record 5-B-27). McGregor believed that Gras rifles like these, smuggled from Thessaly, had become the predominant weapon for *četas* in the Monastir region by April 1903 (FO 195/2156/494: McGregor to Biliotti, April 28, 1903). According to one Ilinden pension applicant, the Ottoman authorities also knew about this traffic; regarding the army attack on Capari that followed the Salonika bombings of April 1903, Riste Zengoski wrote that "the Turks killed 13 people in the village, because they were taking and transporting weapons to the neighboring villages. The Turks intercepted them and killed those 13 men as they were trying to escape" (Record 12-Z-12).

This arms circuit, then, operated very differently from the one involving the Bulgarian army. The organization effectively outsourced responsibility to individuals to equip themselves and left it to local leaders to manage the traffic and distribution. Rifle purchase in Greece was therefore ideologically less problematic than the Bulgarian route. There were pragmatic disadvantages: the accuracy and range of Gras rifles were considered inferior to others that were available. Ottoman authorities knew about the route, and although they could not shut it down, they could and did "profile" the charcoal merchants of Capari, thereby reducing their usefulness as couriers. Additionally, ammunition had to be purchased and smuggled in, or manufactured by the organization itself; it was not readily available from other sources closer at hand. Nonetheless, the channel remained active up to Ilinden and beyond, constituting a running sore for Greek nationalists. In February 1907, Greek paramilitaries killed fifteen charcoal burners in Katerini, most likely representing their own effort to cut off this supply route (Dakin 1966: 308).

Traffic With the Enemy: Albanian Sources for Macedonian Arms

The other three rifle types named by Choublin—Martinis, "Turk," and Snyders [sic]—had diverse origins. Martinis were originally a British design, produced under license by a number of industrialized countries. The largest provider to the Ottoman Empire was the United States. "Turk" rifles were probably locally made versions of the Martini, from a factory in Tetovo. The Sniders had traveled the most complicated route; Turkish Sniders were for the most part retrofitted U.S.-produced Springfields with British-made Snider firing mechanisms. Some came directly to Turkey, others as gifts from Prussia, which had captured many thousands during the Franco–Prussian War of 1870 (Williamson 1952: 64). All three types, then, were in use by the Turkish army and its auxiliaries in Macedonia; the fact that they were found in the organization's arms depots around Skopje was not an anomaly, but was evidence of the MRO's ability to innovate and overcome obstacles to its quest to acquire arms and ammunition. In a supremely elegant twist of counter-counterinsurgency, MRO members began purchasing rifles and ammunition from the sources that were closest at hand: the soldiers, gendarmes, field guards, and local Muslim population who were the embodiment of the oppression that the organization set out to end.

Several accounts in the Ilinden Dossier, as well as accounts from the consular reports, narrate circuits of this kind. M. Tase Bočvarski of Lopatica, Bitola, bought cartridges from Tetovo and Kičevo Turks, while Boris Gruev of Skopje bought guns from Dalip Bičakčija, whom he calls a "friend" (Records 5-B-22; 8-G-37). Dimitar Bojadžiev of Bitola persuaded an Anatolian Turk soldier to bring him army rifles: he writes, "we paid 5–6 liras each, and every 10–15 days he brought one, with ammunition, and left them at Miše Dimov's stables" (Record 4-B-54).[4]

In each of these cases, the organization acquired rifles and/or ammunition from the hands of those entitled to bear them in Macedonia and diverted them into the caches of the local committees. In keeping with its overall commitment to a stealthy, incremental marshaling of resources, it appears that the organization sought to purchase weapons and munitions from Turks and Albanians more often than they stole them. It appears also that they did so on a sufficiently large scale to prompt the Ottoman authorities to investigate and punish Muslim traffickers as well as Christian recipients. Among the 594 political prisoners amnestied in March 1903, most of whom were described as Christian Bulgarians, there were also eighteen Muslims, all arrested for "conveying firearms for the use of the Bulgarian committees" (FO 195/2156/281: McGregor to Biliotti, March 24, 1903).

Buying guns from local Muslims had several practical advantages. In the first place, it created highly efficient and virtually unbreakable circuits of arms trading. The rifles concerned crossed the borders of Macedonia without any risk to the organization's personnel. And because the final transaction was illegal, the risk of the Turk or Albanian betraying the organization to the authorities was low. Additionally, obtaining and using the same rifles as the incumbent regime meant that ammunition was more readily available, either through purchase or theft, which is one of the recommendations contained in Che Guevara's work on guerrilla warfare (Guevara 2007: 24). The Martini had the added advantage that it was possible to fill the cartridges by hand, thereby reducing concerns over the degradation of stored ammunition (Durham 1905: 52–53; see also "Regulations for Village Bands," item #7, in appendix 1).

"Magic" Revisited: Guns and Power

All across Macedonia, then, in the years leading up to the Ilinden Uprising, rifles were changing hands from incumbents to insurgents for money. Nikola Neškov Kondarkoski of Kruševo provides the greatest detail in reporting his purchase of a Martini, including the price and the names of both the recipient and the supplier of the rifle he obtained:

> I received an order to buy a gun for Tome Niklev, and I bought a new gun from the village of Norovo from an Albanian called Meri. The gun, for which I paid 13 Turkish lira, was a new Martini with 200 bullets. There was also an order that everybody who joined the četa should buy a gun, so I bought a gun for the price of 11 Turkish lira and then I bought five more guns. (Record 17-K-59)

Coupled with the data regarding the range of rifles that the organization acquired and the journeys they had traveled, Kondarkoski's account presents an opportunity to flesh out more fully Katardžiev's insights into the impact of arms on the MRO's members. While Katardžiev most likely used the term "magical power" in a metaphorical sense, the influx of guns to Macedonian villages under the MRO's auspices surely had a range of intended and unintended effects. Those that he sketches out—evidence that the organization's goals might be realized, and an increased sense of security—appear at first sight commonsensical and obvious. But comparative work in anthropology and history on the social lives of things in general, and guns in particular, suggests that this project of physical and symbolic empowerment had further dimensions.

Kondarkoski describes buying a rifle for Tome Niklev, a major figure in the organization's leadership in Kruševo, who appears as oath giver, organizer, and member of the military command during the Ilinden Uprising, when the MRO controlled Kruševo. In his hands, a rifle would serve the functions that Katardžiev imagines: a marker of authority and potency. In a context where Christians were banned from owning or displaying firearms, the MRO's personnel represented literal defiance of that Ottoman law. Photographs from the period, in which young men swathed in cartridge belts stare out proudly, often holding their rifles in plain sight, suggest the symbolic significance of this transgression. It was part of the self-fashioning, and representation by others, of the MRO as a new quasi-knightly order, to make public their access to, and familiarity with, modern weapons. Christian village audiences for such performances, whether live, photographically recorded, or narrated in folklore, may have viewed Niklev's breech-loading rifle as a novelty from the outside world, part of the same impressive influx of modern paraphernalia that included sewing machines and phonographs, which in the Balkans and elsewhere generated their own stories of "first contact" and native awe (see for example Brailsford 1906: 71).

Kondarkoski highlights the dramatic importance of this purchase in his emplotment, whereby he distinguishes Niklev's rifle from the other six—one

Figure 6.3. MRO leader Vasil Čakalarov and his staff, well-armed, during the Ilinden Uprising. Čakalarov is seated at reader's left.

for himself, five for use by others—he had a hand in obtaining. Only Niklev's rifle is identified by its make, the standard one-shot Martini design. Though we cannot be certain of this particular rifle's provenance, as Martinis were produced under different licenses by international arms manufacturers, it is statistically most likely that it was one of the 500,000 Peabody-Martinis produced for the Ottoman government by the Providence Tool Company in Rhode Island in the 1870s (Rose 2008: 181–0000; see also Durham 1905: 97). By 1902, the Ottoman Empire was well along in its modernization campaign, as part of which it adopted German-made Mauser rifles, and older weapons like the Peabody-Martinis found their way into reservist units at the margins of the empire. Some, though, might well never have been used in that time; Kondarkoski's note, repeated twice, that Niklev's rifle was "new" hints that perhaps it fell into that category.

So too does the price that Kondarkoski reports paying—thirteen Turkish lira. This far exceeded the reported costs of other rifles. Bojadžiev, for example, paid five to six lira for the Turkish army rifles he purchased, and three to four lira for others obtained from Kozani (Record 4-B-54; see also Perry 1988: 163). Šapardan, a counterpart of Kondarkoski's in Kruševo, paid four to six lira for Greek rifles, obtained via Magarevo (Šapardan n.d.). Consular reports indicate that in early 1904, the organization was buying Martini-pattern rifles manufactured in Tetovo for 150 piastres—that is, roughly one-eighth of the price Kondarkoski reports paying. The closest equivalent in reported price is the twelve Napoleons that an Albanian notable boasted of paying for each of the eight new, repeating Mauser rifles he owned in 1908 (Durham 1905: 62).

In the case of Tome Niklev's rifle, though, the question of value plays out very differently from the Bulgarian situation, where obsolete, Russian-made Krnka rifles may have been substituted for modern Mausers by wily Bulgarian quartermasters. Certainly there were material differences between rifles. Martinis produced in Tetovo were generally acknowledged to be of lower quality than the foreign-made, while the Gras was both heavier and less accurate than other models. Beyond such considerations, though, the price Kondarkoski paid alerts us that, given the status of the recipient of this rifle, he may well have seen this transaction as of a different kind from the mass import of guns from Bulgaria. His task as the supplier of the rifle (and the teller of the tale of the rifle) was to endow Niklev's rifle with all the prestige it could bear. The goal, in other words, was not value for money in a strict economistic sense; instead, Kondarkoski was interested in trading money for value.

This distinction is more often made in Pacific anthropology than in Southeast European history. In the very different context of the mid-nineteenth-century southern Marquesas, for example, Nicholas Thomas describes the musket economy as one in which

> the values of things became entangled with the stories about their sources, about the great things that those outsiders did. . . . A receiving group like this [southern Marquesans] does not want commodities disconnected from their users; it wants artifacts which tell a story. (Thomas 1991: 103)

By extended analogy, part of the value of Niklev's rifle lay in the story of its acquisition, and specifically the story of the larger system of relations by which it reached Niklev's hands. Insofar as the money paid to Meri came from the local MRO treasury—as it most likely did, in line with doctrine—then peasants could see and handle the rifle as a material instantiation of their own agency and commitment. The local treasury, after all, was built from their own contributions to the cause. So one dimension of the "magical power" of Niklev's rifle was the story of the organization's trustworthiness to deliver on its commitments and transform pooled resources into effective results in the world. The cost in this case, thirteen lira, was substantial: equivalent to six months' gross wages from charcoal work, half of a typical village household's gross annual income, or between four and six times the price of one head of cattle. But in this case, the high price further increased the rifle's prestige, simply proving its value.

The price point aside, the very facts of purchase had further significance for the gun's meaning for MRO supporters. There is an apparent paradox at work in this transaction and in all the others described in the dossier in which members of the organization hand over hard-earned cash, assembled through taxation, to representatives of a system of oppression. At first sight, it looks self-destructive. An alternative view, though, would argue that in this and other cases where weapons were bought from representatives of the Ottoman state, the organization pursued a strategy of subversion and destabilization. By offering cash payment for rifles—at a time when Ottoman finances were in a shambolic state and payment to its personnel was many months in arrears—the organization gave Albanians like Meri an economic interest in its survival. Simultaneously, it waged a form of information warfare: while Meri would be unlikely to reveal the nature of the transaction to Ottoman officials—Christians, after all, were not permitted to own weapons—he knew and if pressed would probably share with family and neighbors the extent to which Christians were flouting a law that left them vulnerable, and taking steps to defend themselves.

Monopolizing Violence: Albanians and the Ottoman Empire

Purchases like the one described by Kondarkoski were part of a larger, incremental shift in the security situation in Macedonia. The late 1890s and early 1900s saw the Ottoman Empire under considerable external and internal pressures, especially in its Balkan and Aegean territories. Greece, Bulgaria, and (most recently) Crete had all launched struggles that had prompted foreign intervention and led to some form of autonomy; sanguine international observers asked why Macedonia should escape what appeared to be destiny (French Foreign Ministry 35: July–August 1903, 22). In attempting to bring about a different outcome by embracing reforms, the empire added fuel to the crisis by mobilizing the anti-imperial sentiments of Macedonia's Albanian population.

Across the *vilayets* of Turkey in Europe, people generally referred to as "Albanians" numbered around 1.5 million, compared with around 600,000 "Turks" and 1.3 million Slavs, Greeks and Vlahs (FO 195/2157 /444: Fontana to O'Conor, September 4, 1903). To an even greater extent than these counterparts, the Albanians constituted an internally diverse grouping. Albanian speakers could be Christian, either Catholic or Orthodox (in which case they were often claimed as Greeks). Many were Muslims, members of families that converted during the extended presence of the Ottoman Empire in the Balkan Peninsula. The language itself still has two distinct dialects, Gheg and Tosk, which in this period also served to index different modalities of custom and livelihood. Ghegs lived north of the river Shkumbi, were generally northerners and highlanders, and retained a vibrant clan and tribal structure; Tosks dominated in the southern plains, and included a larger, urban, settled population.

When viewed as a bloc, Albanians also represented ambivalence toward Ottoman rule (Blumi 2011). Over several centuries, they converted to Islam at higher rates than any of the other groups, and many advanced to serve key roles in the maintenance of the empire. As early as the seventeenth century, Albanians had earned a reputation in Turkish circles as good counselors (Brown 1673: 74–75), and in the early twentieth century the grand Vizier was of Albanian descent (Brailsford 1906: 235). This ran alongside a longer legacy of banditry, brigandage, and mercenary soldiering, represented most color-fully in the early nineteenth-century career of Ali Pasha, the so-called Lion of Ioaninna. Ali carved out his own fiefdom from Ottoman rule in the early nineteenth century before his ambitions and schemes attracted the attention of the sultan, who besieged Ioaninna and ultimately had the rebel beheaded (Fleming 1999). Albanian Muslims, or, in the terms of the period, "Arnauts," in western Macedonia operated in similar mode at the turn of the twentieth century, serving the empire as tax collectors, gendarmes, or field guards, while retaining their sense of autonomy and their license to raid their Albanian and non-Albanian neighbors. Although generally content with the status quo, in which they enjoyed considerable privileges, by the early twentieth century many Albanian elites were anticipating the end of Ottoman rule and insisting that by virtue of their numbers and proud history, "the Albanians have the right to be heard, and listened to, in the question of the ultimate settlement of Macedonia" (FO 195/2157 /444: Fontana to O'Conor, September 4, 1903). Their concerns drove the formation of the League of Prizren in 1878, and a broader Albanian national movement united by shared language and aspira-tions for political autonomy (Skendi 1967).

The ways Ottoman central authorities used the principle of "divide and rule" to fragment the Slavic-speaking Orthodox Christian population has been widely noted. The recognition of the Bulgarian Exarchate in 1870, for exam-ple, was a political move that undercut the unique authority the Orthodox Patriarchate had enjoyed for over a century, and it ultimately put Bulgaria and Greece at loggerheads. It was only in this late nineteenth-century context of competition along denominational lines that the intense antipathies between "Greeks" and "Bulgarians" observed during the Second Balkan War of 1912–13 were generated. As a number of historians have observed, the "ancient hatreds" observed by the Carnegie Commission in their inquiry into that war's atroci-ties were in fact very young (Livanios 2008; Mazower 2000; see also Brown 2013). In the wake of Ilinden, the sultan continued with the same approach in recognizing in 1905 the Roumanist millet, set up by Vlahs in Macedonia. As was the case with the Bulgarian Exarchate, it sparked strong reaction from the Greek Orthodox establishment, which was also manifest in physical violence against adherents of the newly recognized faith, including the destruction of their sacred texts (Dakin 1966: 236).

Just as potential Christian unity was disabled by encouraging the proliferation of religious options, so Albanian unity and aspirations toward secession were impeded by the empire's restrictive policy on education in the medium of the Albanian language. This took several forms, including closing schools and a strong reaction against efforts to import Bibles in the Albanian language. The consular reports include accounts of Ottoman authorities prosecuting individuals—in at least one case from the coastal city of Kavala in late 1902, a representative of the British and Foreign Bible Society—for attempting to distribute Bibles in the Albanian language (FO 195/2133/790: Biliotti to O'Conor, November 8, 1902). By means of this policy, combined with a continued permissive attitude to Albanian Muslims who flouted the law they were ostensibly responsible for enforcing, Ottoman policy sought to slow the spread of the ideology of Albanian unity.

This form of ad hoc crisis management, though, was of only limited success, especially as information spread among Albanians of the apparently accelerating process of reforms to empower those Christian subjects who enjoyed the sponsorship and support of external actors. The response was armed demonstrations of force against Ottoman authorities. On several occasions, thousands of Albanians converged on key cities or towns, and in the cases of Mitrovica in early 1903 and Djakova in early 1904, could only be dispersed by artillery fire from imperial forces (FO 195/2156/281; 195/2182/86).

One particular issue that fueled Albanian opposition was the planned phase-in of Christian gendarmes and field guards, and the presumption that these new representatives would be armed, especially in Christian-dominated regions. Such a reform, under discussion in 1903, would have two negative consequences for Albanians. First, over the previous five years they had achieved something close to a monopoly of these two professions. Second, those not employed in this way (as well as some who were) engaged in forms of banditry and extortion at the expense of the Christian population, a livelihood that Christian field guards and gendarmes might threaten. Writing from Salonika in May 1902, Sir Alfred Biliotti described the status quo in the following terms:

[T]he *gendarmerie* in this vilayet [are] one fourth native Moslems, one fourth Ghegs and one half Tosk Albanians.... Up to five or six years ago the Bekchis (rural guards) were natives of the villages in which they were employed, Christians or Moslems according to circumstances. Since then however the *Gendarmerie* colonels, themselves Ghegs, under pretext of protecting the villagers from the Greek bands who were scouring the country, compelled the former to employ Ghegs as *bekchis* [field guards], and it is since this innovation that the Christians have complained of murders and all manner of violence and oppression.

... In addition to the swarms of Ghegs and Tosks who emigrate into Macedonia in search of work and pending its procurement frequently live by cattle-letting, etc., shepherds drive their flocks into the country and pasture them here, from November to May, and instead of four or five per thousand sheep, Gheg (Albanian) shepherds accompany the flocks, forty or fifty of them per thousand sheep, all armed. (FO 195/2133/332: Biliotti to O'Conor, May 17, 1902)

Particularly notorious were the Muslim Albanian tribes of Dibra (modern Debar). Reported by Edith Durham as the second-largest tribe and known as the "Dibra tigers" (Durham 1905: 239; 1909: 317), they attracted the attention of the British consular staff for their repeated raiding down into the Salonika *vilayet*. Well-armed pastoralists, they rustled cattle along the way to market, and lived off the land, terrorizing local populations. Two further forms of extraction, directed by Dibra's Albanians against their Slavic Christian neighbors, were also recorded in another extended consular report, prompted by a petition from the victims. The complaint was that multiple Albanian chieftains—specifically both the nominally Catholic "Latins" or Malessors from Upper Dibra and local Muslim tribes—were exacting tribute from the Christians of the lower town.

The taxation of Christians in general by the Albanians is an established fact and the sums paid to them are heavier than those paid to Government. The Bulgarian agent told me that the Bulgarians did not object so much to taxation by one Albanian chief, since it entails protection by him, but they object strongly to patronage by several, which entails a corresponding increase in expenditure. The marriage tax ... is of general and traditional practice, even in the vilayet of Salonika. Here the steward of the farm exacts his bakshish [tip or bribe] of boots, handkerchief, shirts etc., often amounting to five pounds, as in Dibra his chiefs demand ready cash. Refusal is followed by punishment, which in Dibra is the death of the bridegroom (the rape of the bride alleged in the petition is, I believe, an exaggeration).

... The Malessores also practice brigandage proper, carrying off men and cattle and releasing them on payment of ransom ranging from one hundred to two hundred pounds. (FO 195/2156/331: Biliotti to O'Conor, April 1903)

Such forms of systematic, habitual exploitation were clearly part of the context in which the organization was able to appeal to villagers. These descriptions also provide a clear rationale for evidence of greater allegiance and commitment to the organization in western Macedonia—around Monastir, Prilep, Resen, and Ohrid—than in eastern Macedonia, closer to Bulgaria but without a significant Albanian population. For the circuits of destruction and repression outlined here were both ecologically and politically rooted. They were also not new: in his autobiographical memoir Hristo Tatarčev, the first president of the Salonika-based MRO in 1893, recalled outrages conducted by Albanians against his family in their home in Resen in 1877, when he was a child, and he stressed that they "stayed in his mind and heart" (Nikolov and Baševski 1995: 325).

Arms and Manhood: Feud and the Construction of Solidarity

Nothing symbolized Albanians' superior standing within the Ottoman Empire more visibly than their gun culture, which was in turn closely tied to the *kanun*, the "unwritten law" by which violence was managed (Hasluck 1954). In keeping with decentralized, "tribal" societies in Africa, Central Asia, and the Middle East, at least some Albanians lived in a society governed by a consensually shared code of conduct and system of justice in which the obligations of blood were paramount. In the manner laid out in the classic *The Nuer* (Evans-Pritchard 1940), solidarity was nested; each household identified with a clan, tribal segment, and tribe, and its affiliation determined who its members could marry, and with whom they should ally in any given dispute. Among the aspects that attracted particular attention from outsiders was the manifestation of rugged, agonistic individualism in what appears to be a rigid frame of social constraints. Writing about Montenegro, for example, Christopher Boehm turned the tables on accounts of feud as mechanistic and agency-stultifying by arguing that Montenegrins engage in sophisticated social engineering and calculation:

> To work, the blood-feud system required that this kind of analytic and decision-making competency exists on the part of ordinary individuals, whose intuitive and sometimes very rapidly made decisions deeply affected the welfare of entire clans and tribes. There was also a need for experts to serve as decision leaders, and entire kin groups functioned as collective decision-making units. (Boehm 1984: 157)

Others have pointed out the ways in which the sentiment of solidarity with blood kin built into the tribal system provides the basis for ethnonationalism in the region and beyond. Detailing the way that Albanians would overcome tribal differences and rally to one another in a confrontation with Slavs, for example, Margaret Hasluck wrote:

> National solidarity was recognized in the debatable borderlands where Slav and Albanian lived side by side. If an Albanian was killed by a Slav, any Albanian would kill any Slav in revenge. The crime, it was felt, had pitted the Albanian family against the Slav family. This national sentiment was so strong that though there has never been any love lost between Gegs (north Albanians) and Tosks (south Albanians), no Geg would allow a Slav to kill a Tosk without seeking in return to kill any Slav he could find. The less warlike Tosks did not feel a similar impulse. If one of their number or a Geg was killed by their Bulgarian or Greek neighbors, they left vengeance to the victim's family. (Hasluck 1954: 226)

What Hasluck describes is the variation in the extent to which different Albanian actors extended their own code of conduct and system of justice to create space for others to act meaningfully. In short, among Albanians, patrilineal groups under certain circumstances are "in blood" with other similar groups: There is a long or short history of bloodshed between the two families, the origin point of which is often in dispute, such that at any time the members of one group feel under an obligation to avenge the loss of one of their own at the hands of the other. When a member does so—in an act of homicide that is expected to follow a particular ritualized form—the two groups swap positions, so that the former blood debtor becomes the blood debt seeker. Some feuds are long-running over centuries; others are resolved by the intervention of some mediator, recourse to payment in cash rather than blood, or some act of union between the feuding houses. The existence of such feuds provides a frame for the maintenance of knowledge of kinship and descent, as well as constituting social relationships between different groups.

This vision carries particular resonances about masculinity and the expectations of manhood. In this system political agency, and the management of external relations, is a male domain. Women were not appropriate targets for vengeance; if they took up arms to avenge a death in the family (more often a brother, father, or son than a husband) it was an anomaly, which demanded special provision in the nature of blood debt thus incurred. Such principles can be traced to the tie between the feud and the patrilineal order, in which men's loyalties, ordered by descent, are clear-cut and readily patterned, whereas women's relationships with others and subsequent loyalties are multiple and overlapping, and may shift in the course of a lifetime.[5]

In Albania and the Balkans, the case law of feud was by the end of the nineteenth century voluminous. There were rules regarding the treatment of the body of a victim; formulae for calculating how much blood was owed in the case of a serious wound, or the death of a sheepdog or an unborn child; instructions for how to request and grant a truce; and cautionary tales of how violence could spiral out of control without proper observance of the conventions. The practice of families "in blood" remained much as it had for generations—the designated avenger would seek to ambush an appropriate target from the household which owed blood and try to kill him with a single shot.[6] After an appropriate period of mourning, in the course of which he would pay his respects to his victim's family, he would then be the target for an avenger from the other household. Viewed from this perspective, there was a stately grandeur to the feud. It was deeply entwined with the system of reckoning descent and kinship, so that the pathways of responsibility and participation were usually clear to all concerned, and the escalation or acceleration of violence were precluded.

Testing Solidarity: The MRO, *Honor, and Retributive Violence*

This, then, was the community into which members of the MRO successfully opened channels to buy guns for the organization. The exact motivation of Albanians like Meri to participate in these illegal transactions is not clear. The organization did find sympathizers among socialists in Ottoman service and other supporters of the Young Turks, already preparing the ground for their 1908 coup d'état that was launched in Macedonia. Slavs and Albanians, possibly more than in the contemporary world, did at times call each other friends in this period, and such ties may have played a role. In the absence of other hard evidence, it is easy to assume that motives were primarily financial, but perhaps also nudged along by the growing divergence of interests between the Ottoman government and the Albanian population writ large.

What makes this interpretation insufficient, though, is the uses to which the MRO put these weapons and, perhaps more saliently, the effects of the increased morale and assertiveness of the organization, to which the growing stockpiles contributed. For at the same time the organization was buying guns from Albanians and Turks, it was also issuing orders to selected members to kill them. Alongside the self-designated terrorists of the organization discussed earlier, whose primary duty was the elimination of spies and traitors, a further seven pension seekers, without using any specific term to describe themselves, report carrying out executions of Turkish field guards or gendarmes. Two of the seven explicitly report doing so at the direct orders of the organization.

These seven, all young men, fit closely the profile of "rural terrorists" identified in documents captured in June 1903 and made available to the consuls in French translation. J. Micko Joševski, of Žvan, gives one of the fullest accounts of the process by which a killing was ordered and carried out, and its consequences.

> In 1902 in our village Žvan we had a *poljak* [field guard], a Turk, by name Mesole Bajram, from the Turkish village of Suhodol in the Bitola region. This field guard became a source of great terror and violence . . . people could not endure all that he did in the village, and so they sought through the Revolutionary Committee for the *poljak* to be executed. I was appointed, along with my brother Stojan, by the Committee, to carry out the killing.

On 18 March 1902, when the *poljak* was due to eat lunch at our house, I and my brother Stojan killed him with a hatchet, which is today kept in the Folk Museum in Kruševo. After the killing, I and my brother Stojan became *komitas* and my father went to Bulgaria. (Record 15-J-47: see also appendix 2)

The order of events described here certainly fits that laid out in the organization's principles. The killing was carried out by members of the village community, and the victim had clearly committed repeated offenses against the local population. The village had first to approach the committee to gain their sanction for the killing to take place, and the committee designated who the killers should be and issued the command in writing.[7]

A similar scenario is reported by Milan Milenkov Angelov, of Sopot, in the Sveti Nikola region, who killed two field guards on separate occasions in 1903. He names the second as an Albanian named Kjazim Arnautin, whom he killed for committing outrages against a young Macedonian woman from his village. Like the Joševski brothers, he carried out this execution after written orders had been issued by the organization designating him, together with two others, for the task. In his case, he was afterward caught and jailed for a 101-year term and was only amnestied in 1908 (Record 1-A-43).

Iljo Lokardev, of Setino in the Lerin region (modern Florina), carried out his first assassination, of a Turkish state official named Ahmed, in December 1901, two years after being recruited by his father as a seventeen-year-old. In February 1902 he killed a field guard, and in May 1902 he killed two gendarmes, whom he names as Muslija and Suleiman, who were on their way from Setino to Gorničevo. After this, he became *ilegalen* and entered a *četa,* still only nineteen years old (Record 20-L-59).

Such killings attracted less attention in the consular sources than those where the organization targeted fellow Christians, whether for refusing to contribute to the cause or for betraying secrets to the authorities. But word of the capacity of MRO bands to offer protection against the everyday depredations of low-ranking officials or bandits previously operating with impunity clearly spread. In April 1904—a full eight months after the Ilinden Uprising and after allegedly intensive efforts to recruit Christians to serve as gendarmes and field guards—the British Consul in Salonika wrote that a *četa* had been seen close to Yenidje, which he learned later had been summoned by two

Patriarchist villages to "deal with lawless Albanian field-guards." In a rare piece of editorial commentary, the author continued:

> It is indeed a curious inversion of the natural order of things by which the insurgent band is called in to punish or avenge the crimes of the nominal protectors of life and property, while the last to appear on the scene are the military and police. (FO 195/2182/294: Graves to O'Conor, April 12, 1904; see also Fraser 1906: 203)

Although their pension-seeking killers identify some of their victims as "Turks," it is most likely, following the consular sources, that a majority of these low-ranking Ottoman representatives were Albanian. If so, then the willingness of Meri and numerous other Albanians and Turks to trade with the organization arguably presents a larger paradox than the readiness of rural Macedonians to hand over money to these supposed "enemies." The most striking example of this apparent disconnect comes in a consular report on the very eve of Ilinden, in which McGregor reports that after the engagement at Mogila in which Cvetkov was killed, the Turkish soldiers sold two thousand Martini cartridges to the villagers (FO 195/2157/232: McGregor to Graves, August 2, 1903). Not only did Meri and his fellow traders give Christian villagers the basic materials of self-defense that stripped Albanian field guards, gendarmes, and cattle raiders of an impunity that was already under challenge, but they also put Ottoman soldiers at risk.[8]

It is of course possible that all this was accidental or unintended. Nevertheless, by locating and then exploiting the economic self-interest of individual Albanians, and simultaneously ordering the execution of those who had abused their power over Christians—especially when they had assaulted women—the organization challenged enshrined myths about Albanian militancy and solidarity. By acquiring rifles and ammunition from whatever source, it replaced an existing power asymmetry between Albanians and Macedonian Slavs with a calculated claim to equality, unlicensed by the Ottoman state. By prioritizing arms trading with Albanians and Turks in particular, it made them complicit in this project, thereby demonstrating the bankruptcy of the Ottoman State, both in terms of its capacity to pay its personnel and its ability to command their allegiance, as well as gaps in the vaunted solidarity of Albanians. And finally, by mobilizing young men as representatives of a larger solidarity to carry out retributive violence against those who had challenged the organization's honor—vested, according to cultural norms in the region, in women's bodies—it claimed the role of definer of justice.

Staking Claims: The MRO, Tribal Standing, and the Power of Restraint

Together, these activities can be read as constituting an implicit claim, addressed to Albanian elites, that the organization and its followers deserved the respect and treatment usually accorded to an Albanian tribe by its peers. This attempt, arguably, foreshadows methods adopted or counseled by some counterinsurgency practitioners in imperial contexts, ranging from the practice of T. E. Lawrence, who became an "honorary Arab," to Bing West's advice that the U.S. in Iraq must establish themselves as "the strongest tribe" (West 2008). The MRO, though, subverted rather than adopted the tenets of tribal behavior, seeking to demonstrate that violence against individual violent or transgressive Albanians need not necessarily trigger the invocation of "honor" and swift reprisals. Rifles were Albanian in that they stood for the readiness of a clan to avenge any insult as well as the domination of Christians; by buying them from Albanians, the organization transvalued them, changing their identity to serve, as Katardžiev writes, as tangible proof that security for Christians was possible in the future.

Through its acquisition of rifles, then, the organization pursued the same goal as it did in the other domains discussed in previous chapters. The issue of receipts and bonds, the maintenance of archives, the creation of an elaborated system of modes of membership and training regimes for village četas and militias, and the continuous attention to loyalty and secrecy were all intended to attract and retain members who were, in the typology defined by political scientist Jeremy Weinstein, investors rather than consumers (Weinstein 2007: 8–9). Similarly, rifles were obtained only under orders from the organization, with the instruction, apart from the arms that četas and vojvodas carried, that they were then to be stockpiled and kept hidden.[9] The goal was to control violence tightly—in particular, to manage the single largest potential source of deadly confrontations, tensions between armed Albanian representatives of Ottoman rule and the organization's adherents—and to build instead the potential capacity for violence, to be unleashed only on command.

These were all actions of a body committed to internal legitimacy and with aspirations to constitute the apparatus of a future state. Much of the evidence indicates that the internal, autonomist wing of the MRO made progress toward that goal in the years between the Vinica Affair of 1897 and the Ilinden Uprising of 1903. The Ilinden Dossier, as well as the consular reports, suggests that in this period the organization acted to reduce the overall level of violence. This spirit was observed even in the uprising itself, during which Brailsford, responding to accusations of the MRO's bloodthirstiness or antipathy toward Albanians, Turks, or Greeks, observed that apart from a few isolated incidents, there was no widespread bloodletting or score settling (Brailsford 1906: 153n).

The Salonika bombings and the extreme and symbolically freighted violence that the organization sometimes employed against traitors or spies—the case of Sophia Trencoff, the police chief's mistress in Kruševo, being the obvious example—represent challenges to this interpretation of the MRO as an anti-escalatory institution. But the greater part of the violence ordered by the MRO's leadership was discriminating and responsive rather than provocative. The examples of the killings of Albanians in this chapter were all implicitly or explicitly judicially sanctioned; they represented punishment in response to transgressive or illegal behavior, and in particular to violations of honor. As such, they were concrete expressions—in a language of violence that its intended audiences understood—of the MRO's commitment to foster a sense of security for the Christian population it claimed to represent. By responding to violations of basic human rights with a form of due process and targeted terror, the organization insisted that Albanians take it seriously and treat its constituency with respect. Through the parallel process of identifying pragmatic individuals among their Muslim neighbors, appealing to their interests, and negotiating with them in an atmosphere of trust, MRO members incrementally called into question Albanian and Ottoman solidarity and resolve even as they affirmed their own, one rifle at a time.

CONCLUSION

The Archival Imagination
and the Teleo-Logic of Nation

This book is conceived as an attempt, through the practice of historical ethnography, to respond to the challenge set by Herbert Butterfield's epigraph. It represents the product of an extended attempt to interpolate and imagine—in the spirit expressed by Butterfield's contemporary R. G. Collingwood—the world of Ottoman Europe at the start of the twentieth century (Collingwood 1946: 240–46). In particular, my goal in writing was to combine data with comparative perspectives to shed light on the thinking and actions of some of that world's inhabitants, whose intentionality has generally been interpreted through the lens of ethnonationalism. Whatever their dreams for themselves, their families, and the communities in which they lived, they have been overwritten by the fiction of the nation that, to apply Geertz's observation on the meaning of "fictio," became the dominant mode of fashioning political subjectivity over the subsequent century (Geertz 1973: 15). Already, nation-states had established themselves in the Balkans as the preferred means through which people, or at least those who could shed the stigma of classification as "nonhistoric peoples," might control their own destinies (Rodolsky 1986). As Greece, Bulgaria, and Serbia invested ever more of their resources into gaining rights over territory in Macedonia, the goals stated by the Macedonian Revolutionary Organization, and seemingly shared by a significant portion of the population, shrank out of reach. Even as the organization continued to call for autonomy and solidarity and struggled to maintain institutions to ensure dignity, justice, and security for an expanding, diverse constituency of stakeholders, it was drawn into a multisided and lethal war that would straiten its appeal and its legacy.

Macedonia in Context: Modernity and Anti-Imperialism

In its initial establishment, though, the MRO was one of a worldwide set of movements that often took nationalist form but which were at heart anti-imperial in outlook and appeal. And it is that sense of connectedness with a wider world, then and now, that I have sought to revive here. The terms in which Western media discussed late Ottoman Macedonia at the time—as a place of revolution, terror, insurgency, and guerrilla warfare—were hardly unique to the region. Across the globe, old and new empires found their rule violently rejected by a range of new historical actors, which included the Boers in South Africa, and Bengali and Irish revolutionary forces in India and Ireland, respectively, all opponents of British imperial rule; the Moros in the Philippines, fighting first Spain and then the United States; a variety of anti-imperialist forces in Czarist Russia; a range of other Christian-led movements against Ottoman rule, especially in Armenia and Crete; the Hereros in German West Africa; and the Boxers in European-dominated China.

Innovations in technology played a key role in many of these struggles, mostly serving the incumbent powers, but at times subverting them. Communications technology, for example—the telegraph, the mimeograph, and the photograph—could assist in policing and military actions, and also in the surveillance of organizations perceived as threats to order; but these tools could also bring questionable conduct by armed forces before the court of public opinion at home, generate diplomatic pressure by other powers, or be harnessed by insurgents themselves. Anti-imperialist movements in the United Kingdom and the United States, for example, made use of documented atrocities against Boer civilians (herded into the world's first "concentration camps") and suspected Filipino guerrillas (subjected to waterboarding by U.S. troops). The new technology of communications made it possible for different movements to share techniques and learn from one another's experiences, distribute news of imperial setbacks that could then inspire or enflame further protests, and build their own parallel systems of command and control.

New military hardware—the repeating rifle, the machine gun, and mountain artillery in particular—again generally favored imperial police and military forces, who were generally outnumbered but better-equipped. In the Philippines and Africa, the deployment of firepower overwhelmed indigenous forces in any face-to-face encounters, compelling resort to ambushes, night attacks, and other guerrilla tactics designed to even the odds. Elsewhere, resistance forces sought different means to counteract superior armament. The Boxers claimed immunity from Western bullets; Russian anarchists, Armenian revolutionaries, and Bengali terrorists explored the use of more destructive, if less discriminating, technologies. This was the period in which the hand grenade, the car bomb, and other varieties of "infernal machine" were invented and widely used against the established order (Carr 2007; Davis 2007).

Alongside these material technologies came a conflict of ideas, especially around the idea of progress and civilization. Generally couched in a European or (in the U.S. case) European-derived idiom, and often tied to dominant notions around racial hierarchy, these notions were combined with concepts of legal conduct and mobilized by the forces of counterrevolution. So, for example, with the Philippines, United States president William McKinley emphasized a mission of "benevolent assimilation" that drove initiatives in health, education, and other public goods (Miller 1982). The Boxers of China were demonized by Western powers for their alleged savagery (Phillips 2011: 196). But these conflicts also raised questions about the future of waging war and keeping or imposing peace, and they blurred the distinctions between fighting and policing. This was the period in which William Calwell published Small Wars, which drew heavily on British experience in South Africa and Afghanistan (Calwell 1906). Questions of ethics and pragmatics, and the importance of attention to civilian "hearts and minds," acquired new salience.

As noted earlier, the risings of the period are often analyzed through the prism of the primary documents generated by their imperial enemies, with the result that we know more about the ripostes and the responses of the incumbents than about the motivations of the insurgents. Subaltern historiography has turned such perspectives on their head by treating these elite sources as a distorting mirror in which rebel consciousness can in fact be discerned, and hence the insurgents' own revolutionary project reconstituted (Guha 1999: 333). This analytical virtuosity, embraced within anthropology, has had less influence in mainstream political science. Idioms of realism drive a focus on outcomes; they thus tend to divide these uprisings between success and failure and look to classify the specific characteristics that make the difference. This same emphasis is apparent in the recent surge in interest in comparative studies of insurgencies, arguably driven by U.S. experiences in Iraq and Afghanistan and the wider confrontation with Al Qaeda, and an impulse to apply the lessons of history.[1]

Intellectual Poaching: Political Science,
Anthropology, and Postnational History

This instrumental approach to insurgency contrasts sharply with the scholarly and analytical richness of more recent, ethnographically informed works on civil war by both political scientists and anthropologists. While much of that literature focuses on cases defined as civil wars from the period since World War II, where the battle lines divide fellow citizens of a nation-state or polity, it nonetheless generates a wealth of transferable insight for thinking about Ottoman Macedonia. In particular, a set of powerful political science studies which at first glance appear merely state-centered, identifying camps demarcated as "incumbents" and "insurgents" seeking unitary control, or demarcating the recurring characteristics of "external" and "internal" insurgencies, in fact explore the dynamic human struggle over definition. This struggle is a component of the competition for legitimacy, whether by stressing the importance of organizational analysis or arguing that notwithstanding material self-interest, rigid ideology, or simple coercion, people's participation in rebellion is tied to the "pleasure of agency" (see for example Kalyvas 2006; Weinstein 2007; Wood 2003). And from their separate ethnographic work in different UN-designated "complex emergencies," Carolyn Nordstrom and Steven Lubkemann have introduced the evocative terms "warscapes" and "fragmented wars" to highlight how interaction among multiple planful actors with differential access to resources challenges parsimonious explanations of chaotic political processes (Nordstrom 1997; Lubkemann 2008).

Such far-fetched methodological and theoretical borrowing, of course, risks criticism along several lines of attack. Having decried nationalist history as presentist and, in its inattention to the lived reality of the early twentieth century, a form of "pidgin social science," how do I justify making parallels to other times and places, of which I know little? And in the particular context of Balkan politics, in which Macedonians' passage to nationhood has been bitterly contested and the Republic of Macedonia's sovereign status still challenged by intransigent neighbors, why do I dilute the specificity of the struggle and call into question the status of the MRO's founders and loyalists as nation-building pioneers and visionaries?

I have thought hard about these criticisms, which have also arisen, in different forms, in response to earlier work. I maintain that Macedonia's anti-Ottoman insurgency demands an anthropologically informed approach that recognizes the organic ties with other times and places, and challenges the dogma of uniquely resonant fellow feeling between MRO loyalists then and loyal Macedonians now. That approach is grounded in the exercise of the archival imagination. It is through close reading of diverse sources that I have come to terms with the stubborn experiential gulf that will always separate me from, for example, a butcher from Prilep around 1903. I am relatively confident that in his everyday life and speech he was sometimes serious, sometimes playful, with an ear for irony and poetry as well as the potential to be brutally straightforward, stubborn, or even pigheaded. If he was associated with the MRO, he knew the importance of trust and the impact of terror. But I see little value in speculating on his national consciousness and no basis for definitive truth claims. Even for leaders like Goce Delčev, Pitu Guli, Damjan Gruev, and Jane Sandanski—the four national heroes named in the anthem of the modern Republic of Macedonia—the written record of what they believed about their own identity is open to different interpretations. The views and self-perceptions of their followers and allies were likely even less conclusive.

What is clear, from abundant evidence, is that Macedonia's population was victimized by a variety of alien forces. British consuls of the time described the fervor with which Grecomans (or, in the local idiom, Grkomani), Exarchists, Arnauts, Bashi-bazouks, and other compradors and predators robbed Slavic-speaking Christians of their rights to worship as they chose, their property, and any sense of security. And equally indisputable is that a significant number of these former victims took up the cause of Macedonian autonomy that the organization preached and resisted attempts by states—and their soft-handed servants—to have the last word on who they "really" were (or who they were not).

They waged their struggle however they could—building on the logistical infrastructure established by patterns of labor migration; drawing on the cultural symbols and social systems of brigandage; and seizing opportunities created by Macedonia's peculiar international profile as a European territory where Christians were subject to "Asiatic" Muslim overlordship. They aspired to dignity and autonomy in a dynamic context of agricultural commercialization and legal reforms that altered class relations and urban-rural interconnections. Ideas of radical political transformation, along socialist and communist lines, developed in tandem with pressures for nationally oriented self-determination from subjects of the empire—Albanians, Bulgarians, and Greeks—and Ottoman reform movements. Family structures flexed to meet new needs and various migratory patterns, shifting expectations and social roles both for those who moved and for those who stayed behind.

Bodies of Evidence: Losing the Plot

In all this noise, it is hardly surprising that observers, as well as more recent interpreters, have either retreated to the position that the mysteries of the Balkans are impenetrable (in part because, in Saki's misapplied bon mot, they produce more history than they can consume locally) or have relied on the easy tropes of nationalism to make sense of events. As an example of the richer story revealed by closer engagement with the archival record, which challenges easy closure, I return to the case of the pregnant mother and her baby killed by a "Turk" in January 1903, shortly before the Salonika meeting of the MRO that voted for an uprising. The British consular report included in the introduction was terse; it dwelled not on the double killing, but on the subsequent and shocking career of the child's body, embalmed and presented in turn to the Russian consul, the reforms commission, and the Ottoman administrator. It did, though, report that the perpetrator, identified as "the Albanian, Kiasim," was arrested.

The MRO compiled its own narrative of its first decade and the escalating hardships faced by Macedonia's Christian population, which was published in French for an international readership (VMRO 1904). Brailsford, who was a staunch supporter of the movement, makes reference to this report, calling it "remarkable for its method, its accuracy and its modesty" (Brailsford 1906: 117n). The report includes the following account of the same incident:

> On December 18 [1902] Kiasim Ousko, an agent of Kiamil-Effendi, a tax entrepreneur, came to the village chiftlik (Malech [sic]) to levy what was owed. Among the numerous peasants whom he summoned to appear before him was one poor devil, Arso Sindranoff [sic], who was five years in arrears with his tax. Lacking the means to pay his debt, Arso implored the agent to give him further grace period until the next season. But the Turk [sic] insisted on immediate payment, and threatened poor Arso with his rifle. At this point in their exchanges, Arso's wife arrived, who placed herself between the two men

and took on herself the duty of shielding her husband. The Turk fired, and one bullet passed clean through the unfortunate woman, who died several hours later, and brought into the world a still-born child.

Arso took up the tiny dead creature, carried it to Skopje, and showed it to the Vali and the consuls. The authorities took no steps to punish the murderer. So on December 25, he took the body to Salonika to demand justice from the so-called "Reformer," Hilmi-Pasha. But he was turned back, under armed escort, to his village. (VMRO 1904: 32–33)

The VMRO's own "official" account clearly inflects the story with pathos, apparent from the twice-repeated adjective of "pauvre" to describe Arso. He begins the story materially poor, or even impoverished, by a 7 percent tax on the harvest, or *dîme*, that the VMRO document describes elsewhere as a key factor in the economic exploitation of the rural population. Although this narrative suspends explicit commentary on his state of mind after his tragic loss, that very understatement reinforces the sense of emotional trauma; whether numbed by pain or wild with grief, he is bent on justice as he tries to present his material evidence of the cruel effects of structural violence to those with the power to end it.

In common with the British consul's version, the story lacks any sense of closure. Both also omit the information that in following this path of action, Arso Sindranov was following the spirit of the "Instructions" issued by the MRO to its supporters to present testimony of abuses to the Ottoman authorities and to international representatives. In this particular case, there is no indication that he contemplated, at least in the first instance, taking the law into his own hands, nor that he sought redress from the MRO's terrorist enforcers or avengers. Besides the observation that the perpetrator was a "Turk," there is no hint of nationalist language or sentiment in the VMRO account, which for the most part adopts instead the restrained tone and documentary attention to specificities familiar from contemporary human rights reportage.

This tone and spirit—emphasizing the MRO's focus on justice and basic human rights and its commitment to the enlistment of international sympathy for the cause—was already under strain in early 1903. It was further undermined by the dynamite attacks launched by the Gemidžii in Salonika in April of the same year, in which Turkish and European civilians were killed and wounded. And although pledges to work for peaceful coexistence were made

to and received from Muslim villagers during the Ilinden Uprising, most notably between the insurgents in Kruševo and the village of Aldanci, elsewhere
MRO *četas* launched attacks against Turkish civilians, described in a number of
the pension biographies.

The years 1902 and 1903 marked the turning point when the MRO's work to
expand its circuits of trust and solidarity were first stopped, and then reversed,
in an increasing spiral of terrorist violence. Although the organization had exercised control over its own operatives, authorizing deadly force only against
individual traitors, spies, and abusers of authority, it faced continuous provoca-
tions from a range of adversaries. Ottoman counterinsurgency efforts escalated,
including search and seizure raids which led to thousands of Christian civilians being detained and in many cases subjected to torture. Increased army and
gendarmerie action also generated atrocities like the destruction of Smûrdeš in
May 1903. Armed Albanians, including cattle raiders, brigands, and government
officials, appear to have been given carte blanche to press Slavic Christians
harder. And neighboring states, with their own irredentist agendas, preached
and sponsored violent action by their own proxies in the province.

All these forces threatened the unity of the organization itself, as its more
impetuous and impatient members responded precisely as these different
actors hoped they would, and through their action fed escalating cycles of
violence that the MRO, lacking the government resources of its rivals, could
ill-afford. In the final analysis, a significant number of modern historians in
Macedonia have concluded that the uprising itself took place too early and
represented counterproductive escalation. Arguably, though, the MRO had
lost its struggle to manage the multiple circuits of violence before the uprising, in a plethora of violent incidents that, during 1902 and early 1903, caused
a buildup of deadly energies that overloaded the MRO's circuits of command
and control.

In April and May 1903, the consular correspondence records several overlapping and increasingly lethal chains of action and reaction. In mid-May,
McGregor submitted a list of murders committed in the Monastir region in
April, together with his own interpretation of motivating forces. He included
the following:

16 April—Kruševo. A Turk called Rassim-Bei-Halil, a native of Pressila,
who was in the employ of the Régie [the tobacco monopoly] as a "*Kolji*"

[watchman]—was murdered by Bulgarians, and robbed of his rifle, revolver and dagger which were afterwards found in a wood close by. The victim had numerous relatives in the neighborhood and the following are considered as reprisals.

18 April—At Krushoyani near Kruševo, a relation of Rassim's from Vyr-booftsi killed a Bulgarian named Anghel Joakim and wounded another called Ghiourghi who was brought to Monastir for treatment.

20 April—Vyrbyani—a Bulgarian was killed by Turks from Pressila. Some women who were concealed close by heard the assassins refer to the murder of Rassim.

22 April—At Potmol the Turkish watchman was killed by the Bulgarian villagers. The watchman had himself killed one of the villagers and wounded another a few months ago. (FO 195/2156/576: McGregor to Graves, May 1903)

In the first two cases, McGregor indicates that relatives or fellow villagers of Rassim took action—each acting independently in accordance with the principles of feud. In the last, however, he does not make explicit his evidence for including this killing in the sequence and in fact links it to a different chain of action-reaction, self-contained and separate. What McGregor suggests, though, that in this case there was a contagious quality to killing; the assumption is that the Bulgarian villagers considered that the watchman had earned his fate, but the chain of events started by Rassim's murder served as direct trigger.

The situation is further complicated, though, by data that McGregor provided in his previous list of murders, which covered the period April 3–10 and included, in a longer list, the following two cases:

3 April—Ostrilci, near Kruševo. Two Bulgarians named Dimko Nedelkoff and Stoyan Domazet were murdered by Turks from Pressila in revenge for the murder of Rassim Kokié (14 March).

9 April—Potmol. A Bulgarian villager and his son murdered by Sug-areff's band for having refused to supply them with rifles. (FO 195/2156/454: McGregor to Biliotti, April 1903)

Assuming that a single Régie employee named Rassim is referred to in both cases, McGregor appears to have lost track of the timing of the original murder, which in this accounting occurred in March and had already been avenged twice over before April. In addition, McGregor here records two previous organization-sanctioned murders in Potmol which would have served notice to the villagers of the deadly consequences of disobeying orders. This short sequence of murders back and forth, then, features a set of different kinds of corporate bodies—Rassim's family, "Turks" from one village, "Bulgarians" from another, and Sugarev's band, representing the organization—and reflects wider trends of escalating violence apparent in the consular records.

The Salonika bomb attacks of April 1903, launched by a young group of activists only partly under the MRO's control, triggered a different scale of escalatory violence. The responses included vigilante action by Muslim civilians against Christians in Salonika and Monastir, and government-organized attacks on the villages of Capari (where MRO supporters defended themselves successfully) and Smûrdeš. Consular reports again provide more vivid, micro-sociological detail of how the violence spread. According to a report in the French archives, the violence in Monastir began with a perceived insult:

> Around 1 o'clock on the afternoon of 6 May, St. George's Day, two Bulgarians in a drunken state were passing near a fountain, where a Musulman [sic] was in the act of washing. This last, seeing them, remarked in a loud voice "Ghiaour lara bak" (Look at the Ghiaours [an offensive term for non-Muslims]). Hearing these words, one of the Bulgarians fired a shot from his revolver at the Turk, wounding him seriously; this Turk responded and killed the Bulgarian. The second one took flight, but was pursued by some soldiers and many Turks, who caught up to him and killed him. This was the start of a general panic. Everyone started running in all directions, closing their shops: the soldiers opened fire on those fleeing, wounding a dozen and killing 22, of whom 12 were Greeks. Next day, in the course of arrests, four Bulgarians were killed. (Turquie-Macédoine Volume 33 (1903): From a report by M. Cartali, May 9, 1903, p. 233)

The British version offered different detail, but told much the same story. McGregor refuted the Vali's version that it began with some drunken Bulgarians in the horse market district disparaging the empire, but reported that the flashpoint was a dispute between a Bulgarian butcher and an ex-kolji of the woods and forests department, Shukri, in the course of which both used revolvers. Shukri was badly wounded and the Bulgarian was killed. Shukri's relatives then killed two more Bulgarians before the broader Muslim population "set about Bulgarians and other Christians." (FO 195/2156/557: McGregor to Biliotti, May 7, 1903).

These two accounts, again, blend the personal, familial, governmental, and confessional in explaining the contagion of violence. In this case, the contingencies are especially striking, and they pose questions about the motivation and state of mind of the "Bulgarian" at the heart of what became a religious riot. He was celebrating St. George's Day—a Christian festival and the traditional start of the *hajduk* and *četa* season. Though we cannot know if he was also toasting the self-sacrifice of the Salonika boatmen, alcohol clearly played a part in precipitating the incident. So too did the fact that he was carrying a revolver—suggesting that he was a member of the organization, as does his professional status as a butcher and member of the skilled urban artisan class from which the MRO recruited heavily (Gounaris 2001: 54). In the French version, he responds to a spoken insult with immediate violence, but in firing at a Muslim who was in all likelihood preparing to pray, he ignored the niceties of feud. In the British version, it is Shukri's relatives who take up the obligation or opportunity to escalate the initial dispute. There is no question of a truce or pause in the action; any rules are in abeyance as the Ottoman military also joins in.

Again, the consular records also provide a larger context for the incident, in which the news from Salonika clearly affected all parties, but especially Monastir's Muslim population. But the chain of provocation starts earlier; as noted in the previous chapter, the horse market was the neighborhood where an MRO cartridge factory had exploded in early April, undoubtedly sparking concern and talk of the need for self-defense among Muslims. McGregor's careful reporting also flags a consequence of this particular incident: at the time of the Ilinden Uprising, the rumor in Monastir was that the fellow guildsmen of Shukri's victim, the butchers, had volunteered to launch Salonika-style bomb attacks in the city, perhaps in solidarity with their dead colleague (195/2157/232: McGregor to Graves, August 2, 1903).

These examples from spring 1903 demonstrate both the increasing assertiveness of the MRO and its members and the reprisals that such action prompted from an Ottoman regime that, despite international surveillance, conducted counterinsurgency with few constraints. In both cases, the body count was one-sided. Rassim's execution prompted at least two and as many as four deaths among potential MRO supporters, while Shukri's wound cost at least nine Christian lives. For all its success in recruitment and organization, then, the MRO found itself by the spring of 1903 facing similar dilemmas to those of all partisan movements where an incumbent power commits to calculated terror as a means to suppress resistance—declaring, for example, that it will kill a certain number of civilians for every soldier lost in counter-insurgency operations (Kalyvas 2006: 150). The Ottoman Empire was not as systematic as other regimes in following such policies; nonetheless, the fierce reprisals carried out by its military and paramilitary forces made the MRO's policy of proportionate retaliation, in the spirit of enforcing justice in the face of an unjust regime, unsustainable.

This, though, was not the limit of the failure of the MRO's mission to secure a monopoly of legitimate violence. For just as its sophisticated, multipronged efforts to rein in systematic depredation by Albanians were defeated by deliberately excessive reactions, so its project of enforcing solidarity and obedience among its Christian constituency provoked neighboring nation-states to intervene to undo its efforts by escalating the level and scale of violence. This became clear only after the Ilinden Uprising, but here again, the consular records reveal the microprocesses by which the MRO was slowly but surely eliminated as a distinctive, future-oriented political actor in the Balkans.

During the fall of 1904, "Greeks" in Monastir reportedly declared to "Bulgarian" residents their commitment to such reprisals: for every Patriarchist murdered in the countryside, they would kill two "Bulgarians" in the town (Fraser 1906: 207). They soon made good on this threat. On October 12, in the town of Brod, a "Bulgarian Patriarchist" priest, Stojan, and his wife, together with two headmen named Veljan and Koča, were killed at the order of the organization (FO 195/2183/284: Shipley to O'Conor, October 12, 1904). "Greek" retaliation followed in Bitola within two weeks, including a knife attack by eight young "Greeks" on Lazar Tsouneff, a "Bulgarian" described by the vice consul as an "inoffensive professor" (FO 195/2183/329: Shipley to O'Conor, October 27, 1904).[2]

By this point, earlier constraints on the use of deadly force had clearly been eroded. But this particular incident also marks a more profound and radical change in the patterns of violence among the Christian population. As noted earlier, the organization was initially scrupulous in the discrimination of its use of violence; aside from the anomalous attacks on Salonika, those that they targeted had operated directly against the MRO's interests and in most cases had been warned of the price they might pay before the death sentence was carried out. As was the case with Sophia Trencoff's murder, or other reported cases of mutilation of convicted traitor's bodies, the organization's methods were frequently and deliberately brutal, but they were used only against those who were, in some sense, knowing participants in the life-or-death struggle being waged. Though the organization demanded total allegiance from its sworn members, its primary demand was obedience when called to action; bystanders who had not yet been invited or coerced to join, and who were not actively working against the MRO, had less to fear.

The Monastir Greeks' decision in 1904 demonstrates a different, and differently discriminating, logic of violence. The MRO targeted only established, conscious "players"; the Greek reprisals in the Brod case, though, extended the domain of risk to anyone they judged belonged to the same ethnoreligious group as the majority of the MRO's members. This is the enactment of nationalism, in the sense that primordial sentiments—the aspects of personhood that one cannot help—are assumed to fully describe one's political loyalties and to override all individual characteristics or aspirations. Tsouneff died at the hands of eight young Greek assailants not because he supported or sanctioned the MRO, but because of the language in which he taught. He died alone, scared, unarmed, and in all likelihood utterly unaware of the reason for his death.

Lazar Tsouneff was, of course, far from the last of the victims of the protracted process by which the European territory of a morally and financially bankrupt imperial administration came to be divided between three imperfect and extractive nation-states. All the parties involved continued to enhance their killing capabilities; in 1906, for example, a Greek military officer formed a "Greek Organization in Thessaloniki" in which he administered an oath to ten followers, stressing secrecy, obedience, and faith in God, and then, behind the "front" of a sewing machine store, orchestrated assassinations and other activities against the more established Macedonian Revolutionary Organization (Dakin 1966: 204–205).

Tsouneff's death, though, as imagined here through the archival record, offers a poignant parallel with the Sindranovs' stillborn baby whose father's circuit among the authorities expressed the hope that the tragedy of a life thus cut short, begun and ended prematurely, might prompt decisive action to improve conditions in Macedonia. In both deaths, violence overstepped existing boundaries; a Christian mother was shot by a member of a culture where the lives of women and children are sacred, and a professor who had offended no one was surrounded and stabbed to death by eight students.

The first death, the baby's, was a function of a broader system of licensed exploitation; in itself a tragic accident (at least in the 1904 VMRO account), it was one act in a larger tragedy that drove the MRO's attempt to acquire rifles from "Albanians" and "Turks" and transfer them to its membership, in order to put an end to the structural violence perpetrated by "Albanians" and "Turks" against the Slavic Christian population. This policy was ambitious in scope and ingenious in its simplicity. It was also deadly in its effects. For despite the MRO's efforts to establish and police the legitimate bounds of violence, deploying it only against those who acted in violation of the organization's interests or rules, an array of adversaries instead opted to categorize people according to criteria they could not control and then to pursue policies of indiscriminate and deadly violence against those they identified as "other." The second death, Lazar Tsouneff's, came about when the constraints of feud, waged against intimate adversaries according to basic shared principles, were displaced by the license of total war against socially distant enemies. The MRO had created circuits of belonging and coercion to mobilize the disenfranchised subjects of a dysfunctional empire around the shared goal of autonomy. The antipathies of nation short-circuited the experiment in solidarity, erasing a future path now only glimpsed in tales half-told. But through the exercise of the archival imagination—our own and that of the record keepers of the past—we can still retrace the circuits of trust and terror to think past the nation.

Documents of the Macedonian Revolutionary Organization

This appendix contains translations of two documents that were captured by Ottoman forces during their counterinsurgency operations in 1903. The first, referred to elsewhere in this book as "Instructions," was taken from the body of the MRO *vojvoda* Cvetkov after he and most of his band were surrounded and killed in the village of Mogila in May 1903. The British vice consular in Monastir (Bitola), James McGregor, obtained a copy of the regulations, and this translation was included in his dispatch to the consul general, Sir Alfred Biliotti, in Salonika on June 10, 1903 (FO 195/2156/731).

The second, referred to elsewhere in this book as "Regulations," was included in McGregor's dispatch to Biliotti's successor, R. W. Graves, in a dispatch sent on October 31, 1903 (FO 195/2157/737).

Instructions for the Macedonian Revolutionary Bands and the Affiliated Peasants

It is the responsibility of each village and each agent to monitor the movement of patrols—that is, who comes and who goes. The courier will make every effort to alert the village toward which a patrol is heading, at least five or ten minutes ahead.

The village residents should be compelled, by arguments or by force, to go to the capital of the *vilayet* [district] and, in front of the consuls and then in front of the *vali* [governor], to protest the abuses committed by the detachments committed to pursuing [our bands].

The villagers should make the necessary steps to gain compensation for any crops—even the most insignificant—trampled over by troops and other state agents, at the rate due according to the import title. Should the authorities refuse to agree, the complaint should be lodged with the consuls.

Unsupportive and noncompliant Christians should be killed in any village, and the blame put onto the field guard, if it can be, or any other representative of Ottoman authority, and to this effect two pieces of testimony should be presented which seek to persuade tribunals that the assassination was committed by tyrants of this kind. In these cases, people should give testimony with full conviction and assurance.

The first duty of a band when it enters a village is to establish outposts of their own men and two or three villagers who should monitor traffic to warn of danger. One of the more experienced among the band members will monitor all the outposts to ensure they don't fall asleep.

After the necessary rest the band must question the notables of the village, each separately if possible, on the general situation. They should also arrange the provision of weapons and other contributions from everyone, except those who are not in a financial position to contribute.

The band will let peasants know where they can purchase arms, and the means by which to transport them. The band will audit the accounts of those local treasurers responsible for arms. If local funds not available, they should arrange with a nearby band to find a means of arming them. Arms should be sought from smugglers, and also among Albanians who would not hesitate to sell their weapons for profit. Put simply, it is necessary to take all measures possible to arm all recruited members in the villages. Regarding ammunition, we should encourage the practice of buying empty cartridges, and filling them ourselves

The band must appoint in each village committed members who will take individual vengeance on the oppressors. One member should be instructed to eliminate a bey or a denouncer in the village or a nearby village. By this measure we'll achieve the following results:

—We'll create agents who are committed and ready to sacrifice themselves one after the other for the common good.

—We'll establish a body of recruits who after already committing one murder, will keep their courage and their sangfroid in critical moments.

The chief of the band must always be surrounded by his men, just as a state surrounds and safeguards its capital city.

The band should not waste its time committing assassinations unless the opportunity only appears then.

During a conflict the band should not by any means leave, and if within a certain distance, it should enter a village to reawake the courage of the peasants, just like a mother who does not abandon her children in the most critical moment. If a band is blockaded, each member should try to escape in the first night, between midnight and two and three in the morning. Delay is not useful, as the enemy will be reinforced. The band must quickly return to the village to punish the informers, if their discovery was not due to chance.

The Vlahs who live in tents, being born smugglers, should be employed for the transport of arms.

No active member should reveal to another that he possesses arms; even less should he reveal to another the place where arms are hidden. This secret is also imposed on members of the member's family.

Regulations for Village Bands
CHAPTER 1

Art. 1. In every village a band of seven to ten persons is formed.

Art. 2. The most experienced and capable of the villagers shall be appointed as *vojvoda.*

Art. 3. The village band shall be for the village what the *rayon* band is for the rayon (see regulations for bands).

Art. 4. The band shall consist of the most ardent and active workers in the village.

Art. 5. Every member of a band must possess a good, clean rifle and a dagger, knife, or bayonet. He must also have a revolver, felt leggings, and a sheepskin coat.

[NB. Indigent members who have distinguished themselves are equipped by the village treasury.]

CHAPTER 2

Art. 6. The members are bound to leave even the most urgent private affairs and rally to the *vojvoda* when summoned, and they must render him unconditional obedience.

Art. 7. Members of the bands who commit any offense are liable to much more severe punishment than ordinary workers.

Art. 8. Generally speaking, the bands are required to be always ready to defend the interests and authority of the organization and they, together with the *rayon* band, form the standing military force in the *rayon.*

Art. 9. The relations of the village band with regard to the village administration are in every respect analogous to those existing between the band and the administrative council of the *rayon,* but in regard to military matters the village band is under the immediate command of the *vojvoda* of the *rayon.*

Art. 10. Similar bands are to be formed likewise in the towns.

Art. 11. When the *rayon* band (or any portion thereof) is in danger, the neighboring village bands shall come to its help. In such cases not only the village band but all the armed villagers (the natural militia) must turn out, especially at nightfall. The revolutionary movement is so far advanced that no villager must think of turning back or abandoning his band on seeing that he is discovered.

Art. 12. Every villager, shepherd, or other person who sees that a band is in danger must find means of informing the nearest village. Contravention of this regulation will involve punishment.

Art. 13. Any villager who, in such a case, does not come to the assistance of the band will be punished. This offense will be punished with death in the case of members of the village band.

Art. 14. In order that the members of the village band may be inured to fatigue, the *vojvoda* should take them out with his band in small parties for five or six days. (This is done in the *vilayet* of Adrianople).

Art. 15. The *vojvoda* should also occasionally alarm the villages for the same purpose.

Biographies from the Ilinden Dossier

The fourteen personal statements included here are taken from the Ilinden Dossier, housed at the National Archives of Macedonia in Skopje. This set of materials is stored in forty-three boxes, and individual files are catalogued by box number, first letter of surname, and sequential number among pension recipients under that letter. I have included a mixture of biographies, which were usually included in initial applications, and petitions, appeals, or complaints, which were submitted by unsuccessful or dissatisfied applicants and often provide more specific detail.

These fourteen records, composed by eleven men and three women, constitute only a small sample from the 3,500 applications, and also from the 375 awardees on whose records I took detailed notes. I selected them with an eye to geographical range (they represent twelve different birthplaces) and diversity in status and roles in the organization (including several self-styled *četniks* and couriers, and a *vojvoda,* a terrorist, a *jatak,* and a cashier or *blagajnik*). They offer rich descriptions of different kinds of mobility associated with unfree and paid labor, trade, marriage and education, and the ways the MRO harnessed those patterns of movement. A majority provide detailed and consistent information about key personalities and places.

Also included are detailed accounts of the practices analyzed in individual chapters of the book: the symbolic importance of oath and archive, the production and transmission of messages, the care and concealment of *četas,* the tactics of espionage and subterfuge, the manufacture of munitions, and the purchase and storage of rifles. I have edited to make the prose more readable in English. I have also, in most cases, omitted descriptions of activities conducted after the Balkan Wars of 1912–13, the exception being the biography of Velika Hristova Dimitrova, who describes drawing on the techniques she learned during the Ilinden era to assist the next generation of insurgents during World War II.

The statements are presented in (Macedonian) alphabetical order.

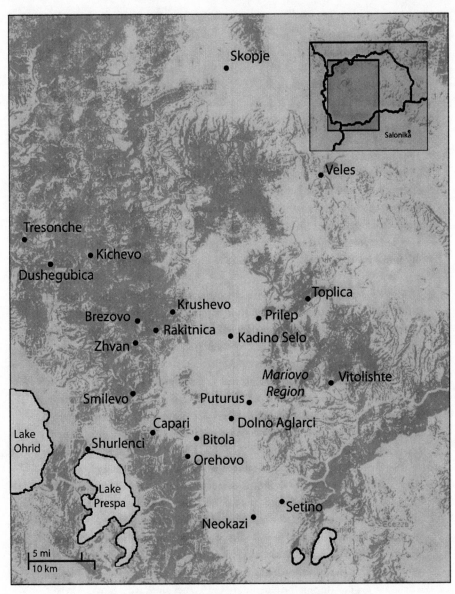

Figure A 2.1. Birthplaces, residences, and sites of transformative
activism of fourteen Ilinden pension seekers.

Dame Hristov Aldžikočovski, of Prilep. Record 2-A-72.
Petition submitted December 23, 1948.

Regarding my participation in the national revolutionary movement and the struggles for the liberation of the Macedonian people, I present the following evidence.

In 1896 I swore an oath and became a member of the Macedonian revolutionary organization. First I was a terrorist, but afterwards I was assigned as a *desetar* of terrorists.

When Goce Delčev was traveling around Macedonia he passed through the Prilep region too and visited the city. He stayed at the house of the Peškovs. Somebody had recommended me to him and he sent for me and made me a member of the governing body of the organization in Prilep. From that time on, I was always chosen as a member of the governing body of the Macedonian organization in Prilep.

In 1902 when Metodi Pačev's *četa* was slaughtered in the village of Kadino, their archive was captured and the code was broken, which led to my arrest together with my comrade Rampo Peškov. He and I had gone to Bitola in order to serve as members of the Bitola *rayon's četa*, led by Gjorgi Sugarev. The plan was to make a circuit through the Prilep region, to lift the spirits of the villagers, which were flagging after the destruction of Pačev's *četa*. But the Turkish police were tracking me, and they captured us—Rampo Peškov and myself—in Bitola. We resisted arrest with whatever weapons we had at hand, but nevertheless we were overpowered and imprisoned. At the trial we were both convicted: I was sentenced to life imprisonment as a member of the leading body of the organization in Prilep and another three years for resisting arrest. After we had spent ten months there, the sultan issued an amnesty for all political prisoners. All the other organization-affiliated prisoners were released. Only the two of us, myself and Rampo, remained in prison, to serve the shorter sentence for resisting the police. I spent two years in jail, during which time comrade Rampo died. There were still other prisoners, and one day, thirty-two of us resolved to escape. We dug a tunnel in the prison and one night we escaped and joined the *četas* that were still active . . .

Some time after this a special amnesty was issued by the sultan for those who had escaped from prison. At the command of the regional committee in Bitola, I took the amnesty [and returned to legal status], as I was needed in Prilep.

Around that time there was another incident. An archive was captured in the village of Toplica, in the Prilep region, and the entire leadership became outlaws (*nelegalni*). I did not leave the city with them, but remained in my post to direct the organization's business. But after a couple of days the police came and surrounded my house and took me into custody. I managed to escape from the Turkish police and joined the *četa* of Mirče Svakarov. When I fell ill, they sent me to Sofia to undergo treatment. After my recovery I returned in Macedonia as a member of the *četa* of Krste Germov (aka Šakir).

After the Huriet all members of the *četas* returned to regular life as *legalni,* and the Turks began to disarm the population. Then I was apprehended, detained and interrogated, as they were trying to locate the organization's arms caches. They tortured and beat me, but I didn't say a thing. They then sent me to the military court in Bitola, but the court released me.

With every arrest I was tortured and beaten by the Turks and I still suffer the consequences of that ill-treatment.

Malinka Najdova Veljanovska, of Rakitnica, Bitola region. Record 6-V-37. Biography submitted August 5, 1952.

I was born on February 20, 1875, in the village of Rakitnica to extremely poor parents. When I was young, and before I was married, we lived only on our income as hired laborers for the Turkish beys in Novo Selo. I still carried the thought that the day would come when I would not be a slave, but would live free. In 1900 I married Najdo Veljanovski from Rakitnica. Because my husband Najdo was a member of the Macedonian revolutionary movement, I myself became a member and brought weapons, food, shoes, clothing, correspondence, and other items to the *četas.* Our house was the first in the village, and so I was frequently charged with receiving and sending *četas.* In 1902 [during the engagement in Rakitnica], Velko Vojvoda's *četa* was stationed in our house; six men died, and the house was set on fire by the Turkish soldiers and the *bashi-bazouks.* Because we were suspected of receiving members of the organization on a regular basis, and my husband Najdo, under threat of state terrorism, had gone illegal, I was the primary target of Turkish abuses after this.

I responded by working even more intensively with the *četas* to prepare for the Ilinden Uprising, which earned me three visits to the house of the district commissioner in the village of Pribilci, where I was beaten. But since I didn't admit to working with the *četas,* I was released.

The thought of liberation that I had cherished since my youth wouldn't leave my mind, and I remained in contact with the *četas* until 1912, when our brother nation of Serbia liberated this region from the five-hundred-year Ottoman tyranny. But that wasn't true freedom, because both the Great Serbian hegemony and the two periods of Great Bulgarian oppression were unbearable. When the partisan units began operations in our region in 1942, they came first to our house, knowing that I was and remain a true revolutionary. So even though I was old, I once again started to work as a courier, carrying letters to the partisan headquarters in Kruševo, carrying food to the partisans, and receiving and sending off the partisan detachments until 1944. It was then that our direct struggle, in concert with all the Yugoslavian peoples under the leadership of our dear Tito, finally secured our complete freedom.

Naum Vrčkovski, of Capari. Record 6-V-71. Biography submitted April 20, 1950.

I was born in 1889 in the village of Capari, Bitola region. I come from a middle-rank farming family and was educated up to third grade in the elementary school in the village of Capari.

I started elementary school when I turned eight but studied for just three years, until I was eleven. Initially I stayed home and carried out household chores and farm work. Then when I turned fifteen I went to work charcoal in Vodena Buka in the Ohrid region, in Oteševo and other places. I was a charcoal worker for five to six years, spending several months each year on the work, and for the rest of the time working at home.

As a charcoal worker and seller, I transported charcoal to Bitola, and in Bitola I was given gunpowder and ammunition to carry into the mountains. I would be there with my horse, and a man would come and tell me to go to a particular place, usually a house, where I would load up with ammunition and other cargo. I took would then take it from Bitola to Capari. I carried out this duty five to six times and gave the supplies to Simon Trajkov, a teacher in the village of Capari, who was killed at the time of the uprising.

Before Ilinden 1903 I was working charcoal in Šurlenci, in the Resen region, when a man came to gather all of us workers, and we all went to my village one day before Ilinden 1903. We formed a četa, and our vojvoda was Acko from the village of Bazdernik. On the eve of Ilinden we received an order to attack the Turkish village Ramna, Bitola region, and so during the night we went there and attacked the village. Some of us had weapons, others who were unarmed were carrying firebrands, axes, and such like. A fight began, and we didn't succeed in setting fire to any houses, because of their defense. Then on Ilinden itself we went up into the mountains near Capari, and the next day we left to attack the Turkish village of Vratin Dol. But before we even got there somebody had told the Turkish forces of our plans and they were prepared, so we didn't press our attack. Instead we returned to the mountains. Several days later the Turks besieged the village of Gjavato; there was heavy fighting, and the village was burning. Our *četa* moved from the Capari mountain through the village of Malovište and took up position on the upper side of Gjavato, and opened fire. The Turks recognized they were at risk, and they retreated, and we entered the village, where Sugarev was leading the defense. Our *četa* took charge of the civilians and some of the domestic animals and evacuated them. We headed first for Gopeš, [a Vlah village], then went on from Gopeš through Nakazi, in the Resen region, and then, still with the families from Gjavato, we arrived in Malovište, and went to the monastery of St. Ana in the Capari mountains. One or two women actually gave birth along the way. Some families we then housed in Capari, others in another village, while the *četa* stayed up in the mountains.

After a few days our *četa* was given another assignment, to go and to cut down the telegraph wires from their poles, and so we went to the telegraph line between Capari and Rotino, and pulled all the wires down, and I took one length of cable [as proof] to our *vojvoda* Acko, who had stayed behind in the mountains.

After the fighting in the Turkish villages and the sabotage of the telegraph wires, Turkish forces came looking for us in the mountains. They had artillery; we were forced to leave our stations close to Capari and move down through Malovište to Vrtuška, for if we had stayed there they would have surrounded and wiped us out.

The Turkish army came on, and joining forces with the Vrtuška *četa* we turned toward the village of Bolno, Resen region, where we found Arsov and other *vojvodas* with their *četas*. We stayed there several days, and then our unit was commanded to go to the mountain village of Izbišta, Resen. Capari was still the target of Ottoman forces, but it was by now harvest time, and so we were stood guard for the Izbišta villagers while they were threshing and harvesting. Those *četniks* who were from Izbišta gave us their weapons and worked alongside their fellow villagers, since the grain was dropping to the ground and there weren't enough people to thresh it. We stayed there for twenty days; after we left, the Turks came and killed everyone there, both those fighters who stayed behind, and civilians.

We were now in a composite unit commanded by the *vojvoda* Trifun, from the village of Izbišta, and we made our way back through the mountains to Capari. I was sick by this time, and my throat was burning, but I could not return home openly because the mayor of our village had declared those of us who had left as refugees, and the Turks had surmised that we were *četniks*. I came home in secret and stayed there in hiding, so that no one would recognize me, and I remained sick in bed until the end of the uprising.

After a certain period of time I purchased a horse and began work as a *kiradžija* (transporter), making regular trips between Ohrid and Bitola. I then returned briefly to my former trade of working charcoal, then in 1905 I left for *pečalba* in America. I did three stints of three years there, returning between each stint to spend a few months at home; then I left again for America and stayed there until 1920, when I returned home for good, to work as a farmer.

Mate Petrov Boškoski, of Kruševo. Record 5-B-27.
Petition Biography, submitted April 17, 1953.

I was born in 1875 in Kruševo to a poor working-class family. In 1895 I owned one small shop in Kruševo and because of that I traveled on purchasing trips to Bitola, Kičevo, Tetovo, and Solun (Salonika), and other places, and thus made acquaintances in all of these towns. In Kruševo I was acquainted with Dimitri Lapu and he put me in touch in Bitola with the Skoevci; all of them were active members of the movement for the liberation of Macedonia and involved in the preparations of the Ilinden Uprising. So the movement harnessed my trips for its own ends, and following their orders I started making more trips and to perform courier duties between local branches of the organization and became a man trusted by the organization.

To guarantee complete security the letters I carried were written on cloth and hidden in different parts of my clothing. Afterwards, when I had become a trusted person for the organization, my shop became a cache for weapons and ammunition for the insurgents. I went to Salonika with Kosta Hertu from Kruševo, and bought there eighteen rifles with two or three rings. The money for purchasing the rifles and ammunition was collected voluntarily among the inhabitants of Kruševo; I transported the rifles personally, hidden in the freight among the other wares for my shop. The rifles stayed with me in the shop until 1900. Then I started to buy and transport rifles from Kičevo, as I received a directive from the organization in Kruševo. Again, I stored the weapons I purchased in my shop, along with the rest of the munitions.

I did not purchase only rifles, but also gunpowder and other necessary things for the rebels. Thus in 1900 I bought bullets for different amounts of money, from 2.5 *grosha* to 7.5 *grosha* from the Turks in Tetovo and Kičevo. I stored these initially with Phokion Piha in Kičevo and afterwards transported them from there to Kruševo.

One Sunday before the uprising in 1903, Pitu Guli came to my house to make the final preparations for the uprising. My house became the headquarters, and all the *vojvodas* came there and laid out the plans for the uprising, and I helped them by performing different duties upon their orders. I was preparing my wedding at that time, which was to be on Ilinden. Pitu revealed to me that instead of a wedding the uprising itself was in the making, which would be on the very same day. . . .

At the time the rebels had four hundred Greek [Gras] rifles, three hundred [Turkish-manufactured] "Martinki" rifles from Tetovo, and eighteen Mannlichers, but more weapons were needed for the uprising to start. As my house was close to the woods, it served perfectly for the rebels' meetings and other work, for the distribution of the various weapons and ammunition, and for coordinating the activities of members of the *četa*. On the eve of Ilinden, Pitu came to Kruševo once again with horses, loaded with supplies—grain harvested from the field, flour, lard, and other things—for the insurgents.

Then in the evening at around 18:30 the insurgents arrived and the Turkish garrison, both infantry and cavalry, hid themselves in different houses and shops. During the night I took the weapons and ammunitions from the store and distributed them to the insurgents, and then some Turkish soldiers saw that the store was unlocked and open, and took refuge there. When I realized that there were Turks inside, I emptied a can of kerosene into the store, and then set it on fire, and the Turks were left to burn.

After this, following an order from the insurgents, I went to Dinu Vangel's café, along with some other comrades, and we set the café on fire, because there were Turks hiding there too. Afterwards I arranged the collection of food and money to supply the insurgents, and also scrap metal for the manufacture of munitions. In this way close to 4,800 golden "liri" and napoleons were collected, which were taken by Tome Niklev and Nikola Karev. When Pitu Guli left for Mečkin Kamen, and the other *vojvodas* left the town with their men, I found myself with the *vojvoda* Gjurčin, who took position on Kale and was the first to confront the Turkish army in the field.

After the failure of the uprising, I and twelve other men were taken to Bitola and thrown in prison. I stayed there three months and underwent water torture; we were scheduled to be exiled for a term of 101 years in the infamous prison of Diyar bakir in Asia Minor. But the committee and our people petitioned the Russian consul on our behalf, and after his intervention I was released, along with Gligur Prdišikla. The Russian consul kept his faith with the organization and after our release made it possible for us to work further for the revolution in secret and continue to contribute to the insurgency, by helping us get close to the regular Ottoman soldiers and win their trust. I established contact with Akif Aga from the village of Pribilci in this period, and thanks to that friendship I was able to supply *četas* with shoes, food, medicine, and other things. As one example I treated and took care of Hristo Matev for three months until he got better, after which I put him in touch with certain people.

In this period I also fed and supported Pitu Guli's children, as [with his death] they were left hungry and without anybody to take care of them. So they joined my children and family.

In 1908 I had once again stored weapons and ammunition, but was found out. The Turks came to my house and searched it, but my mother concealed the weapons and refused to reveal where. For this reason they maltreated and tortured her, so that she fell gravely ill and died soon afterwards.

Such was my activity for the period from 1895 until the Balkan war. All of my testimony will be confirmed by two living Ilindeners, Vančo Andre and Petra Pare, and I request that the municipal public committee call them as witnesses, and then convey my petition along with their testimony to the National Assembly's Ilinden pension board.

Donka Bučakovska, of Kruševo. Record 5-B-52.
Biography submitted February 11, 1952

I was born in Kruševo, on November 24, 1880, to parents Sekula and Marija Trajko Lokvenoski. At the beginning of 1901, I joined the ranks of the "Common" [sic] Macedonian Revolutionary Organization, which was working for the liberation of the Macedonian people from Turkish oppression. I swore an oath, crossing myself, in the presence of Kosta Škodra, the teacher; Tirču Kare, the *bajraktar* (flag bearer); and Tome Nikle, all three from Kruševo. Initially I was made a courier, tasked with carrying correspondence and weapons. I remained in this role until the siege of Rakitnica in 1902, in which twelve men were killed, including Velko Vojvoda and Dame Novev, both teachers, as well as Tirču Kare, the flag bearer. I don't recall the names of the other nine who were killed.

After Rakitnica, I was given a different duty, to collect in the villages and in Kruševo tin and lead, as well as old cartridges and tinware, and to store those in my house. Once we had collected a substantial quantity of this raw material for the manufacture of cartridges, the order came from the headquarters of Pitu Guli, Dimitrije (the director in Ohrid) and Metodija Stojčev (the painter) for a foundry to be opened in my house, to manufacture cartridges and distribute them to the *četas*.

Early on July 20, 1903 [O.S.], at around two o'clock in the morning, the foundry began production in my house. Vele Kalinoski, the watchmaker, prepared the molds for the casting of bullets, and I kept a record of the distribution of the materials. We stopped manufacture at midday on July 31 [O.S.].

On the same day, Todor "the officer," from Veles, came and handed to me a bag with the archival records of our entire revolutionary organization and told me to hide it somewhere safe. At that moment I was covering the traces of the foundry with earth, and he told me to finish up quickly as the Turks had reached the town. I took the archive and buried it in the garbage dump near the fountain Proja, and ten days later when everybody was back in their houses, after the burning of Kruševo I told Kosta Škodra the teacher about the bag and he went to retrieve it. What became of it after that I don't know.

After the Kruševo uprising I got married a second time and because of that wasn't able to work in the organization, since I moved to Bitola. But from the very beginning of 1901 until July 31, 1903, I worked tirelessly for the Popular Revolutionary Organization. Our goal was liberation from the grave oppression of the Turkish authorities, under which Macedonia and the Macedonian people had groaned for centuries, and for that reason I gladly swore the sacred oath. [The promise of] the first People's Republic and the glorious Ilinden Uprising of the Macedonian people, as well as my anger toward our age-long oppressors, prompted me to take up this cause.

Velika Hristova Dimitrova of Bitola, born Dolno Aglarci. Record 9-D-57. Biography submitted April 12, 1952.

I was born in 1875 in the village of Dolno Aglarci in the Bitola region. My father was Gjorgi Apčevski, and ours was a poor farming family. As a young girl, I worked with my father and the rest of our family members as hired hands and sharecroppers on the local *chiftlik* in order to feed ourselves.

In 1889 I married Hristo Dimitrovski, and we remained together until 1930, when he died a natural death. When I was married I moved to the village of Puturus. My life of financial hardship continued, and I still worked for hire or as a sharecropper, but my husband's family was a revolutionary one and participated actively in the struggles for the liberation of the Macedonian people.

The head of the then committee in Puturus was my father-in-law Dimitrija. As I was the closest at hand to carry out confidential and other tasks, he recruited me into this organization, and as a consequence I transported weapons on a regular basis from the committee in Prilep, delivering them to the *vojvodas* of the *četas,* as well as to the heads of the various [village] committees. I remember, for example, delivering weapons to Ilinden rebels, including Trajko Kralot ["the king"] and Petko Mladenov from the village of Makovo, Krste (whose family name I don't recall) from the village of Mogila, and Tole Jovan Pašata. These were all *vojvodas* at the time. I also provided food and refuge for many others, arranging their accommodation and their onward travel, and I also kept watch vigilantly against any mishap that put our fighters at risk.

I started work for this organization very willingly, in part because of my hard past. My active participation began in 1901 and continued throughout the preparation of the Ilinden Uprising. I remained an active contributor in "underground" service until the Huriet in 1908, transporting weapons, concealing fighters, providing food and clothing, doing laundry, and ensuring *četas* safe passage as a woman of the revolution.

I remained loyal and true to the revolutionary struggles of our people after that and never betrayed the Macedonian people neither during the time of former Yugoslavia nor during the occupation. On the contrary, I have always remained [politically] progressive, and have defended the interests of our people.

During the occupation of 1941, right up until liberation [in 1944], not only did I never collaborate with the [Bulgarian] occupying forces, but I was in fact an active contributor to the national movement for liberation. Through his profession as a rugmaker, my late son Blaže got in touch with Stiv Naumov, who proposed to come and live incognito in our house, so as to have a permanent place of residence and be able to work as an organizer. We were to present him as being in the transportation business of *kiradžija,* under the alias Trajko Monopolski. When my son Blaže suggested this to me I gladly agreed and stated that I would not only house him, but also help him, as I had helped in the Ilinden struggle. I transported bombs from our house to other places, wrapped in paper and hidden under a loaf of bread, and from one day to the next our house became the headquarters—a fact that others who are still alive, and I'll mention later, will confirm. When Mirče and Stiv were betrayed I hid them in among the rugs and saved them from being discovered. In 1942, when we were ordered to go to the village of Orehovo to mark May Day, I took active part and took receipt of bombs and revolvers. Following the orders that were given me I took them to Temelko the baker from the village of Lahci. And all this had an impact for me because when the Orehovo plans were betrayed by Cane Kotleto, my son Blaže fell into the hands of the Fascists. They sentenced him to death in July 1942 and I was left alone. My other child, a daughter, was married, and I moved to live with her and my son-in-law from 1942 to 1943. One day he asked me whether I was willing to receive *ilegalni* in our house as before. He thought that because of my prior experience I wouldn't want to do this, but I replied that I had only one son and I had already given him up: now I wanted to take revenge on the enemy. So I agreed to receive *ilegalni* then and in the future.

Nikola Drnev, of Skopje. Record 10-D-52. Biography submitted February 21, 1954

I was born in 1878 from poor parents in Skopje, where I live now. My father Gjorgi Drnev was a farmer, and my mother Anuška Boceva was a housewife. After me they had another son Koce, a tailor, and two daughters, Penka and Mara, both housewives.

I finished elementary school in Skopje and one grade of high school, but because of the poverty of my parents I couldn't continue studying. In 1890, I started learning the trade of tailor: I was apprenticed for three years to Mijalče Šiševski and three years to Stojan Janev, then worked four years as *kalfa* [journeyman] for the Ginalevi brothers. I acquired the right to be a *majstor* and in 1900 I opened an independent tailoring shop where I have worked my whole life. But now I am seventy-six, and because of old age I am incapable of doing any kind of work.

For this entire time I've practiced my trade and supported myself from it, but now this source of income has ceased on account of inability to work. In the past I've had two or three apprentices and journeymen but now I don't have any.

Even in my youth I couldn't endure the injustices and outrages committed against the Macedonian people, and I fought openly. Because of my activism I was under constant suspicion and surveillance and frequently harassed, detained, and arrested.

I entered the ranks of the organization in 1896. I was a *desetar,* collected the contributions and the fees from the members, worked with the *vojvodas* Efrem Čučkov, Andreja Kojuharov, Bobeto, Vasil Adžalarski, Ordan Besnikov, Dame Martinov, and others. I was in prison in 1900 with Spiro Gligorov and Gligor Cvetkov, after I was betrayed by the spy Atanas Temelkov when I was collecting money for the organization. I was imprisoned again in 1903 in connection with the affair of Stojan Colev, because he wounded Todor Kašmakov. I was a member of the governing body for the Skopje district together with Trajan Trpkov, Spiro Stefanov, and Spiro Gajdaštiev, and for all that time I was under the scrutiny of the authorities and constantly was followed and maltreated.

Božin Stefanov Ilievski, of Bitola. Record 13-I-36.
Appeal submitted December 13, 1951.

Before, during, and after the Ilinden Uprising I assisted the cause of liberation of the Macedonian people, carrying out the orders issued by the commanders. I fulfilled these duties when I was stationed in Bitola and also in Kičevo. Following orders I did courier work, transporting weapons, and also took part in all the meetings of the local committee in Kičevo, as part of the preparations for the Ilinden uprising.

After the uprising, again on the orders of the leaders of the organization in Bitola, I took on the duties of a gendarme in the then Turkish police station in Bitola; my mission was to monitor police activities and provide timely information on any operation planned against the organization in that region. More generally, my role was to be of service to the organization and to do whatever was possible to advance the struggle, in particular by preventing the discovery of *četas* or organization leaders, and where possible, misdirecting the work of the police. I accomplished these objectives with complete success and to the satisfaction of my commanders in the organization.

I was doing additional service to the organization and its commanders in Bitola, because, having won the trust of the Turkish authorities, I had access to important information of interest to the organization itself, which I supplied to the commanders. I was able to keep them informed of any operation planned against this or that *vojvoda* or *četa,* or against this or that illegal fighter or legal activist from the city or the region.

In terms of specific contributions I made, I can list the following. In 1904, when I was a Turkish gendarme, the *četnik* Taško Šiškov, from the village of Surovič, in Aegean Macedonia, hid in my house for three months recovering from his wounds.

In 1905 I held the post of police superintendent in Kičevo. Because there was a break in the ranks of the local organization, there was a risk that the archive might fall into Turkish hands, so it was given to me for safekeeping by the head of the local committee, Angele Bongurov. I kept it safe and secure for a whole year, which averted the danger of further damage to the organization.

I provided clandestine lodging, and arranged safe passage, for the *vojvodas* Petar Acev, Pandil Šiškov, Naum Bufčeto, Eftimov, and others.

While I was working for the police in Bitola, entry to Yeni Maale, the bastion of the Bitola organization, was coordinated by Tale Bašarmiš and Lazo Asazot, both trusted people from the organization, and couriers. Their task was to meet and guide every illegal *vojvoda* or *četnik* who had to come in or out of Yeni Maale, to or from a meeting of the regional command in Bitola; they either arranged accommodation for them or took them safely to the assigned house.

These two men were in constant contact with me, on the orders of the command, and also because they knew who I am and why I serve in the Turkish police. Whenever they were bringing *vojvodas* or *četniks* into the neighborhood, or escorting them out, they informed me exactly when and where their mission would be starting and ending. During those times, I would be sure to direct the police patrols in a different direction and to another location in the city and quarter. And when I knew that the police were planning a search in the Yeni Maale, in a certain house, I would immediately let Bašarmiš and Asazot know, so that any illegals could be moved to different houses and avoid discovery. Our goal was to prevent the police from discovering anything regarding the organization and thus to thwart, at their very inception, the attempts of the authorities. . . .

I was placed in this position quite deliberately. I was obliged to take a position with the Turkish authorities, so that I might serve the organization by supplying information in its interest and guiding the activities of the police in directions that were harmless to the struggle, or by taking under my protection in my house or in some other safe place *vojvodas* and *četniks* who otherwise would have been discovered and destroyed. My actions and sacrifices at the time posed great risks and dangers not only for myself but for my entire family. They were such an important contribution to the struggles for the liberation of this nation that they mark my Ilinden activity as greater than that of many others in Bitola who have already been granted Ilinden pensions.

Micko J. Jošeski, of Žvan. Record 15-J-47. Biography submitted December 20, 1956.

I was born on October 15, 1884, in Žvan, in the Bitola district, to a poor village family. My father was a farmer and had ten children. Because the land we owned could not feed our family, my father had to go to earn money in neighboring countries, most often Bulgaria.

In 1902 in Žvan there was a Turkish field guard (*poljak*) named Mesole Bajram, from the nearby Turkish village of Suhodol in the Bitola region. This field guard was terrorizing the village and committing outrages against the Christian population, including extortion, rape, and more. The people of the village could not bear it any longer, and for that reason they petitioned the committee which later organized to authorize the field guard's execution. The committee then chose me and my brother Stojan to carry out the assassination.

On May 18, 1902, when the field guard came to our house to take food, my brother Stojan and I killed him with an axe. The axe is now kept in the national museum in Kruševo.

After the assassination my brother Stojan and I became *komitas,* and my father fled to Bulgaria. When the Turks found out about the murder, they came to the village, but in our house they found no adult men, only my mother with six children under the age of ten years. They sent my mother to the Turkish prison in Bitola, where she was kept for six months. Because she had children, the Turks released her. They also confiscated all our property.

My brother Stojan and I joined the *četa* of the *vojvoda* Veljko, a teacher from Selce in the Kruševo region. This *četa* was operating in the Kruševo region, in the vicinity of the villages Pusta Reka, Radovo, Korenica, [Dolno] Divjaci, Rastojca, Rakitnica, and others.

In May 1903 our *četa* was in the village of Rakitnica, 3 km from the Turkish village of Pribilci, where a Turkish army unit was stationed. A traitor in Rakitnica—Petre, a Turkish servant from Novo Selo—betrayed our *četa*. Turkish forces surrounded us and a bloody fight ensued. In the fighting, ten *komitas* fell dead, among them my brother Stojan and the *vojvoda* Veljko. (There is a song about that struggle, which I very much like.) The other survivors and I traveled up to the immediate environs of Kruševo, to the *vojvoda* Nikola Karev; he then sent me and a couple of other comrades to Mariovo.

During the Ilinden Uprising I was in the region of Mariovo in the *četa* of the *vojvoda* Tase Paša, where I remained until the Huriet from 1908. Our *četa* was operation in the region of the villages Dunje, Vitolište, Makovo, Toplica, Belovodica, and others.

In that region we waged a long and steadfast struggle against Greek *četas,* whose central post was in the villages Staravina and Gradešnica. Many *komitas* died in the struggles with the Greek *četas,* including our *vojvoda,* Marko, from the village of Vitolišta. He was succeeded as *vojvoda* by Trajko Zajkata from the village of Živovo, in the Mariovo region.

Our *četa* maintained order and enforced [organization] laws among the locals. For example, we did not permit people to take their grievances to Turkish courts, and we forbade young women from making elaborate embroidery for their weddings. Additionally, fathers were not allowed to solicit or receive large sums of money or gifts from prospective sons-in-law. The display and presentation of excessive jewelry was also prohibited, as well as many other practices that were considered important at the time.

Jovan N. Jurukovski, of Skopje, born in Tresonče, Galičnik region.
Record 15-J-54. Biography submitted October 5, 1951.

In 1901, at the age of twenty-nine, I was in Sliven as a hired worker. Sympathizing with the socialist party in Sliven, I met with the high school teacher Mihajlo Kantardžiev and others who were leaders in the party, and they accepted me as a member. Afire for the liberation of Macedonia, and seeing with deep sorrow that there was a split among the Macedonian people between the *vrhovisti* and *centralisti,* I entered the Internal Secret Revolutionary Organization—the *centralisti.* Working for the organization in Sliven I met Petar Vaskov, a high school teacher in the Sliven secondary scientific school who was from the town of Veles, and also Peho Jahorov. Those two vouched for me with Goce Delčev and he called for me in May 1901. At his request I presented myself in Sofia at the Hotel Battenberg. He questioned me thoroughly and finally said, "Jahorov recommends you highly and yesterday I also received a letter from Vaskov, who reckons that you will be an asset in our work for Macedonia. We Macedonians have many enemies, and must combat them all, wherever they come from. In the first place the *vrhovisti* are our enemies. They are loyal servants of King Ferdinand, and even though they are Macedonians, they do not work for Macedonia, but for him. So I will give you full powers, and write to the Bitola central committee. You should present yourself there, and you'll be assigned a četa of roughly twenty-five men, with which you'll begin work."

After this meeting with Goce Delčev, I returned home as a regional commander for the Galičnik region, and after ten days' break, I went to Bitola, met with the necessary people and they gave me what was needed (including the regulations, pledge forms, receipts, and the seal), and they wrote to the *vojvoda* Janaki Janev to come to me. He came to me in Tresonče, we took council and made a decision regarding the organizing of the population in the Galica region.

First we organized the villages Tresonče, then Gari, Lazarapole, Osoj, Rosoki, Galičnik, Selce, and the monastery St. Jovan Bigorski as well as Bituše.

In 1902, Maksim Ninev Boškoski (a relative of mine) came to our region with nine *četniks*, sent by the Vrhovist committee with an order from Generals Končev, Protugerov, Nikolov, and Jankov, to come in our region and to take over the organization in order to establish his own Vrhovist organization. I called him to me and told him, "we have an organization and if you want to work for Macedonia you have to enter our organization, otherwise we will be defeated; tomorrow our local *četa* will arrive. I will introduce you so that you can join them together." That is what happened, so that Maksim became second *vojvoda*. Later on Maksim was sent to Bulgaria to gather people and weapons, which he did, gathering forty well-armed *četniks*. But on May 29, 1903, on the way back at the place called Čavkite, he was betrayed by spies. He fought a life-or-death battle, and died along with nineteen *četniks*. The survivors were attached to the *četa* of Janaki Janev.

I continued with my work and we carried out preparations for the uprising, about which only we, the regional commanders, had information. We knew that it would be in that year 1903, while the day would be given to us later. All of us in the region worked for that end.

The long-awaited day arrived; the Macedonian Secret Revolutionary Committee gave an order to all regional and village commanders to announce by ringing of the [church] bells the beginning of the uprising in the Bitola region. For that task on July 19 (in the old calendar), I was summoned to the village of Dušegubica, where the mountain commanders and the central committee were located. I went there accompanied by my courier, Jovan Terziev Vrleski, Jovan Ginoski from Galičnik, and seven *četniks*. We presented ourselves to the command and saw the house where there was a flag with the embroidered words "Death or Liberty."

Afterwards Luka Jerov told us, "Brothers, we are starting the uprising tonight at twelve o'clock midnight. You are not to start operations in the Galičnik region, but to provide us with moral and material assistance. Anyone who wants can stay and participate." Jerov then ordered me, as a regional commander, and also my courier, to go back in order to supervise the preparation for these tasks. He put together supply train of twenty horses for the delivery of military materials, and the village of Tresonče was to serve as a point for connection and redirection. I received these orders and during the uprising I organized one *četa* for service with the command in Dušegubica, which included Janaki Janev, Krsto Aleksov, Tale Cerča, Toško from Sušica, Jovan Pendor, Jovan Trpkov Ginoski, Pavle Kara-asan, and the surviving *četniks* from Maksim Ninev's band. I also sent to them twelve cannons made in the monastery of St. Jovan Bigorski, and served as the instructor of the all of the above-mentioned *četniks*.

After the uprising was put down, I remained for a while among the populace to continue the work of secretly organizing and supporting the fighting spirit and general morale in the region. I continued these illegal activities right up until the revolution of the Young Turks in 1908. I played a leading, public role in the Federal Macedonian Party under the leadership of Jane Sandanski, which lasted for six months: after that, because of the change in the program of the Young Turks, I found myself wanted by the police again for illegal activities. This state of affairs continued until 1911, when I had to leave my place of birth and flee to Bulgaria because I was under suspicion.

On September 28, 1904, Dame Gruev was in Tresonče with me, as well as the *vojvodas* Hristo Uzunov, Arso from Podviš, Dejan from Ohrid and Janaki Janev. We held a conference in connection with the reorganization of my region and this continued for two days. On September 29 we housed them in the village of Selce, half an hour away from Tresonče. I returned to the village with an order from Dame Gruev to send some letters by courier, which he gave me for Kičevo and Debar. On the way back the army captured the courier and discovered Gruev's letters as well as newspapers that he was carrying. They took the courier to Lazarapole and interrogated him there to uncover the whereabouts of Gruev. Under duress, he told them that Gruev was in Tresonče, but that he didn't know in which house exactly. During the night of September 30, 1904, some Turkish officers with an armed force took this man to lead them to me in Tresonče. Instead, he led them to the regional courier, Jovan Terziev. After a long period of torture Terziev finally agreed to take the Turks to Selce. When they got close to the village, though, Jovan cried in a loud voice, "Run, brothers! You are betrayed!" When the soldiers heard this they put out his eyes with hot irons and then killed him. A battle then started, in the course of which, at around two o'clock in the early morning, all the *vojvodas* managed to save themselves and escape.

The above is the brief statement of my work for the Macedonian cause.

Angel Korobar, of Veles. Record 17-K-61. Biography submitted July 19, 1952.

I was born in 1885 in the city of Veles from an established patriotic lineage, which played a role in the foundation of the Internal Macedonian Revolutionary Organization in Veles and the district of Veles. When the founders of this organization came from Štip and other towns to Veles they sought out our family, and the director of the Veles and village schools in the district, Velko Dumev, lodged with us, as well as the teachers Petre Pop Arsov, Dimitar Hadži Dinev, V. Ačkov, Dimitar Bitrakov, and Krstev.

When I was still a student in first grade elementary school these teachers assigned me the task of carrying letters, different written documents, and various packages, the contents of which I myself did not know, to certain members of the organization. This responsibility, given me when I was still young, made me take my own actions more seriously. In addition, reading the revolutionary literature they gave me, and listening to the conversations they had in my presence, gave me wings to fight against the Turkish sultan's tyranny.

In second grade I carried out the same duties and also witnessed the abduction of the child from the wealthy Vesov family. I was told to stand right next to him so that at the time of the abduction the *četniks* (who were disguised, masked members of the organization), who knew me, would be sure to kidnap the right child by taking the fellow next to me. In connection with this case the teacher Prnarov and some other members of the organization were arrested, and there was a real danger of even more arrests.

After finishing second grade I went to Salonika. There I had the opportunity to read revolutionary literature from the progressive writers of the time. During the vacation two fellow students, Kosta Kirkov and Todor Bogdanov, and I decided that when we were to return to Salonika we would surrender ourselves to Goce Delčev's *četa*, so that they could extort ransom from our parents for the benefit of the organization. The unexpected decision of my father to send me to school in Bitola foiled my intentions, but my other two fellow students followed through; they gave themselves up to the *četa* and were taken to Sofia, and their fathers gave the requested amount of money.

Because of the aggravated conflict between the [Exarchist] bishop Gligorija and the organization, a plan was made to discredit him in the eyes of the people, and the task was given to local organization personnel. Two hundred students began a protest in the high school boarding house, and the people rallied in support of the organization's plan, leaving the bishop isolated. But the Exarchate, in order to restore the ruined reputation of the bishop, fired seven of the high school teachers and expelled twenty students, and at the same time they reported these persons to the authorities as rebels. I was one of the students expelled and was no longer able to continue with my education [at the Exarchate school]. I was also unable to cross the border [out of the empire], and I was thus forced to return to Salonika again, and to enroll in the French college as a boarder. I was able to make the condition that at the end of the school day I would be free to go around town, so that in this way I could establish connection with the Salonika student revolutionary circle, while benefiting from the extraterritorial status of the French school's boarding house.

This continued till 1901 when affairs in Salonika were affected by the arrest of the teacher Nikov from Serres. This led to to the arrest of two members of my immediate circle, Milan Rizov and Koce Lazarov Arsov from Štip, who were sentenced and sent into exile to Asia Minor. I was confined to the boarding house till the end of the school year, and during the vacations I returned to Veles.

In the next year I was scheduled to graduate. I went back to Salonika in the boarding house with the same conditions—the right to go about freely in the town. However, I found that revolutionary activity had been largely crushed as a result of the affair. I got in touch with my former classmates from Veles, Kosta Kirkov, Orce Pop Jordanov, Ilija Trčkov, and Pavel Šatev, and offered them my services, telling them of the privileges I had in the college and its exterritorial status. They accepted my proposition and started using me in the same way as the circle had done in the past. The administration of the school did not suspect anything because relatives were constantly coming to visit me there who were already known to them. I received, stored, and passed on a number of heavy suitcases and packages, and in return for a modest bribe the gatekeeper did not report to the administration what I was doing. This continued until 1902, with me going back and forth [delivering explosives] between the boarding house and the barbershop of Vlada Pingov, on Kolombo Street. When that barbershop was closed, Marko Stojanov opened a grocery store with the same purpose; and on

April 14, 1903, the Messageries Maritimes ship the *Guadalquivir* was bombed, and on the evening of April 16 the Ottoman Bank was bombed. At sunrise, I was arrested after being reported, and detained at the town hall, where there was already a multitude of dead, wounded, and deranged people. After a few days they took approximately two hundred of us as prisoners to Bejaz-Kule [the White Tower] during the night. Among the arrested were Garvanov, Pop Stamat, and other members of the leadership of Macedonia.

After six months of interrogation and torture in Bejaz-Kule, and thanks to the intervention on my behalf of the school administration, they sent me under guard to Skopje, and from there to Veles, where I was assigned to the custody of the chief of police. He would not allow me to graduate, but after a long correspondence between Skopje and Salonika he gave me a passport to leave for Switzerland. Then I went to Geneva, but because I didn't have graduation documents from high school, I enrolled as a student in chemistry with the condition that in one year I would present a diploma. There I circulated among leftist student groups, which was easier for me thanks to my knowledge of French, as the members of these groups were from different nationalities. I was most influenced by acquaintance with the students from Russia, and I found no antagonism among Russian, Polish, Armenian, and Ukrainian students. They were all working with great effort for the upcoming revolution.

The Ilinden Uprising and the terror in Macedonia prompted many French newspapers to publish different reports and opinions. The expansionist propaganda of the Balkan states had been stoked to a fever pitch by the uprising, each attacking the other, so that public opinion, especially among the students, was in confusion. For that reason we, the Macedonian students, asked the distinguished Macedonian supporter [Victor] Bérard to give a lecture in the main hall of Geneva University on the Macedonian problem. He, in turn, asked Georges Gaulis, the head correspondent of the Parisian daily magazine (the same man had been the chief correspondent during the uprising in Macedonia, and until the end had traveled along with Sandanski's *četa*).[1] He accepted our invitation, and in his speech, illustrated by photographic slides, he gave a full and detailed description of the Macedonian movement, the outrages of the Turkish army, and the self-sacrifice of the rebels in the battles. At the same time he explained that the Ilinden Uprising was a national uprising according to the statute of the VMRO, in which all nationalities were called to the struggle against the sultan's absolutism and tyranny, for liberty, fraternity, and equality of all nationalities in Macedonia. He thus exposed the Vrhovist propaganda that portrayed the movement as purely Bulgarian. A great number of newspapers covered the occasion, but he was also the target of an attack from a Greek Professor at Bern University.

We ordered *komita* uniforms from Sofia and borrowed rifles from the police and gave a performance of the play "Macedonian Bloody Wedding," which was attended by large numbers of citizens and students.[2]

As I couldn't present a high school diploma, I left my studies and went to Bulgaria, where I made contact with the *vojvoda* for Veles, Stefan Dimitrov, a socialist by conviction. I was determined to join his *četa*. At that time they brought to Geneva from London Boris Sarafov, Ljapov, and Mišel Gerdžikov, who had visited the European capitals and had been collecting aid for the Macedonian movement. At the meeting in the Hotel Bellevue, where princes, the high aristocracy, and the wealthy would stay, I commented on the luxuriousness of the place, and questioned the use of the people's money for this purpose. Sarafov replied, "Since I am about to die, there is no need to be frugal with the money." He also berated us for what had happened to George Gaulis. This was due to the hostility that had already appeared between the external leading body of VMRO and Sandanski; this was the same time that the murder of Daev took place.

Not long afterwards I received a message from Veles that my father and uncle were in prison because of a receipt for thirty napoleons that had been intercepted, that was issued to the Korobar brothers by Sarafov's Vrhovist organization for the receipt of terrorist money. I reported this to Dimitrov, who approved that I go back to Veles, from where I continued to be in touch with him, as a *vojvoda* of the Veles district.

In October 1907 my relatives were released from prison and I left for Salonika to get my diploma. I took the school-leaving examination and was planning to go back to Geneva, but the situation had changed entirely. On June 12, 1908, the Huriet was declared and triggered new political alliance making. The supporters of Bulgarian imperialism joined forces with the Constitution Club, while the members of the VMRO allied with the Democratic Federative Party, which was supported by the workers' club. I changed my plans for further study and instead became a teacher and an active member of the Federative Party and the workers club . . .

Lazar Hristov Svetiev, of Bitola. Record 31-S-15.
Biography submitted March 17, 1952.

I was born the son of Hristo and mother Meglena, on March 13, 1860, in Bitola. I studied in elementary school and had reached fourth grade of high school when Slavic schools were instituted. The principal in the high school was Gligor Prčilev, from Ohrid. After finishing high school, as I did not have any material means of support I stayed in Bitola. Afterwards I apprenticed myself as a tailor and studied the craft for one year.

I was chosen to be a teacher by the people who were in charge of education in Saints Kiril and Metodi school at the church of Sveta Bogorodica [Virgin Mary] in Bitola, where I started as a teacher with the movement from 1877. I also volunteered for the duties of *blagajnik* [cashier] and served continuously until 1895, during which time I supplied the schools for their teaching and overhead expenses from the church funds at Sveta Bogorodica and Sveta Nedela in Bitola. In connection with my work I came into contact with the organizers of the Macedonian committee, which was just launching its secret national revolutionary work against the Turkish empire. I met with the following persons: Dame Gruev, Pavel Hristov, Gjorgi Pop Hristov, Tašku Lozančev, Ace Dore, Gjorgi, and Petre Popev, the terrorist Trifun "Resenčeto," and many others whom I have forgotten, as sixty years have passed since then. These people, since they saw that I was honest and loyal, invited me to join their organization. I accepted without hesitation and with great joy.

This was at the beginning of 1896, when I gave my oath on the cross in the presence of the following persons: Dame Gruev, Tašku Lozančev, and Gjorgi Pop Hristov. On the same day, February 2, 1896, I was assigned to be the regional head for the entire Pelagonija region, in the field along with the *vojvodas* Dimko Mogilčeto, Gjorgi Sugarev, Džon Pasha from the village of Logovardi, and others whom I have forgotten. I sent them weapons, clothes, shoes, and medications through people whom I and they trusted. My correspondence was anonymous and coded, and I signed with the name of ADAM, an alias which was known to only the *vojvodas* and those who were witnesses of my oath on the cross. My letters were intercepted a number of times by the Turkish police, but because I used this alias they were not able to identify me.

In 1898, the existence of the local revolutionary organization led by Dame Gruev came to light when it was betrayed by the traitor Pop Stavre. Stavre was unwilling to contribute money for the organization, and the affair began when his contributions were due. He said that he did not have the funds available that day and that we should come the next day in the evening. The task of collecting the dues was assigned to the terrorist Trifun Resenčeto. Stavre, though, had invited the Turkish police to await Trifun's visit, and so when he came to collect, he found not the money but a detachment of Turkish policemen. As a result of Pop Stavre's betrayal close to thirty people were arrested, including Dame Gruev, Ace Dore, Gjorgi Pop Hristov, Gjorgi and Petre Popev, Spiro Kostov, Trifun Resenčeto, Trajko Petrov Gazibara, and myself.

We were each held each in separate cell and were given only a tin pot for a toilet. After a while they imprisoned us in the basement of the guardhouse, which had a low ceiling and was damp, where we were left for twenty days. Because of the damp our feet were affected and then they sent us to a military doctor who told them to move us with the other prisoners. There we found all the organizers and Dame Gruev at their head. There we were left for seven months, and then they led us all in chains to the chief of the police for a hearing. When he was interrogating me, he said that he knew that I had been a cashier for the committee, and that that is why I should not lie to him.

After seven months in prison they had assembled cases against twenty of us, and they led us out in the prison courtyard and sentenced us: some to be hanged, others to serve 101, 20, 15, or 10 years in prison. I was among the latter with 10 years, because the traitor had said, "I think that Lazar Svetiev was in the organization." After the trial, they took photographs of those of us who had been sentenced and led the others to be tried. After few months of appeals, an amnesty was declared and we were released.

After our release from prison I returned to my previous work with even greater resolution and expanded my activism in my post as a regional overseer.

In 1903 the uprising was to begin and I wrote to the *vojvodas* instructing them to set fires in the fields at the same hour on the appointed day, July 20 [O.S.], as a signal for the uprising. At the time Bitola was under military blockade, but I had to give a letter to the courier Sekule Kantar, from the village of Mogila. We were in the market, and he was standing right at my side: but a Turkish officer was looking directly at us and we had to wait for him to go away in order to pass the letter. When the officer had left I gave the letter to Sekule and he headed off through the burned-out shop beside us. But suddenly the Turkish officer reappeared and shouted after Sekule: "Stop there, old man!" But Sekule replied, "Ah, let me meet you at the other side." At that instant Sekule threw the letter in a gutter filled with water and stepped on it and then continued to meet the officer. The officer took Sekule to the police garrison, and there they undressed him completely in order to find the letter, but couldn't find anything and so Sekule was released.

This event put my life at great risk. The same officer subsequently passed by my shop each day with a group of soldiers to check up on me and confirm that I wasn't away somewhere.

After the uprising I was frequently detained in prison, but each time I was released without trial. Sometimes I was released almost immediately, on other occasions I was held for a few days or a couple of weeks. This went on until the

1908 Huriet, when a general amnesty was given for all political criminals of the Macedonian revolutionary movement.

Today, the ideals of our heroes have been fulfilled and Macedonia is free.

From the people who were sentenced with me only Trajko Petrov Gazibara is still alive; the others were either killed in action, or executed by hanging, or have died. There are other contemporaries of mine in Bitola who can vouch for my work for the organization.

Riste Kolev Stamboldžijovski of Smilevo. Record 32-S-54.
Biography submitted August 14, 1951.

I, Riste Kolev Stamboldžijovski, was born January 7, 1886, in the village of Smilevo. I am the son of Kole Stamboldžijovski, who was regarded in the village as an honest and modest man and who at the time of the formation of the VMRO worked ceaselessly for the organization. In 1906 he was murdered in his house by Greek *andartes* when they attacked the village of Smilevo.

As early as my seventh birthday, while still in school, I started helping my father in his comb-making trade. I left elementary school after fourth grade in Smilevo, and from that point on I started working full-time in my father's trade. By the time I was fourteen, listening to my parents and other villagers talking the monstrosities and outrages committed by the Turkish *baši-bazouks* and police, I began to understand the extent of the Turkish tyranny. Hatred grew inside me, and I craved freedom for our enslaved Macedonian people. As a young and spirited member of the working class, fired by progressive ideas, I became a member of the organization at the age of seventeen [in 1903]. I was given the oath by the leadership, by which I was charged to keep the secrets of the organization and of the *četas*, and I gave my promise that I would fight against Turkish tyranny, for freedom or death. After taking the oath, I became an active member of the VMRO and was placed at the disposal of the Smilevo committee. . . .

I worked as a courier, delivering the letters of the organization whenever it was necessary. After I gained the trust of the local committee, they sent me in the mountains to carry letters, food, and other things to the *četas*. From that time my hunting skills improved and now I am one of the most distinguished hunters in the town of Bitola.

Not long after after beginning work I bought a Gras rifle and enlisted myself in the fighting force of the organization, in which I was made a *desetar*. When the Turkish forces surrounded some *četas*, I went immediately with the other [village] *četniks* to help our surrounded comrades. I actively participated in this way, in the encircling of Turkish army units, on many occasions. For example, when the četa of Jordan Piperkata was surrounded in the village of Brezovo, approximately fifty of us from the village of Smilevo went to help them, and we operated for five to six days in the mountains, during which time Piperkata's četa broke out of Brezovo and was pursued by the Turks. Another time we came to the aid of the četa of the vojvoda Penčo when they were surrounded in the village of Izbišta, in the Resen region. We, the četniks who had come to help, charged the flanks of the numerous Turkish military personnel, and after a long, fierce, and bloody fight, we succeeded in breaking the blockade of Penčo's četa.

On Ilinden itself in 1903, when the uprising of the people in Smilevo started, I was positioned by the leaders in ambush at the house of the Miloševci, and with my comrades we waited for the beginning of the action. Our group was led by a senior četnik whose name now I cannot recall, as a lot of time has passed since then. At six o'clock in the evening [by the Turkish clock around noon], we attacked the Turkish administrative building, as well as the detachment of soldiers that had been stationed in our village ever since the execution of the bloodsucker Ismail from the Turkish village of Obednik. The fight was cruel and terrible and went on throughout the entire night and the day after. We did not back down, and as no reinforcements came for the Turkish forces they broke off the engagement and escaped with their lives. When their relief column finally arrived in Smilevo, the new forces burned and captured close to fifty houses.

On the third day after the beginning of the uprising a large Turkish force came toward Smilevo from the neighboring Turkish village of Obednik. At that point I was in the četa of the fearless vojvoda Stojan Donski. We stormed down out of the village and after a prolonged and bloody fight, managed to repel the attackers, and force them to retreat. We captured four horses from the cavalry, which afterwards were taken from us.

After the first few days of the Ilinden Uprising, local četas were formed led by the vojvodas Dame Moskov, Pavle K. Krstevski, Dimče Kromidarovski, Dame I. Kasapovski, Petar Žapčevski, Gligor Pop-Pavlov, and Kočo Grujevski. I joined the četa of Dame Moskov, who is now dead; his lieutenant Mito Kolev Krstevski, who now lives in Skopje, can confirm the details of my activity and participation in the above-mentioned četa. At the time the Turkish counteroffensive was in full swing, and we fenced off our fields, made ditches, and stood ready day and night for their forces to come for retribution. On the feast of Sveta Bogorodica 1903 a major Turkish force surrounded us and attacked from all sides. After a cruel and prolonged fight we were forced to retreat and our četa retreated in good order to the mountain of Bigla, leaving the Turkish army the master of the field.

Afterwards almost all of the četas were dispatched to different locations, while we with our četa remained as a guard for the headquarters, which included

Dame Gruev, Anastas Lozančev, Boris Sarafov, Dečev, Stojan Donski, and Gjorgi Sugarev.

Two or three months after the unsuccessful uprising of 1903 our *četa* was disbanded and I returned to work in my trade, which I continue to this day.

Atanas Dimitriev Cucukov, of Skopje, formerly Setino, in the Florina region. Record 39-C-47. Biography submitted April 5, 1954.

I am Atanas Dimitrijev Cucukov, a refugee from Aegean Macedonia. I was born in 1883 in the village of Setino, Lerin region, where I lived until I turned fourteen, when we moved to the village of Krušoradi, fifteen minutes away. We moved because the Turks burned our house, as my father was a member of the national organization for the liberation of Macedonia from the centuries-long Turkish tyranny, under which our people were being ground down and broken.

My father was an activist who worked tirelessly for the organization, preparing for the Ilinden Uprising. He enlisted me, as well as our entire family, in the Macedonian national organization for the liberation of our people from the Turks.

During the year of 1901 I was working with the members of the local committee of Setino, who were the comrades Stefo Trpčevski, Vasil Malev, Vanjo Čokrev, Kosta Bažarov, Čole Včkov, Gele Gudov, and Giče Lakardov, and with other *vojvodas* who visited Setino. I was in charge of the guard and also the account books, following decisions made by conferences of all the villages in our region (which included Neokazi, Krušorado, Jurukovo, Ovčarani, Papadija, Sovič, and Živojna).[3]

From the very beginning of my membership in the national Macedonian organization I was known because of my father and worked with the members of nearby local committees. In Krušoradi I worked with Krste Konzulov and Risto Cucukov (my uncle), and in Juruko with Dine Kostenčev, Čole Veseev, and others. I also worked with the surviving *vojvoda* Cvetko Šalapanov from the village of Hasanovo, and with Stojan Konzurov and the *vojvoda* Iljo Dimov from Popadino. I also collaborated with other people from the local committees of Sovič, Stojče, and Živojna, including the *vojvoda* Trajko Piranov.

Beside these local collaborations, I also worked with Jordan Piperkata from the regional committee, especially when my father and uncle, and other members of the local committee, were in detention or under surveillance. I also became acquainted and collaborated with the comrade Iljo Bojadžiev, who was a member of the regional committee in Lerin and who would come down to our region. I had more frequent meetings with these two than with other members of the Regional Committee. But I did meet three times with Gjorgi Pophristov and Boris Sarafov, who came from Bitola by train and held meetings with the local committee.

One of the meetings with Pophristov, I remember, was in 1896, when he came down with comrade Pajančev, when the organization began its operations in our village, to meet with the committee. Later there was a meeting with Boris Sarafov and Jordan Piperkata in 1900, when they came from the village of Ovčarani to Krušoradi with the *vojvoda* Leko Jarlev. There was a conference with the local committee where I was present as well. At the conference we received account books.

Along with my moral and material support for the organization, I also performed the illegal duties that were assigned to me. I murdered the bey Dajlan and his dervish in the locality Šapurkata in 1902. Less than a month later, in the same year, I killed Selafo, who was spying on the members of our organization. I committed that murder close to the Venkov's mill, with cold steel.

In September of 1902 I killed the Turkish policemen Džedžip and Arif from Živojna, after which Turkish soldiers burned down ten houses in Jurukovo as a reprisal.

When it became known that I had committed the murder of the above-mentioned Turkish officials, I was persecuted by the Turkish authorities and went illegal. I went out to join the *četa* of the *vojvoda* Iljo Popadinski, and during the time I was gone, in May 1903, Turkish forces burned down my barn.

During the Ilinden Uprising I took part in many battles as a member of Popadinski's *četa*, including one forty-eight-hour engagement that involved also *četas* led by the *vojvodas* Cvetko Šalafanov, Iljo Gegov, Tane Klancov, Cole Grčev, Trajko Pirganov, and Lečo Creovčeto. In that battle we inflicted heavy losses on the Turks.

The next fight in which our *četa* took part was in Čukurov, where I also participated and where we lost many of our comrades, including the *vojvoda* Iljo Gegov and Lečo Creovčeto. I was wounded in the right shoulder, which to this day does not work because of numbness and paralysis. After the battle in Čukurov I was taken back first to Stalkov Grob, where our headquarters was located, and then to the field hospital at Stračka.[4] I stayed there three months because of my shoulder, but I was impatient and before it was fully healed I went back to the *četa* in which I had served previously. I then took part in the battle our *četa* fought in the village of Čegan, where we inflicted heavy losses on the Turks.

Later I took part in the battle in Jurukovo, where the fight was cruel and lasted for three days and we inflicted great and terrible losses on the Turkish army and police. In this fight my comrades Krste Čanev and Najdo Kojcev were killed, and the Turks burned down the village. I also took part in a battle our *četa* fought in the village of Zabrdeni in 1904, where a cruel fight ensued and the village was burned down, and many Turkish families were trapped in their houses.

Then I took part in the battle in the village of Neokazi, where many of our Macedonian villagers were slaughtered after the fighting of 1904, and many other fights until 1908, when the Huriet was issued. I then returned home where I was pardoned and lived as a free citizen till 1909, when with the change in Turkish government and the takeover of the so called "Young Turks" I was exiled again, and I left for America. I came back from America with the *vojvoda* Petre Neolčeto in early 1912, and we again took up arms as *četniks,* and in September 1912 I took part in the fight at Ovčarani, where at the time the Turks were fighting against the Allied forces of Serbians, Bulgarians, and Greeks for the final destruction of the Turks in Macedonia.

After the expulsion of the Turks, our fight was against the Greek *andartes.* I took part in a battle between our *četa* and the *andartes* in Sulšajanova [*sic*], in which the village was burned down. It became evident that our revolution could not succeed, as it has been put down earlier and now was impeded by the Greek, Serbian, and Bulgarian armies and by politics, and so I gave myself up to the Greek authorities, who had confiscated our land after the *vojvoda* Petre Neolčeto left for Bulgaria and we were disbanded. I was pardoned and granted Greek citizenship by the authorities. But later, as a freedom fighter for our country and people, I provided all the material help I could to the national liberation struggle from 1941 to 1948. My son Ruse was killed in the battle in 1946 at Rajčeva Buka, fighting against the [Greek] monarcho-fascists.

Now I am a resident of Skopje and I and my wife are both weighed down by our old age and unable to work.

GLOSSARY

andartes (pl.)	Greek equivalent of *komitas* or *četniks*.
arnaut	Alternative (now derogatory) term for Albanian, used in consular sources and by Macedonian speakers.
bajraktar	Literally, flag bearer. Designated the head of an Albanian clan, or a middle-rank leader in an MRO *četa*.
bey	Ottoman era Turkish landholder.
blagajnik	In MRO usage, treasurer or cashier. Could also designate the treasurer of a church.
četa	Armed band.
četnik	Member of a *četa*. During and after Second World War, the term also described noncommunist Serbian forces, whether resisting Axis occupation or fighting against Tito's partisans. In Yugoslavia, the term had a derogatory force. Plural form *četnici*.
čiftlik	A large farm or estate, owned by a landlord.
čirak	Junior apprentice of a *majstor*.
comitadji	See Komitadži.
desetar	MRO term for the leader of a local committee, cohort, or *četa* with ten (in Macedonian, *deset*) members.
dragoman	Translator, guide, or "fixer."
esnaf	Trade guild.
Exarchists	Orthodox Christians who, in Ottoman period, pledged allegiance to the Exarchate, an alternative church organization created in 1870 and identified as Bulgarian. See Patriarchists.
gurbet	Labor migration.
gemidžii(te)	Literally, "boatmen." In definite form, the name of a group of VMRO activists who conducted dynamite attacks on

	a French steamship and public buildings in Thessaloniki during April 1903.
Gheg	Dialect of Albanian, spoken in Northern Albania, Kosovo, and most of the northwestern part of the Republic of Macedonia around Tetovo. See also Tosk.
giaour	Derogatory term for Christian, in colloquial Turkish.
hajduk	Brigand or rebel.
han	(Turkish) Inn or hotel.
Huriet	Young Turk Revolution to restore constitutional rule in Ottoman Empire, June–July 1908. The movement initially won support from Christian Ottoman subjects, including progressive elements in the MRO.
ilegalen (pl. ilegalni)	Oathed member of the MRO whose membership and activism are known to the authorities and who has taken refuge, most likely as member of a *četa,* and left behind his or her civilian life.
jatak	Literally "bed" (Turkish). Person who hides, houses, and materially assists brigands; in MRO usage, a category of member with the task of providing logistical support for *četas.*
kaimakam	Local administrator in Ottoman period.
kalfa	Senior apprentice or journeyman of a *majstor.*
kanun	The traditional, oral honor code by which Albanian tribal life was governed.
kiradžija	Person engaged in carting, mule driving, or general transport trade.
kleft	Literally "thief" (Greek); bandit.
kletva	Oath or curse.
kjumurdžija	Person engaged in charcoal cutting, burning, and selling trade.
kolji	watchman (Turkish kolcu).
komita	Member of Revolutionary Organization, which was organized into local and regional committees. Often used to describe armed activists of the organization, and therefore overlapping in meaning with *četnik.*
komitet	Local or regional MRO committee.

Konak	Ottoman-era local government offices.
kum	Godfather or wedding sponsor.
kumstvo	The relationship between two individuals or families, where one is *kum* to the other.
kurier	In MRO usage, courier, responsible for conveying messages, material, and *četas*.
legalen (pl. legalni)	Oathed member of MRO whose activities remain undiscovered by Ottoman authorities and who maintain a parallel life in the civilian world. See *ilegalen*.
majstor	Master of a skilled trade, or *zanaet*, usually owning his or her own business.
millet	Religious community recognized by Ottoman administration.
momok	Contract laborer or domestic servant.
narod	Nation or people.
Patriarchists	Orthodox Christians in Ottoman period who maintained their allegiance to the Patriarchate, the long-established religious authority, identified as "Greek." See Exarchist.
pečalba	Temporary labor migration, undertaken by *pečalbari*.
poljak	Field guard.
rayah	Peasantry in Ottoman Macedonia.
rayon	Region. Designates an intermediate level of authority, between village and central committee, by MRO; designates a district of a *vilayet* by the Ottoman Empire.
Rum	Name of "Greek" Orthodox Christian millet in Ottoman Empire until 1870, when its unity was challenged by the creation of the Exarchate.
terorist	Self-designation used by VMRO activists in 1903 period, who carried out executions of spies, traitors, or other enemies condemned to death.
Tosk	Albanian dialect of southern Albania and southwestern part of Republic of Macedonia, up to Bitola. See Gheg.
vilayet	Ottoman administrative province.
vojvoda	MRO military leader.
zanaet	Skilled artisanal trade.
zaptieh	Ottoman policeman or gendarme.

NOTES

Introduction

1. The consular report did not include the photograph. The identification of the two men, and acknowledgment that their bodies too were mutilated, is provided in a caption to the photograph in an illustrated volume compiled in Sofia in 1931. The caption in this volume reads, "The Bidinovs, father and son, from Kruševo, blinded and murdered" ("Comité de Redaction" 1931: Picture 481). The picture is reproduced in Stoyan Christowe's *Heroes and Assassins*, inflected differently again by the caption "Innocent victims of the Macedonian revolution. Perhaps because they would not tell where the comitadjis were hiding" (Christowe 1935: 173).

2. In this book, I use either the generic acronym "the MRO" or the term "the organization," to refer to the Macedonian Revolutionary Organization. This represents a hybrid approach: my use of "the MRO" modifies the convention established by Duncan Perry, who used the same acronym as shorthand for the Macedonian equivalent, *Makedonskata Revolucionerna Organizacija*, which contains the definite article. Many of the pension applicants referred simply to "the organization"—*organizacijata*. Both naming strategies reduce the potential confusion generated by multiple changes in the organization's official name, several mergers between potential rival organizations, and frequent infighting and contestation among leaders, in the period between 1893 and 1903. For a list of title changes and a more detailed account of the changes and the stakes involved, see Perry 1988.

3. Here, and in general, I use the modern calendar rather than the old Julian calendar to date events. In modern Bulgaria, St. Elijah's Day (Ilinden) is celebrated on the anniversary of its Julian calendar date, July 20; the Republic of Macedonia commemorates August 2.

4. "Macedonia" had no governmentally authorized referent on the ground. The term was in general usage to refer to the administrative regions of Uskub (modern Skopje), Selanik (modern Thessaloniki), and Manastir (modern Bitola). This book uses a mixture of Turkish, Slavic, and Greek terms for place names similar to that used in the various sources used here. So I call these three provinces and

the cities that housed their administrative offices Skopje, Salonika, and Monastir, respectively.

1. Terminal Loyalties and Unruly Archives

1. Ilinden occupies a less central role in Turkish historiography on Macedonia, which has been influenced by the Annales school of history, and so tends to take a longer view and pay particular attention to economic concerns. See for example Adanir 1979.

2. For documentary evidence of the key role played by Bulgarian military personnel in the uprising, see Noneva et al. (1984).

3. More recently, sociologist Rogers Brubaker has expressed similar sentiments with regard to a tendency toward unreflective "groupism" among scholars of nationalism, and in his own work he has sought to engage closely with the making of ethnicity through everyday practices, painstakingly traced through archival research (Brubaker 2004, 2006). Political scientists analyzing the working of violence in civil wars demonstrate similar respect for the ethnographic perspectives gleaned through extensive fieldwork (see for example Wood 2003; Kalyvas 2006; Weinstein 2007).

4. In this regard, I part company with Marshall Sahlins' more radical localism to permit borrowing of insight across space and time, so long as the here and now, and its particular political and ideological concerns, are not privileged as a reference point.

5. Stathis Kalyvas shrewdly refers to such cases of malicious denunciation among intimates as "the dark side of social capital" (Kalyvas 2006 :332).

6. This is not to discount other anthropologists' approaches to the employment of non-narrative and narrative sources in our attempt to get at historical experience; notably, John Davis's account of grappling with fourteen thousand marriage records in Libya, photographed in 1979, where he irreverently refers to the gleanable base of data as "turdish aides-memoire"; Janet Hart's use of narrative analysis in her inquiry into the Greek Civil War; and Ann Stoler's more recent work, where she deploys the metaphor of the "archival grain" that the ethnographer, as metaphorical carpenter, does well to respect (Davis 1994; Hart 1996; Stoler 2009).

7. There were gaps in this international surveillance. Britain, for example, did not maintain a vice consul in Monastir between 1898 and early 1903; James McGregor arrived in post on March 15, 1903. Additionally, R. W. Graves succeeded Sir Alfred Biliotti in Salonika in mid-July 1903, so that for the two weeks immediately before the declaration of the Ilinden Uprising, consular staff were dealing with a transition in leadership.

8. British officials were especially vigilant in reporting Russian efforts to extend influence in the region. They monitored the activities of the Russian consul in Monastir, M. Rostowski, who was generally viewed as an active supporter of the revolutionary movement. The archives also include a fascinating intelligence analysis of reported efforts by Russia to extend the borders of the territory of Mount Athos in order to gain access to the deep-water anchorage of the Bay of Platy and therefore extend the range of her naval forces in the Aegean. When the Russian gunboat *Teretz* visited Athos in June and July 1902, her movements and activities were faithfully reported to London. British suspicions were not unfounded; in his role as war correspondent, Leon Trotsky reports a former Russian consul casually acknowledging that the Russian government had armed insurgents in Macedonia (Trotsky 1980: 127; cited in chapter 5, page <X-REF>).

9. In the immediate aftermath of the uprising, McGregor was sufficiently undiplomatic to express his regret in a dispatch to Graves that the Ottoman commander Bakhtiar Pasha, whom he judged responsible for "the excesses attending the recapture of Krushevo" and who, in McGregor's view, "presided over the destruction of Smilevo and the massacre of the inhabitants," received a prestigious award from the sultan (FO 195/2157/660: October 15, 1903).

10. Some applicants were substantially older than the mean age of sixty-seven. One applicant, born in 1858 in the Prilep village of Vitolište, refers to himself as being in "deep old age"—*dlaboka starost* (Jovan Gjiroski, Record 11-Gj-34)—while another, in more dramatic terms still, describes himself as being "at the gates of the grave" (Petre Bubeski of Gjavato, Record 5-B-39).

11. The archival record is unclear on the total number of pensions eventually awarded. Almost all of the sample of 375 were awardees. The geographical concentration is matched in the archive as a whole: of 2,594 recipients listed in the early 1950s (when a number of applications were still under review), the contiguous areas of Bitola, Prilep, Kičevo, Kruševo, Demir Hisar, Resen, and Ohrid contributed 1,581 or around 60 percent. A further 299 traced roots to the areas of Lerin (modern Florina), Kostur (modern Kastoria), and Voden (modern Edhessa) in Aegean Macedonia and were among the larger population displaced by the Greek Civil War. These applicants filed either from the formerly German villages in Vojvodina where they were settled, or from towns in Macedonia, but recorded their birthplaces, which were also where their revolutionary activity took place.

12. Her pension number from the Bulgarian regime was 4183, indicating that the earlier pension scheme had benefited more individuals that its successor. One reason for that was that the Bulgarian scheme paid "survivor" benefits to widows, as in this case, where the Macedonian scheme did not.

2. The Horizons of the "Peasant"

1. Although in many cases conscious that the uprising and the subsequent Ottoman reprisals had conspired to devastate the local economy, most observers still attributed the region's visible wretchedness to aspects of local character rather than the specific effects of trauma.

2. Scott also draws attention to a less-cited two-article argument he published in *Theory and Society* in 1977, in which he extended the approach of moral economy to pay closer attention to the moral, spiritual, and religious world of peasants (Scott 1977a, 1977b).

3. An account of the legal proceedings by which Kruševo passed into the hands of its occupants is given in Matkovski and Bitoski 1978: 25–28.

4. These were the terms used by applicants in the 1940s. *Majstor* is a substitution for the Turkish word *usta* (Victor Friedman, personal communication).

5. The examples presented here were not selected for their statistical representativeness. In terms of overall trends suggested in the pension requests, while some male children received education and professional training, most of those who sought pensions had from their early teens been wage-laborers, either for other families, Turkish landowners, or as *pečalbari* in foreign cities.

6. It should also be noted that Bulgaria, Greece, and Serbia were also concentrating on training citizen armies in this period and spent long periods at a state of near-full mobilization or at war with one another or with Ottoman Turkey. Statistics are hard to come by, but it seems likely that this also contributed to the demand for Macedonian labor in the new capitals of Sofia, Athens, and Belgrade.

7. Ottoman authorities also learned from the South African experience: Nazir Pasha, who took over command of the counterinsurgency campaign in Macedonia on August 25, 1903, reportedly boasted of adopting the methods of the British in his assault on villages (Brailsford 1906: 61; Dakin 1966: 103n).

8. The date of Hampson's letter confirms the enduring seasonal pattern of *pečalba*, in which young men would typically depart in the spring and aim to return in the fall.

9. In a second irony, the Gemidžii were acting independently of the MRO and in defiance of at least some of the organization's leaders. Although they had the support of Boris Sarafov and (reportedly) Goce Delčev, other leaders correctly anticipated that European public sympathy for the cause would be eroded by attacks that put civilians, including Europeans, at risk and that were directed at institutions in which international capital was heavily invested.

3. The Oath and the Curse

1. Another firsthand account appears only obliquely in Reginald Wyon's journalistic account, where he provides the text of a letter received from an MRO member imprisoned in Asia Minor. The letter's author, reporting on the tortures he is suffering, reaffirms his commitment to the organization, which has continued "from the day we consecrated our lives to the holy cause, from the day on which we kissed the holy revolver and the twice-holy dagger, we have ever been ready to die for it" (Wyon 1904: 143).

2. Branov was sworn in by Atanas Fermanov and Gjorgji Markov, both leading military figures in the uprising.

3. Some pension applicants, indeed, remained tight-lipped about the organization and their membership, even fifty years later, denying knowledge of the organization or stating that it was secret. Such accounts lend themselves to different interpretations: genuine ignorance or an enduring commitment to honor an oath of secrecy sworn almost half a century earlier, of the kind that Caroline Elkins encountered in her work in Kenya, referenced in chapter 1 (Elkins 2005: 27).

4. Pop Stamat was an Exarchist priest and longtime member of the organization, whose role in recruiting was widely known. He was eventually killed in October 1904 by Greek operatives on the doorstep of his house—a significant loss for the organization reported in both the consular reports of the time and in the Ilinden Dossier fifty years later.

5. The cultural significance of kissing sacred objects as a somatic/stomatic additive to the power of words in a pledge of faith is discussed in Mikhailova and Prestel 2011: 3–5.

6. Among those who recalled taking the oath in Constantinople were Jovan Lazarev Stojanov, from Ramna, who adds that he took it "along with many other villagers," and Temelko Lazarov Iliev from Bitola (Records 33-S-20; 13-I-34).

7. The three-person team was also, of course, a key artifact in Russian revolutionary practice, where assassinations were the designated work of *trojkas*.

8. For Greek Civil War examples see Vasiliadis (1989: 109) and Brown (1998). All these reported behaviors are very much in line, of course, with the argument made by Samuel Popkin regarding peasant rationality (Popkin 1975).

9. Vrhovists were adherents of the Sofia-based Supreme Committee that had been largely co-opted by Bulgarian state interests. See appendix 2 for Jurukovski's full biography.

10. The particular risks for an organization moving to mass swearings-in—as it appears the MRO did in 1901–1902—are discussed in the Mau Mau context by David Anderson (2005: 42).

11. Njama went on to take the second Mau Mau oath, the so-called Batuni or platoon oath. Where he took the first oath with several others under pressure and in the face of a group of well-armed Mau Mau members, he reports taking the second oath willingly with just one other initiate and that it was administered by a single oath administrator (Barnett and Njama 1966: 130–33).

12. The reference here is to Evans-Pritchard's discussion of faulty psychologism and crude literalism among analysts of "primitive" thought. He takes as a specific case the assumption that when Nuer speak of a cucumber as an ox in a context of sacrifice, they are asserting a false identity between a cucumber and an ox, which reveals a prelogical way of thinking. In a spirit similar to Sahlins' later critique of "pidgin anthropology," Evans-Pritchard urges fellow anthropologists to recognize the poetic sensibility evident in other cultures' discussions of underlying relations between the material, spiritual, and social domains of life (Evans-Pritchard 1974: 128–29, 140–43).

13. The point of comparison here is with the various anti-imperial movements in the Philippines, China, Latin America, and Africa in the same time period. The organization's leaders drew parallels in particular between their own struggle and that of the Boers in South Africa against England. In the latter case, of course, the English were unfettered by international outrage and implemented practices that enable them to destroy the commandos; it was in that war that the concentration camp was invented, as villages were depopulated to remove the supply echelon of the Boer movement. The Ottoman Empire could only have prevailed against the Macedonian Revolutionary Organization by similar means, but the humanitarian pressure imposed by Western Great Powers with significant interests in the Balkans prevented them from doing so, thereby contributing to the MRO's survival.

4. The Archive and the Account Book

1. The notion of *communitas* deployed here is drawn from the work of Victor Turner (1969).

2. Perry estimates MRO's membership at no more than fifty in 1894 and notes that even after *četas* began to operate as a "standing army" in 1896, there were only two armed confrontations with Ottoman forces before the end of 1900, and then only a further eight in 1901, as opposed to fifty-three in 1902 (Perry 1988: 145, 154).

3. The Kadino engagement, 10 km east of Skopje, occurred in April 1902 and was one of several defeats inflicted on the organization that spring (Dakin 1966: 73n). The Peškov family was centrally involved in the revolutionary movement in Prilep. As well as hosting oathing ceremonies in the family home, they also accommodated Goce Delčev when he visited Prilep. Rampo Peškov is named by several pension applicants as a fellow *četnik*, and Kolo Peškov is reported as an oath giver by Boris Gruev.

4. The three self-identified secretaries were Petar Kolarević in Tašku Karev's *četa*, Krste Germov (Šakir) in the Mariovo region under Tole Pašev, and Risto Domazetovski in Vrbeni, close to Lerin (modern Florina) (Records 17-K-49; 7-G-54; 10-D-48). Named secretaries included Stavre Andrevski in Kruševo, identified by Tale Ristev Vezenkoski of Svetomirci in the Prilep district (Record 6-V-15).

5. Even if taken as a purely pragmatic administrative device, the institution of the *arhiv*, and in particular the inclusion of members' names in it, does not sit easily with Perry's view of the MRO. For if viewed in this way, it suggests an organization with a large number of members who do not know each other.

6. For Foreign Office sources on receipts, and a longer discussion of their significance, see the section Money Matters: *Blagajniks* and the Circuits of Taxation below.

7. Peterson and Smith thus lean toward a reading that would suggest, in the terms laid out by Ranajit Guha, that Mau Mau did not in fact break out of a subaltern mode of thinking. Their willing adoption of forms of writing, in this regard, also parallels certain characteristics of "cargo cults" (Worsley 1968) in which native peoples ostensibly presume that by appropriating the signs of the colonizer, they will receive the material bounty that appears to be the colonizer's reward.

8. For Gjakerkoska's full biography, see chapter 5.

9. Riste G. Zengoski, for example, reports that his brother was jailed and severely beaten during Ilinden when carrying supplies from their village, Capari, to the insurgents. After a fee (supplied by the organization) was paid to the local Turkish judge, he was released within a month, despite the apparent objections of the Turkish gendarmes who were convinced—rightly—that he would immediately make the transition from *kurier* to *četnik* (Record 12-Z-12).

10. A few weeks before Smûrdeš's destruction, Turkish forces had been forced to retreat from an armed engagement close to the village. An MRO band headed by Boris Sarafov had been located and surrounded in Smyrdesh, but Sarafov had successfully mobilized neighboring village militias, who had outflanked the Turkish forces. The sack of the village could be seen as reprisal for this reverse; additionally, there were contemporary reports that Smyrdesh was a bomb making center for the MRO (Anastasoff 1938: 321).

11. The fact that a majority of applicants, like Stefan Ilioski here, nonetheless focused on what they actually did, rather than merely claiming to have followed a *vojvoda* into the field during the Ilinden Uprising, serves again to lend the dossier authenticity.

12. The strength of the organization in Prilep is attested by a letter in the consular archives from McGregor, who reports that the residents (whom he refers to as Bulgarians) are reputed to belong to the most advanced revolutionary school (FO 195/2156/535: May 5, 1903, No. 43).

13. Dimko I. Ačkovski, of Prilep, for example, reports collecting money for the

committee in the United States, while Kirjako Andrevski from Dûmbeni in the Kostur (Kastoria) region reports going to Athens, "Asia," and the island of Rhodes to explain the organization's goals and to form societies (presumably among *pečalbars*) to collect of funds for the organization (Records 2-A-69; 2-A-15).

14. The MRO's acquisition of arms is discussed more fully in chapter 6.

5. The Četa *and the* Jatak

1. In another work, Doolaard suggests that the metaphor of an underground republic took literal substance, reporting that beneath every village was a set of underground residences and throughways (Doolaard 1932: 34).

2. The dead man carrying these and other papers was reported to be P. Cvetkov, a leading figure in the organization who was variously reported as a former lieutenant in the Bulgarian army (Chotzidis et al. 1993: 34n) or as a former music teacher (Dakin 1966: 52; Brailsford 1906: 142).

3. This instruction offers one way to interpret the intention behind the dispatch of the dead baby's body to the European consuls, reported in chapter 1. The case is discussed further in the conclusion.

4. Marko Lerinski was the alias, or nickname, for Gjorgi Ivanov, a native of Bulgaria who had served in the Bulgarian army as a noncommissioned officer.

5. Again, the reportage from the British vice consul in Monastir, James McGregor, reveals his understanding of the logistical planning of the organization. Writing in early July 1903, he reported that "several shoemakers of Monastir have since left for the villages where they are said to be engaged in preparing footwear for the insurgents" (FO 195/2157/136: McGregor to Biliotti, July 10, 1903).

6. Upper and Lower Balvan are just to the north of Štip, on the road to Kočani, approximately fifty kilometers or thirty-one miles from Veles, giving some indication of the significant level of commitment a *kurier*'s tasks might demand.

7. As was the case with "terrorist" as a term of self-designation, a number of further pension applicants beyond these six also describe the same kinds of activities—receiving *četas* and sending them on. Antona T. Anastazija reported her revolutionary activity in hiding *četniks* in her Skopje house, while Božin Stefanov Ilievski of Bitola, whose biography is included in appendix 2, reports that in 1904 he hid Taško Šiškov in his house when wounded. Ilievski was himself in the Turkish gendarmerie, thus taking the additional risk of being misidentified as collaborator when in fact working for the organization. Nikola Neškov Kondarkoski of Kruševo, as well as his role as treasurer and group leader, describes having the task of housing any *četa* that came through (Records 2-A-34; 13-I-36; 17-K-59).

8. A different perspective on Turkish treatment of churches is presented by Edith Durham, touring after the Ilinden Uprising. She found the church in

Nakolec, on Lake Prespa in the Resen region, had been defiled and smeared with animal manure, and the eyes scratched out of all the saints. A Muslim gendarme told her, "We must do these things to frighten them. They would kill us and take our land" (Durham 1905: 152).

9. Guevara adds to this list the role of teaching children basic literary skills.

10. For a fuller account of the lives and afterlives of Nikola Karev and Pitu Guli, see Brown 2003: 189–210.

6. Guns for Sale

1. Lokardev is not explicit as to whether he and his father brought these rifles in a single shipment—which would have required a substantial number of men or mules to carry them and therefore would have increased the risk of interception—or over a period of time. Perry indicates that most shipments were small (Perry 1988: 166–67): given the sheer number of rifles that did make their way into Macedonia from Bulgaria, though, some major shipments must have been involved, adding to the plausibility of Lokardev's claim.

2. Their rarity is confirmed anecdotally in the pension application of Jankula Kostov Jovčevski of Skopje, who reports being issued a Mannlicher and one hundred rounds in 1902, which he then had to pass on to another member during 1903 (Record 15-J-19). This was the case for the internal organization's *četas*, as frictions with Bulgaria increased and that supply route was cut off. The Vrhovist *četas*, based in Bulgaria and supportive of Bulgarian policy aims, were increasingly better equipped than their internal organization counterparts, and so would be more likely to have modern Bulgarian army-issued Mannlichers.

3. Instances where *četas* donned Bulgarian-issued uniforms, as sometimes reported, had an even more dramatic impact in this respect.

4. It is plausible to assume that Dimov's stables were located in Bitola's horse market, identified in other sources as a key site for the MRO's illicit activities.

5. In Catholic areas, priests—also outsiders to the patrilineal order—were exempt from *kanun,* which allowed them to serve as mediators.

6. The emphasis on the importance of the first shot explains in part the continued popularity of the single-shot Martini over the repeating Mannlicher or Mauser. The Martini was larger caliber and therefore shot a heavier ball; Edith Durham reports extended conversations among Albanian tribesmen complaining that the Mauser, despite its accuracy, lacked stopping power (Durham 1909: 53, 176).

7. A contemporaneous source reports a similar case, where Nurredu-Aga, of the village of Sv. Nedelja, near Kastoria in Modern Greece, was killed on instructions from the regional committee. The letter ordering the assassination was left behind by one of the killers in his hat (VMRO 1904: 51).

8. Christ Anastasoff cites Slaveiko Arsov's memoirs to report that MRO buyers did an especially good trade with Turkish soldiers after a firefight, because in that context the soldiers did not have to account to their officers for every bullet—they could claim to have fired more than they actually did. Arsov paid half a *piastre* per cartridge; again, the logic appears to work in favor of the MRO, in that each bullet they buy is one fewer fired at them (Anastasoff 1938: 85).

9. This point is made by Brailsford, one of the best-informed analysts of the organization, who indicates that the rifles were kept buried. He goes on to explain, "They are for use when the hour of insurrection comes, and they cannot be worn or displayed or used to prevent or to resent [*sic*] a personal injury. It is really more dangerous for a Christian to have a rifle than to be without one" (Brailsford 1906: 48n).

Conclusion

1. See for example Nagl 2005; Moyar 2009. The thrust of these lessons, of course, is directed by contemporary interests. The U.S. military, tasked with fighting and winning the nation's wars, has sought to identify the ingredients of successful counterinsurgency and has consequently engaged in a dialogue with past military and political practitioners like Robert Thompson, who devised and led Britain's campaign in Malaya, and David Galula, who participated in and analyzed France's attempt to maintain control of Algeria.

2. Pop Stamat, the MRO stalwart and autonomously minded Exarchist priest, was also killed in this period in Thessaloniki. He died on October 18, 1904, shot on the threshold of his house—one more sign of the increased disregard for the distinctions of public and private domains in the execution of deadly violence. The consular reports do not link his death to the Brod murders; it is clear, however, that part of the workings of escalatory violence in this period was the accelerated transmission of information among organizations committed to launching swift and decisive counterattacks to ensure that their losses were amply avenged.

Appendix 2

1. Georges Gaulis and Victor Bérard both authored books supportive of the Macedonian cause. See Bérard 1904; Gaulis 1905.

2. *Macedonian Bloody Wedding* was written by Vojdan Černodrinski in 1900 and depicted Turkish abuses against Macedonian villagers, focusing on the abduction of a young woman by a bey. It was staged as part of fund-raising and propaganda campaigns by advocates of both reform and revolution.

3. Cucukov's document, in keeping with his Aegean Macedonia dialect, loses some of the consonants in several of the standardized versions of these village names. So he renders Jurukovo as Juruko, Papadija as Papadi, Sovič as Sojič, and Živojna as Žuina.

4. Some of the toponyms Cucukov uses are not traceable. I have not been able to correlate Čukurov, Stračka (which literally translates as "magpie"), or Sulšajanova with any named settlements in this geographical area. Stalkov Grob is a peak close to the modern Macedonian-Greek frontier.

BIBLIOGRAPHY

Adanir, Fikret

    1979   *Die Makedonische Frage: Ihre Entstehung u. Entwicklung Bis 1908.* Wiesbaden: Steiner.

Andonov-Poljanski, Hristo

    1985   *Documents on the Struggle of the Macedonian People for Independence and a Nation-State.* Skopje: Kultura.

Alexopoulos, Golfo

    2003   *Stalin's Outcasts: Aliens, Citizens, and the Soviet State, 1926–1936.* Ithaca, N.Y.: Cornell University Press.

Amery, L. S., John Barnes, and David Nicholson

    1980   *The Leo Amery Diaries.* London: Hutchinson.

Amin, Shahid

    1995   *Event, Metaphor, Memory: Chauri Chaura, 1922–1992.* Berkeley: University of California Press.

Anastasoff, Christ

    1938   *The Tragic Peninsula; a History of the Macedonian Movement for Independence since 1878.* St. Louis, Mo.: Blackwell Wielandy Co.

Anderson, Benedict R.

    1983   *Imagined Communities: Reflections on the Origin and Spread of Nationalism.* London: Verso.

Anderson, David

    2005   *Histories of the Hanged: The Dirty War in Kenya and the End of Empire.* New York: W. W. Norton.

Appadurai, Arjun

    1993   "Patriotism and its Futures." *Public Culture* 5(3):411–29.

Axel, Brian Keith (ed.)

    2002   *From the Margins: Historical Anthropology and Its Futures.* Durham, N.C.: Duke University Press.

Banfield, Edward C.

    1958   *The Moral Basis of a Backward Society,* Glencoe, Ill: Free Press.

Barkey, Karen

  1994   *Bandits and Bureaucrats: The Ottoman Route to State Centralization.*
          Ithaca, N.Y.: Cornell University Press.

Barnett, Donald, and Karari Njama

  1966   *Mau Mau from Within: Autobiography and Analysis of Kenya's Peasant
          Revolt.* London: Macgibbon & Kee.

Barry, Tom

  1973   "The Importance of Civilian Support." In *Revolutionaries on Revolu-
          tion: Participants' Perspectives on the Strategies of Seizing Power,* ed.
          Philip Springer and Marcello Truzzi. Pacific Palisades, Calif.: Good-
          year Publishing.

Beames, Michael

  1983   *Peasants and Power: The Whiteboy Movements and their Control in Pre-
          famine Ireland.* New York: St. Martin's Press.

Bérard, Victor

  1904   *Pro Macedonia: L'Action Austro-Russe.* Paris: A. Colin.

Berman, Bruce, and John Lonsdale

  1991   "Louis Leakey's Mau Mau: A Study in the Politics of Knowledge. *His-
          tory and Anthropology* 5(2):143–204.

  1992   *Unhappy Valley: Conflict in Kenya and Africa.* London: J. Currey.

Blok, Anton

  1975   *The Mafia of a Sicilian Village, 1860–1960: A Study of Violent Peasant
          Entrepreneurs.* New York: Harper & Row.

Blumi, Isa

  2011   *Reinstating the Ottomans: Alternative Balkan Modernities, 1800–1912.*
          Basingstoke: Palgrave MacMillan.

Boehm, Christopher

  1984   *Blood Revenge: The Enactment and Management of Conflict in Montene-
          gro and Other Tribal Societies.* Philadelphia: University of Pennsylva-
          nia Press.

Bracewell, Wendy

  1992   *The Uskoks of Senj: Piracy, Banditry, and Holy War in the Sixteenth-
          Century Adriatic.* Ithaca, N.Y.: Cornell University Press.

Brailsford, Henry Noel

  1906   *Macedonia; its Races and their Future.* London: Metheun & Co.

Branch, Daniel

  2009   *Defeating Mau Mau, Creating Kenya: Counterinsurgency, Civil War, and
          Decolonization.* Cambridge, U.K.: Cambridge University Press.

Bringa, Tone

    2005   "The Peaceful Death of Tito and the Violent End of Yugoslavia." In *Death of the Father: An Anthropology of the End in Political Authority,* ed. John Borneman, 148–200. Oxford, U.K.: Berghahn.

Broche, François

    1977   *Assassinat De Alexandre Ier Et Louis Barthou: Marseille, Le 9 Octobre 1934.* Paris: Balland.

Brown, Edward

    1673   *A Brief Account of some Travels in Hungaria, Servia, Bulgaria, Macedonia, Thessaly, Austria, Styria, Carinthia, Carniola, and Friuli as also some Observations on the Gold, Silver, Copper, Quick-Silver Mines, Baths and Mineral Waters in those Parts: With the Figures of some Habits and Remarkable Places.* London: Printed by T. R. for Benj. Tooke.

Brown, Keith

    1998   "Whose Will Be Done? Nation and Generation in a Macedonian Family." *Social Analysis* 42: 110–31.

    2000   "A Rising to Count On: Ilinden Between Politics and History in Post-Yugoslav Macedonia." In *The Macedonian Question: Culture, Historiography, Politics,* ed. Victor Roudometof, 143–72. Boulder, Colo.: East European Monographs.

    2003   *The Past in Question: Modern Macedonia and the Uncertainties of Nation.* Princeton, N.J.: Princeton University Press.

    2004   "Villains and Symbolic Pollution in the Narratives of Nation: The Case of Boris Sarafov." In *Balkan Identities: Nation and Memory,* ed. Maria Todorova, 233–52. New York: New York University Press.

    2013   "'Wiping out the Bulgar Race': Hatred, Duty, and National Self-Fashioning in the Second Balkan War." In *Shatterzone of Empires: Ethnicity, Identity, and Violence in the German, Habsburg, Russian, and Ottoman Borderlands,* eds. Omer Bartov and Eric D. Weitz, 298–316. Bloomington: Indiana University Press.

Brubaker, Rogers

    2004   *Ethnicity without Groups.* Cambridge, Mass.: Harvard University Press.

    2006   *Nationalist Politics and Everyday Ethnicity in a Transylvanian Town.* Princeton, N.J.: Princeton University Press.

Butterfield, Herbert

    1924   *The Historical Novel.* Cambridge, U.K.: Cambridge University Press.

Calhoun, Craig

    1988   "The Radicalism of Tradition and the Question of Class Struggle." In

Rationality and Revolution, ed. Michael Taylor, 129-78. Cambridge: Cambridge University Press.

Callwell, C. E.

1906   *Small Wars: Their Principles and Practice.* London: HMSO.

Campbell, John

1964   *Honour, Family, and Patronage: A Study of Institutions and Moral Values in a Greek Mountain Community.* Oxford, U.K.: Clarendon Press.

Carabott, Philip John

1997   "The Politics of Integration and Assimilation Vis-à-Vis the Slavo-Macedonian Minority of Inter-War Greece: From Parliamentary Inertia to Metaxist Repression." In Ourselves and Others: The Development of a Greek Macedonian Cultural Identity Since 1912, ed. Peter Mackridge and Eleni Yannakakis, 59–78. Oxford: Berg.

Carpenter, Teresa

2003   *The Miss Stone Affair: America's First Modern Hostage Crisis.* New York: Simon & Schuster.

Carr, Matthew

2007   *The Infernal Machine: A History of Terrorism.* New York: New Press.

Čepreganov, Todor, ed.

2008   *History of the Macedonian People.* Skopje: Institute of National History.

Černodrinski, Vojdan, and Goce Stefanoski

1969   *Makedonska Krvava Svadba.* Skopje: "Prosveta."

Chaliand, Gérard

1982   *Guerrilla Strategies: An Historical Anthology from the Long March to Afghanistan.* Berkeley: University of California Press.

Chandler, David Leon

1975   *Brothers in Blood: The Rise of the Criminal Brotherhoods.* New York: Dutton.

Chatterjee, Partha

2002   *A Princely Impostor?: The Strange and Universal History of the Kumar of Bhawal.* Princeton, N.J.: Princeton University Press.

Chernilo, Daniel

2007   *A Social Theory of the Nation-State: The Political Forms of Modernity beyond Methodological Nationalism.* London: Routledge.

Chotzidis, Angelos, et al.

1993   *The Events of 1903 in Macedonia as Presented in European Diplomatic Correspondence.* Thessaloniki: Museum of the Macedonian Struggle.

Christowe, Stoyan

1935   *Heroes and Assassins.* New York: R. M. McBride & Co.

1947   *My American Pilgrimage.* Boston: Little, Brown and Co.

1976   *The Eagle and the Stork.* New York: Harper's Magazine Press.

Clough, Marshall S.

1998   *Mau Mau Memoirs: History, Memory, and Politics.* Boulder, Colo.: L. Rienner.

Cohn, Bernard S.

1987   *An Anthropologist among the Historians and Other Essays.* Delhi; New York: Oxford University Press.

1996   *Colonialism and its Forms of Knowledge: The British in India.* Princeton: Princeton University Press.

Collingwood, R. G.

1946   *The Idea of History.* Oxford: Oxford University Press.

"Comité de Redaction"

1931   *Album-Almanc "Macedoine."* Sofia.

Connor, Walker

1978   "A Nation Is a Nation, Is a State, Is an Ethnic Group, Is a . . . " *Ethnic and Racial Studies* 1(4):379–88.

Corfield, F. D.

1960   *Historical Survey of the Origin and Growth of Mau Mau.* London: H. M. Stationery Off.

Coser, Lewis A.

1974   *Greedy Institutions: Patterns of Undivided Commitment.* New York: Collier Macmillan.

Cowan, Jane

2007   "The Supervised State." *Identities* 14(5):545–78.

Crenshaw, Martha

1978   *Revolutionary Terrorism: The FLN in Algeria, 1954–1962.* Stanford, Calif.: Hoover Institution Press, Stanford University.

Cvijić, Jovan

1906   *Remarks on the Ethnography of the Macedonian Slavs.* London: Printed for the author by H. Cox.

1966   *Balkansko Poluostrvo i južnoslovenske Zemlje: Osnovi Antropogeografije.* Beograd: Zavod za izdavanje udžbenika.

Dadrian, Vahakn N.

1995   *The History of the Armenian Genocide: Ethnic Conflict from the Balkans to Anatolia to the Caucasus.* Providence, R.I.: Berghahn Books.

Dakin, Douglas
  1966   *The Greek Struggle in Macedonia, 1897–1913.* Thessaloniki: Institute for Balkan Studies.
Daraul, Arkon
  1961   *A History of Secret Societies.* New York: Citadel Press.
Davis, John
  1994   "Events and Processes: Marriages in Libya, 1932–79." In *Social Experience and Anthropological Knowledge,* ed. Kirsten Hastrup and Peter Hervik, 200–23. London: Routledge.
Davis, Mike
  2007   *Buda's Wagon: A Brief History of the Car Bomb.* London: Verso.
Davis, Natalie Zemon
  1987   *Fiction in the Archives: Pardon Tales and their Tellers in Sixteenth-Century France.* Stanford, Calif.: Stanford University Press.
Dimevski, Slavko
  1971   *Nikola Karev.* Skopje: Misla.
Dirks, Nicholas
  1993   "Colonial Histories and Native Informants: Biography of an Archive," in *Orientalism and the Postcolonial Predicament,* eds. Peter van der Veer and Carol Breckenridge, 279-313. Philadelphia: University of Pennsylvania Press.
  2002   "Annals of the Archive." In *From the Margins: Historical Anthropology and Its Futures,* ed. Brian Keith Axel, 47–65. Durham: Duke University Press.
Djordjevic, Dimitrije, and Stephen A. Fischer-Galati
  1981   *The Balkan Revolutionary Tradition.* New York: Columbia University Press.
Doolaard, A. den
  1932   Quatre Mois Chez Les Comitadjis; Meurtriers patentés. Paris: Bossuet.
  1935   *Express to the East,* New York: H. Smith and R. Haas.
Doubt, Keith
  2000   *Sociology after Bosnia and Kosovo: Recovering Justice.* Lanham, Md.: Rowman & Littlefield Publishers.
Durham, M. E.
  1905   *The Burden of the Balkans.* London: Edward Arnold.
  1909   *High Albania.* London: Edward Arnold.
Edwards, David B.
  2002   *Before Taliban: Genealogies of the Afghan Jihad.* Berkeley: University of California Press.

Edwards, Lovett Fielding

1938   *Profane Pilgrimage; Wanderings through Yugoslavia.* London: Duckworth.

Elkins, Caroline

2005   *Imperial Reckoning: The Untold Story of Britain's Gulag in Kenya.* New York: Henry Holt.

Elliott, Paul

2008   *Brotherhoods of Fear: A History of Violent Organizations.* London: Blandford.

Emerson, Rupert

1960   *From Empire to Nation: The Rise to Self-Assertion of Asian and African Peoples.* Cambridge, Mass.: Harvard University Press.

Engerman, David C.

2003   *Modernization from the Other Shore: American Intellectuals and the Romance of Russian Development.* Cambridge, Mass.: Harvard University Press.

Evans-Pritchard, Edward

1940   *The Nuer.* New York: Oxford University Press.

1974   *Nuer Religion.* New York: Oxford University Press.

Finnegan W.

2010   "Silver or Lead: The Drug Cartel La Familia Gives Local Officials a Choice: Take a Bribe Or a Bullet." *New Yorker,* May 31: 38–51.

Fischer-Galati, Stephen

1973   "The Internal Macedonian Revolutionary Organization: Its Significance in 'Wars of National Liberation.'" *East European Quarterly* 6: 454–72.

Fitzpatrick, Sheila

1994   *Stalin's Peasants: Resistance and Survival in the Russian Village After Collectivization.* New York: Oxford University Press.

1999   *Everyday Stalinism: Ordinary Life in Extraordinary Times: Soviet Russia in the 1930s.* New York: Oxford University Press.

Fitzpatrick, Sheila, and Robert Gellately

1997   *Accusatory Practices: Denunciation in Modern European History, 1789– 1989.* Chicago: University of Chicago Press.

Fleming, K. E.

1999   *The Muslim Bonaparte: Diplomacy and Orientalism in Ali Pasha's Greece.* Princeton, N.J.: Princeton University Press.

Foster, George

1967   "What Is a Peasant?" In *Peasant Society: A Reader,* ed. J. M. Potter, M. N. Diaz, and G. M. Foster, 2–14. Boston: Little & Brown.

Fraser, John Foster

1906   *Pictures from the Balkans.* London: Cassell.

Galt, Anthony H.

1994   "The Good Cousins' Domain of Belonging Tropes in Southern Italian Secret Society Symbol and Ritual, 1810–1821." *Man (New Series)* 29(4):785–807.

Garnett, Lucy

1904   *Turkish Life in Town and Country.* London: G. P. Putnam's.

Gaulis, Georges

1905   *Les Questions d'Orient.* Paris: Librairie de Pages Libres.

Geertz, Clifford

1973   *The Interpretation of Cultures: Selected Essays.* New York: Basic Books.

1983   *Local Knowledge: Further Essays in Interpretive Anthropology.* New York: Basic Books.

1994   *Primordial Loyalties and Standing Entities: Anthropological Reflections on the Politics of Identity.* Budapest: Collegium Budapest, Institute for Advanced Study.

Geifman, Anna

1993   *Thou Shalt Kill: Revolutionary Terrorism in Russia, 1894–1917.* Princeton, N.J.: Princeton University Press.

Ginzburg, Carlo

1980   *The Cheese and the Worms: The Cosmos of a Sixteenth-Century Miller.* Baltimore, Md.: Johns Hopkins University Press.

Ǵorǵiev, Vančo

2003   *Sloboda ili Smrt: Makedonskoto Revolucionerno Nacionalnoosloboditelno Dviženje vo Solunskiot Vilayet 1893–1903.* Skopje: Tabernakul.

Gjorgiev, Dragi

2003   *Amnestiranite Ilindenci Vo 1904 Godina.* Skopje: Državen arhiv na Republika Makedonija.

Gladstone, William

1897   "On the Macedonian Question. Letter to the President of the Byron Society, 19 January." Reprinted in *Documents on the Struggle of the Macedonian People for Independence and a Nation-State,* ed. Hristo Andonov-Poljanski et al., 406–407. Skopje: University of "Cyril and Methodius."

Gounaris, Vasilis K.

1989   "Emigration from Macedonia in the Early Twentieth Century." *Journal of Modern Greek Studies* 7: 133–53.

1993 *Steam Over Macedonia, 1870–1912: Socio-Economic Change and the Railway Factor.* Boulder; New York: East European Monographs; Distributed by Columbia University Press.

2001 "From Peasants into Urbanites, from Village into Nation: Ottoman Monastir in the Early Twentieth Century." *European History Quarterly* 31(1):43–63.

Graham, Stephen

1972 *Alexander of Yugoslavia: The Story of the King Who Was Murdered at Marseilles.*New Haven, Conn.: Yale University Press.

Grave, Jean

1893 *La société mourante et l'anarchie.* Paris: Tresse & Stock.

Green, Sarah F.

2005 *Notes from the Balkans: Locating Marginality and Ambiguity on the Greek-Albanian Border.* Princeton, N.J.: Princeton University Press.

Gruev, Damian, Boris Sarafov, Ivan Garvanov, and Liubomir Miletich

1927 *Spomeni Na Damian Gruev, Boris Sarafov i Ivan Garvanov.* Sofia: Pečatnitsa P. Gluškov.

Guevara, Ernesto

2007 *Guerrilla Warfare.* BN Publishing.

Guha, Ranajit

1999 *Elementary Aspects of Peasant Insurgency in Colonial India.* Durham, N.C.: Duke University Press.

Gurr, Ted Robert.

1970 *Why Men Rebel.* Princeton, N.J.: Published for the Center of International Studies, Princeton University [by] Princeton University Press.

Haddad, William W., and William Ochsenwald

1977 *Nationalism in a Non-National State: The Dissolution of the Ottoman Empire.* Columbus: Ohio State University Press.

Halpern, Joel Martin

1987 "Yugoslav Migration Process and Employment in Western Europe: A Historical Perspective." In *Migrants in Europe: The Role of Family, Labor and Politics,* ed. H. C. Buechler and J-M. Buechler, 91–115. Westport, Conn.: Greenwood Press.

Hammel, Eugene

1968 *Alternative Social Structures and Ritual Relations in the Balkans.* Englewood Cliffs, N.J.: Prentice-Hall.

Hanioglu, M. Şükrü

2001 *Preparation for a Revolution: The Young Turks, 1902–1908.* Oxford; New York: Oxford University Press.

Hart, Janet

    1996   *New Voices in the Nation: Women and the Greek Resistance, 1941–1964.* Ithaca, N.Y.: Cornell University Press.

Hart, Peter

    1998   *The I.R.A. and its Enemies: Violence and Community in Cork, 1916–1923.* Oxford: Clarendon Press.

Hashim, Ahmed

    2006   *Insurgency and Counter-Insurgency in Iraq.* Ithaca, N.Y.: Cornell University Press.

Hasluck, Margaret

    1954   *The Unwritten Law in Albania.* Cambridge: Cambridge University Press.

Heehs, Peter

    1994   "Foreign Influences on Bengali Revolutionary Terrorism 1902–1908." *Modern Asian Studies* 28(3):533–56.

Herzfeld, Michael

    1985   *The Poetics of Manhood: Contest and Identity in a Cretan Mountain Village.* Princeton, N.J.: Princeton University Press.

Hobsbawm, E. J.

    1959   *Primitive Rebels: Studies in Archaic Forms of Social Movement in the 19th and 20th Centuries.* Manchester: University Press.

    1969   *Bandits.* New York: Delacorte Press.

Hopkins, James Lindsay

    2009   *The Bulgarian Orthodox Church.* Boulder, Colo.: East European Monographs.

Horgan, John

    2005   *The Psychology of Terrorism.* London; New York: Routledge.

Hull, Isabel

    2005   *Absolute Destruction: Military Culture and the Practices of War in Imperial Germany.* Ithaca, N.Y.: Cornell University Press.

Hutchinson, Sharon Elaine

    1996   *Nuer Dilemmas: Coping with Money, War, and the State.* Berkeley: University of California Press.

Inalcik, Halil

    1991   "The Emergence of Big Farms: Cifliks, State, Landlords and Tenants." In *Landholding and Commercial Agriculture in the Middle East,* ed. Çağlar Keyder and Frank Tabak 17–34. Albany: State University of New York Press.

Isaacman, Allen J.

1990   "Peasants and Rural Social Protest in Africa." *African Studies Review.*
        33(2) (September):1–120.

Kalyvas, Stathis N.

2006   *The Logic of Violence in Civil War.* Cambridge, U.K.: Cambridge University Press.

Kanogo, Tabitha M.

1987   *Squatters and the Roots of Mau Mau, 1905–63.* London: J. Currey.

Kanter, Rosabeth Moss

1972   *Commitment and Community: Communes and Utopias in Sociological Perspective.* Cambridge, Mass.: Harvard University Press.

Karakasidou, Anastasia

1997   *Fields of Wheat, Hills of Blood: Passages to Nationhood in Greek Macedonia, 1870–1990.* Chicago: University of Chicago Press.

2000   "Transforming Identity, Constructing Consciousness: Coercion and Homogeneity in Northwestern Greece." In *The Macedonian Question: Culture Historiography, Politics,* ed. Victor Roudometof, 55–98. Boulder, Colo.: East European Monographs.

Karpat, Kemal H.

1973   *An Inquiry into the Social Foundations of Nationalism in the Ottoman State: From Social Estates to Classes, from Millets to Nations.* Princeton, N.J.: Princeton University, Center of International Studies.

2002   *Studies on Ottoman Social and Political History: Selected Articles and Essays.* Leiden: Brill.

Katardžiev, Ivan

1993   *Sto Godini Od Formiranjeto Na VMRO—Sto Godini Revolucionerna Tradicija.* Skopje: Misla.

Kazazes, Neokles

1904   *Hellenism and Macedonia.* London: Thomas.

Keen, David

2008   *Complex Emergencies.* Cambridge, U.K.: Polity.

Keyder, Çağlar, and Faruk Tabak

1991   *Landholding and Commercial Agriculture in the Middle East.* Albany: State University of New York Press.

Kitson, Frank

1960   *Gangs and Counter-Gangs.* London: Barrie and Rockliff.

Koliopoulos, Giannēs S.

1987   *Brigands with a Cause: Brigandage and Irredentism in Modern Greece, 1821–1912.* Oxford, U.K.: Clarendon.

Koljević, Svetozar

1980 *The Epic in the Making*. Oxford, U.K.: Clarendon Press; Oxford University Press.

Kofos, Euangelos

1993 *Nationalism and Communism in Macedonia: Civil Conflict, Politics of Mutation, National Identity*. New Rochelle, N.Y.: A.D. Caratzas.

Kosev, Dimitŭr Konstantinov, Voin Božinov, and Liubomir Panaïotov

1979 *Macedonia, Documents and Material*. Sofia: Bulgarian Academy of Sciences.

Kravčinskij, Sergej M.

1883 *Underground Russia: Revolutionary Profiles and Sketches from Life*. London: Smith, Elder.

Krstevski-Kshka, Aleksander, ed.

1993 *Spomeni i Biografii Na Ilindenci*. Bitola: Archives of Macedonia-Bitola.

La Fontaine, Jean

1985 *Initiation*. Harmondsworth, U.K.: Penguin Books.

Lange-Akhund, Nadine

1998 *The Macedonian Question, 1893–1908, from Western Sources*. Boulder, Colo.: East European Monographs.

Laqueur, Walter

1977 *Terrorism*. Boston: Little, Brown.

Lazreg, Marnia

2008 *Torture and the Twilight of Empire: From Algiers to Baghdad*. Princeton N.J.: Princeton University Press.

Le Roy Ladurie, Emmanuel

1979 *Montaillou, the Promised Land of Error*. New York: Vintage Books.

Leacock, Eleanor Burke, and Richard B. Lee

1982 *Politics and History in Band Societies*. Cambridge [Cambridgeshire]; New York; Paris: Cambridge University Press; Editions de la Maison des Sciences de l'Homme.

Leakey, L. S. B.

1952 *Mau Mau and the Kikuyu*. London: Methuen.

1954 *Defeating Mau Mau*. London: Methuen.

Leger, Louis

1904 *Turcs et Grecs contre Bulgares en Macédoine*. Paris: Plon-Nourrit.

LeQueux, William

1907 *The Near East. The Present Situation in Montenegro, Bosnia, Servia, Bulgaria, Roumania, Turkey and Macedonia*. New York: Doubleday.

Livanios, Dimitris
    2008   "Beyond 'Ethnic Cleansing': Aspects of the Functioning of Violence in the Ottoman and Post-Ottoman Balkans." *Southeast European and Black Sea Studies* 8(3):189–203.

Lubkemann, Stephen
    2008   *Culture in Chaos: An Anthropology of the Social Condition in War.* Chicago: University of Chicago Press.

MacDermott, Mercia
    1978   *Freedom or Death: The Life of Gotsé Delchev.* London; West Nyack, N.Y.: Journeyman Press.
    1988   *For Freedom and Perfection: The Life of Yané Sandansky.* London: Journeyman.

Majdalany, F.
    1962   *State of Emergency, the Full Story of Mau Mau.* Boston: Houghton Mifflin.

Mao Zedong
    1963   *On Guerrilla Warfare.* New York: Praeger.

Marinov, Tchavdar
    2009   "We, the Macedonians: The Paths of Macedonian Supra-Nationalism (1878–1912)." In *We, the People: Politics of National Peculiarity in Southeastern Europe,* ed. Diana Mishkova, 107–38. Budapest: Central European University Press.

Marx, Karl
    1963   *The Eighteenth Brumaire of Louis Bonaparte.* New York: International Publishers.

Matkovski, Aleksandar, and Krste Bitoski
    1978   *Istorija Na Kruševo i Kruševsko: Od Postanokot Na Gradot do Podelbata Na Makedonija.* Kruševo: Sobranie na opštinata: Opštinski odbor na Sojuzot na borcite od NOV.

Mazower, Mark
    2000   *The Balkans: A Short History.* New York: Modern Library.

Mazrui, Al-Amin
    1986   "Ideology, Theory and Revolution: Lessons from the Mau Mau of Kenya." *Monthly Review* 39: 20.

Mertus, Julie
    1999   *Kosovo: How Myths and Truths Started a War.* Berkeley: University of California Press.

Mihailoff, Ivan
    1953   *Macedonia's Rise for Freedom 1903: The Great Insurrection.* Indianapolis, Ind.: Central Committee of the MPO.

Mikhailova, Y., and D. K. Prestel
2011   "Cross Kissing: Keeping One's Word in Twelfth-Century Rus." *Slavic Review* 70(1):1–22.

Miller, Stuart Creighton
1982   *Benevolent Assimilation: The American Conquest of the Philippines, 1899–1903.* New Haven, Conn.: Yale University Press.

Misirkov, Krste
1974   *On Macedonian Matters.* Skopje: Macedonian Review Editions.

Moore, Frederick
1906   *The Balkan Trail.* London: Smith, Elder.

Morison, Walter
1929   "Ballad of the Hajduks: Harambaša Ćurta and Bisčanin Ilija. *The Slavonic and East European Review* 8(23):389–99.

Moyar, Mark
2009   *A Question of Command: Counterinsurgency from the Civil War to Iraq.* New Haven, Conn.: Yale University Press.

Mylonas, George E.
1947   *The Balkan States: An Introduction to their History.* Washington D.C.: Public Affairs Press.

Nagl, John
2005   *Learning to Eat Soup With a Knife: Counterinsurgency Lessons from Malaya and Vietnam.* Chicago: University of Chicago Press.

Nalbandian, Louise
1963   *The Armenian Revolutionary Movement: The Development of Armenian Political Parties through the Nineteenth Century.* Berkeley: University of California Press.

Nikolov, Ivan Hadži, and Dimitar Baševski, eds.
1995   *Spomeni: I. H. Nikolov, D. Gruev, B. Sarafov, J. Sandanski, M. Gerdžikov, d-r H. Tatarčev.* Skopje: Kultura.

Noneva, Zdravka, Liubomir Panaĭotov, Doĭno Doĭnov, and Dimitŭr Khristov Mintsev
1984   *Dnevnitsi i Spomeni Za Ilindensko-Preobrazhenskoto vŭstanie.* Sofia: Izd-vo na Otechestveniia front.

Nordstrom, Carolyn
1997   *A Different Kind of War Story.* Philadelphia: University of Pennsylvania Press.

Obeyesekere, Gananath
1992   *The Apotheosis of Captain Cook: European Mythmaking in the Pacific.* Princeton, N.J.: Princeton University Press.

O'Malley, Pat

1979　"Social Bandits, Modern Capitalism and the Traditional Peasantry:
A Critique of Hobsbawn." *Journal of Peasant Studies* 6: 489–501.

Palairet, M. R.

1997　*The Balkan Economies c. 1800–1914: Evolution without Development.*
Cambridge. U.K.: Cambridge University Press.

Panaiotov, Liubomir

1983　*Ilindensko-Preobrazhensko vuštanie, 1903.* Sofia: Septembri.

Panov, Anton

1968　*Pečalbari.* Skopje: Misla.

Papachristos A. V.

2009　"Murder by Structure: Dominance Relations and the Social Structure of Gang Homicide." *American Journal of Sociology* 115(1):
74–128.

Perlmutter, Dawn

2006/7　"Mujahideen Desecration: Beheadings, Mutilation and Muslim Icon-
oclasm." *Anthropoetics* 12(2).

Perry, Duncan M.

1988　*The Politics of Terror: The Macedonian Liberation Movements, 1893–
1903.* Durham, N.C.: Duke University Press.

Perry, Elizabeth J.

1980　*Rebels and Revolutionaries in North China, 1845–1945.* Stanford, Calif.:
Stanford University Press.

Peterson, Derek R.

2004　*Creative Writing: Translation, Bookkeeping, and the Work of Imagination in Colonial Kenya.* Portsmouth, N.H.: Heinemann.

Petroff, Lillia

1995　*Sojourners and Settlers: The Macedonian Community in Toronto to 1940.*
Toronto: Multicultural History Society of Ontario: University of
Toronto Press.

Pettifer, James

1999　*The New Macedonian Question.* New York: St. Martin's Press.

Phillips, Andrew

2011　*War, Religion and Empire: The Transformation of International Orders.*
London: Cambridge University Press.

Piore, Michael J.

1979　*Birds of Passage: Migrant Labor and Industrial Societies.* Cambridge,
U.K.: Cambridge University Press.

Polk, William R.

2007   *Violent Politics: A History of Insurgency, Terrorism and Guerilla War, from the American Revolution to Iraq*. New York: HarperCollins.

Pollard, Hugh B. C.

1922   *The Secret Societies of Ireland: Their Rise and Progress*. London: P. Allan.

Popkin, Samuel L.

1979   *The Rational Peasant: The Political Economy of Rural Society in Vietnam*. Berkeley: University of California Press.

Potter, Jack M., May N. Diaz, and George M. Foster

1967   *Peasant Society: A Reader*. Boston: Little, Brown.

Poulton, Hugh

1995   *Who Are the Macedonians?* Bloomington: Indiana University Press.

Radin, A. Michael

1993   *IMRO and the Macedonian Question*. Skopje: Kultura.

Ramet, Sabrina

1995   *Social Currents in Eastern Europe*. Durham, N.C.: Duke University Press.

Ranger, T. O.

1968   "Connexions between 'Primary Resistance' Movements and Modern Mass Nationalism in East and Central Africa, Part 1." *Journal of African History* 9(3):437–53.

Rapoport, Anatol

1960   *Fights, Games, and Debates*. Ann Arbor: University of Michigan Press.

Reineck, Janet

2000   "Poised for War: Kosova's Quiet Siege." In *Neighbors at War: Anthropological Perspectives on Yugoslav Ethnicity, Culture and History*, ed. Joel M. Halpern and David A. Kideckel, 357–81. University Park: Pennsylvania State Press.

Richards, Paul

1996   *Fighting for the Rain Forest: War, Youth & Resources in Sierra Leone*. Portsmouth, N.H.: Heinemann.

Ricoeur, Paul

2006   "Archives, Documents, Traces." In *The Archive*, ed. Charles Merewether, 66–69. Cambridge, Mass.: MIT Press.

Risal, P.

1917   *La Ville Convoitée – Salonique*. Paris: Perrin.

Rodolsky, Roman

    1986   *Engels and the "Nonhistoric" Peoples: The National Question in the Revolution of 1848.* Glasgow: Critique Books.

Rogel, Carole

    1977   "The Wandering Monk and the Balkan National Awakening." In *Nationalism in a Non-National State: The Dissolution of the Ottoman Empire,* ed. William Haddad and William Ochsenwald. Columbus: Ohio State University Press.

Rossos, Andrew

    2008   *Macedonia and the Macedonians: A History.* Stanford, Calif.: Hoover Institution Press.

Rose, Alexander

    2008   *American Rifle: A Biography.* New York: Delacorte Press

Roudometof, Victor

    2000   *The Macedonian Question: Culture, Historiography, Politics.* Boulder, Colo.: East European Monographs.

    2002   *Collective Memory, National Identity, and Ethnic Conflict: Greece, Bulgaria, and the Macedonian Question.* Westport, Conn.: Praeger.

Routier, Gaston

    1903   *La Question Macedonienne.* Paris: H. Le Soudier.

Sahlins, Marshall D.

    1963   "Poor Man, Rich Man, Big-Man, Chief: Political Types in Melanesia and Polynesia." *Comparative Studies in Society and History* 5(3):285–303.

    1995   *How "Natives" Think: About Captain Cook, for Example.* Chicago: University of Chicago Press.

Sanford, N.

    1953   "Individual and Social Change in a Community Under Pressure: The Oath Controversy." *Journal of Social Issues,* 9: 25–42.

Šapardan

    n.d.   "Spomeni na Kole Zdravev-Šapardan." (Memoirs of Kole Zdravev-Šapardan). Unpublished typescript.

Šatev, Pavel

    1994   *Solunskiot atentat i zatočenicite vo Fezan.* Skopje: Kultura.

Schatz, Edward

    2009   *Political Ethnography: What Immersion Contributes to the Study of Power.* Chicago: The University of Chicago Press.

Schierup, Carl-Ulrik, and Aleksandra Ålund

    1987   *Will They Still be Dancing? Integration and Ethnic Transformation among Yugoslav Immigrants in Scandinavia.* Stockholm: Almqvist & Wiksell International.

Schwartz, Jonathan Matthew

    1996   *Pieces of Mosaic: An Essay on the Making of Makedonija.* Højbjerg, Denmark: Intervention Press.

Scott, James C.

    1976   *The Moral Economy of the Peasant: Rebellion and Subsistence in Southeast Asia.* New Haven, Conn.: Yale University Press.

    1977a   "Protest and Profanation: Agrarian Revolt and the Little Tradition, Part 1." *Theory and Society* 4(1):1–38.

    1977b   "Protest and Profanation: Agrarian Revolt and the Little Tradition, Part 2." *Theory and Society* 4(2):211–46.

    1985   *Weapons of the Weak: Everyday Forms of Peasant Resistance.* New Haven, Conn.: Yale University Press.

    1985   *Domination and the Arts of Resistance: Hidden Transcripts.* New Haven, Conn.: Yale University Press.

    1998   *Seeing Like a State: How Certain Schemes to Improve the Human Condition Have Failed.* New Haven, Conn.: Yale University Press.

    2007   "Peasants, Power and the Art of Resistance." In *Passion, Craft and Method in Comparative Politics,* ed. Geraldo Munck and Richard Snyder, 358–73. Baltimore, Md.: Johns Hopkins Press.

    2009   *The Art of Not Being Governed: An Anarchist History of Upland Southeast Asia.* New Haven, Conn.: Yale University Press.

Shils, Edward

    1957   "Primordial, Personal, Sacred and Civil Ties: Some Particular Observations on the Relationships of Sociological Research and Theory." *The British Journal of Sociology* 8(2):130–45.

Simons, Anna

    1997   *The Company They Keep: Life Inside the U.S. Army Special Forces.* New York: Free Press.

Sinno, Abdulkader H.

    2008   *Organizations at War in Afghanistan and Beyond.* Ithaca, N.Y.: Cornell University Press.

Skendi, Stavro

    1967   *The Albanian National Awakening, 1878–1912.* Princeton, N.J.: Princeton University Press.

Skocpol, Theda

2003   *Diminished Democracy: From Membership to Management in American Civic Life.* Norman: University of Oklahoma Press.

Smith, Arthur D. Howden

1908   *Fighting the Turk in the Balkans; an American's Adventures with the Macedonian Revolutionists,* New York: G. P. Putnam's Sons.

Smith, James H.

1998   "Njama's Supper: The Consumption and Use of Literary Potency by Mau Mau Insurgents in Colonial Kenya." *Comparative Studies in Society and History* 40(3):524–48.

Sonnichsen, Albert

1909   *Confessions of a Macedonian Bandit.* New York: Duffield & Company.

Sowards, Steven W.

1989   *Austria's Policy of Macedonian Reform.* Boulder, Colo.: East European Monographs.

Spivak, Gayatri Chakravorty

1985   "The Rani of Sirmur: An Essay in Reading the Archives." *History and Theory* 24(3):247–72.

Springer, Philip B., and Marcello Truzzi

1973   *Revolutionaries on Revolution: Participants' Perspectives on the Strategies of Seizing Power.* Pacific Palisades, Calif.: Goodyear Publishing Co.

Stalin, Joseph

1942   *Marxism and the National Question, Selected Writings and Speeches.* New York: International Publishers.

Stead, Alfred

1909   *Servia by the Servians.* London: W. Heinemann.

Stead, W. T.

1896   "The Eastern Ogre: Or, St. George to the Rescue." *The Review of Reviews* 14: 576–81.

Stepniak

1885   *Underground Russia: Revolutionary Profiles and Sketches from Life.* New York: Charles Scribner's.

Stoianovich, Traian

1960   "The Conquering Balkan Orthodox Merchant." *Journal of Economic History* 20(2):234–313.

1992   *Between East and West: The Balkan and Mediterranean Worlds.* New Rochelle, N.Y.: A. D. Caratzas.

Stoler, Ann Laura

    2009   *Along the Archival Grain: Epistemic Anxieties and Colonial Common Sense.* Princeton, N.J.: Princeton University Press.

Stone, Ellen Maria

    1902   *Six Months among Brigands.* New York: S. S. McClure Co.

Sugarman, Jane

    1997   *Engendering Song: Singing and Subjectivity at Prespa Albanian Weddings.* Chicago: University of Chicago Press.

Sullivan, Stacey

    2004   *Be Not Afraid, for You Have Sons in America: How a Brooklyn Roofer Helped Lure the U.S. Into the Kosovo War.* New York: St. Martin's Press.

Taylor, Keith

    1982   *The Political Ideas of the Utopian Socialists.* London: Cass.

Taylor, Michael

    1988   *Rationality and Revolution.* Cambridge, U.K.: Cambridge University Press.

Thomas, Nicholas

    1991   *Entangled Objects: Exchange, Material Culture and Colonialism in the Pacific.* Cambridge, Mass.: Harvard University Press.

Thompson, E. P.

    1966   *The Making of the English Working Class.* New York: Vintage Books.

Todorova, Maria N.

    1997   *Imagining the Balkans.* New York: Oxford University Press.

    2004   *Balkan Identities: Nation and Memory.* New York: New York University Press.

Tomašić, Dinko

    1948   *Personality and Culture in Eastern European Politics.* New York: G. W. Stewart.

Trotsky, Leon, George Weissman, and Duncan Williams

    1980   *The Balkan Wars, 1912–13: The War Correspondence of Leon Trotsky.* New York: Pathfinder Press.

Tsanoff, Corrinne Stephenson, and Radoslav Andrea Tsanoff

    1914   *Pawns of Liberty; a Story of Fighting Yesterdays in the Balkans.* New York: Outing Publishing Co.

Tsing, Anna Lowenhaupt

    2005   *Friction: An Ethnography of Global Connection.* Princeton, N.J.: Princeton University Press.

Turner, Victor Witter

1969   *The Ritual Process: Structure and Anti-Structure.* Chicago: Aldine Publishing Co.

Udovički, Jasminka, and James Ridgeway

1997   *Burn This House: The Making and Unmaking of Yugoslavia.* Durham, N.C.: Duke University Press.

U.S. Department of State

1954   "Macedonian Nationalism and the Communist Party of Yugoslavia." Typescript: Washington, D.C.

Upward, Allen

1908   *The East End of Europe; the Report of an Unofficial Mission to the European Provinces of Turkey on the Eve of the Revolution.* London: J. Murray.

Vasiliadis, Peter

1989   *Whose Are You?: Identity and Ethnicity among the Toronto Macedonians.* New York: AMS Press.

Venturi, Franco

1966   *Roots of Revolution; a History of the Populist and Socialist Movements in Nineteenth Century Russia.* New York: Alfred Knopf.

Veskoviḱ-Vangeli, Vera

1995   *Borbata za Nezavisna Makedonska Republika od Ilinden do ASNOM.* Skopje: Makedonska Kniga.

Vivian, Herbert

1904   *The Servian Tragedy, with some Impressions of Macedonia,* London: G. Richards.

VMRO (Vutrieshnata Makedonska Revoliutsionna Organizatsiia).

1904   *La Macedoine Et Le Vilayet d'Andrinople, 1893–1903.* [Paris]: [s.n.].

Walton, John

1984   *Reluctant Rebels: Comparative Studies of Revolution and Underdevelopment.* New York: Columbia University Press.

Warren, Kay B., and Jean E. Jackson

2002   *Indigenous Movements, Self-Representation, and the State in Latin America.* Austin: University of Texas Press.

Weber, Eugen

1976   *Peasants into Frenchmen: The Modernization of Rural France, 1870–1914.* Stanford, Calif.: Stanford University Press.

Weinstein, Jeremy M.

2007   *Inside Rebellion: The Politics of Insurgent Violence.* New York: Cambridge University Press.

West, Bing

2008 *The Strongest Tribe: War, Politics and the Endgame in Iraq.* New York: Random House.

West, Rebecca

1941 *Black Lamb and Grey Falcon: A Journey through Yugoslavia.* New York: Viking Press.

Wiessner, Polly

1982 "Risk, Reciprocity and Social Influences on !Kung San Economics." In *Politics and History in Band Societies,* ed. Eleanor Lee and Richard Lee, 61–84. Cambridge, U.K.: Cambridge University Press.

Williamson, Harold

1952 *Winchester: The Gun that Won the West.* Washington, D.C.: Combat Forces Press.

Wimmer, Andreas, and Nina Glick-Schiller

2002 "Methodological Nationalism and Beyond: Nation-State Building, Migration and the Social Sciences." *Global Networks* 2(4):301–34.

Wood, Elisabeth Jean

2003 *Insurgent Collective Action and Civil War in El Salvador.* Cambridge, U.K.: Cambridge University Press.

Worsley, Peter

1968 *The Trumpet Shall Sound: A Study of "Cargo" Cults in Melanesia.* New York: Schocken Books.

Wyon, Reginald

1904 *The Balkans from Within.* London: J. Finch & Co.

Yosmaoğlu, İpek K.

2006 "Counting Bodies, Shaping Souls: The 1903 Census and National Identity in Ottoman Macedonia." *International Journal of Middle East Studies* 38(1):55–77.

Živković, Marko

2011 *Serbian Dreambook: National Imaginary in the Time of Milošević.* Bloomington: Indiana University Press.

INDEX

KEITH BROWN is Professor (Research) at Brown University's Watson Institute. He is author of *The Past in Question: Modern Macedonia and the Uncertainties of Nation* and editor of *Transacting Transition: The Micropolitics of Democracy Assistance in the Former Yugoslavia.*

CPSIA information can be obtained at www.ICGtesting.com
Printed in the USA
LVOW130148200313

325078LV00004B/5/P